MW01596796

LIFE IS A METAPHOR
The Definitive Book of Self-Help

NEIL KATZ

BALBOA.
PRESS
A DIVISION OF HAY HOUSE

Copyright © 2012, 2013 Neil Katz.

All rights reserved. No part of this book may be used or reproduced by any means, graphic, electronic, or mechanical, including photocopying, recording, taping or by any information storage retrieval system without the written permission of the publisher except in the case of brief quotations embodied in critical articles and reviews.

Balboa Press books may be ordered through booksellers or by contacting:

Balboa Press
A Division of Hay House
1663 Liberty Drive
Bloomington, IN 47403
www.balboapress.com
1-(877) 407-4847

Because of the dynamic nature of the Internet, any web addresses or links contained in this book may have changed since publication and may no longer be valid. The views expressed in this work are solely those of the author and do not necessarily reflect the views of the publisher, and the publisher hereby disclaims any responsibility for them.

The author of this book does not dispense medical advice or prescribe the use of any technique as a form of treatment for physical, emotional, or medical problems without the advice of a physician, either directly or indirectly. The intent of the author is only to offer information of a general nature to help you in your quest for emotional and spiritual well-being. In the event you use any of the information in this book for yourself, which is your constitutional right, the author and the publisher assume no responsibility for your actions.

Any people depicted in stock imagery provided by Thinkstock are models, and such images are being used for illustrative purposes only. Certain stock imagery © Thinkstock.

ISBN: 978-1-4525-7481-3 (sc)
ISBN: 978-1-4525-7483-7 (hc)
ISBN: 978-1-4525-7482-0 (e)

Library of Congress Control Number: 2013909338

Printed in the United States of America.

Balboa Press rev. date: 06/28/2013

TABLE OF CONTENTS

DEDICATION

For Jack, Eunie, Ellie, Harriet, Tarren, Kira, Hayley, Jenessa, Madeline, and all manner of Katz, past, present, and future. This is what you have created.

PREFACE:
CREDENTIALS

I am perfect.

Contrary to what you may think, there is not one conceited bone in my rather well-defined body. I am what I am: perfect. If you consider me pompous, I've every right to be—perfect people are, you know.

My parents would have told you how perfect I am. They positively beamed with pride at my excellence. And why shouldn't they have? They raised me to be an intelligent, independent, compassionate, ambitious, perceptive, and, well, perfect person. That's because they never ordered me around, never had inflated expectations, always balanced the right amount of discipline and tenderness at just the right time. I grew up in an ideal familial environment.

Ask my kids; they'll tell you: I'm perfect. Of course, my kids are perfect, too. What an ideal relationship we all have. They always listened to me; they always picked up after themselves; they never argued with one another. Their rooms sparkled! Exemplary students, all of them. Talented beyond belief. Little darlings!

But then what would you expect with perfect parents as their role models? We also pick up after ourselves and never argue. We support each other at all times; we fulfil our spousely needs both lovingly and devotedly. Our wide range of friends admires us for this.

I have numerous friends because that is the kind of easy-going, fun-loving, likeable person I am. I am willing to lend an ear, eager to lend a hand, happy to lend a shoulder and any other body part that is required. Being quite skilled at problem-solving I am able to thwart obstacles even before they materialize. I am never immobilized and no one ever victimizes me. Naturally, I have all the answers.

Of course I do. I am perfect.

Well, isn't that why you bought this book?

PREFACE: CREDENTIALS REVISED (THE TRUTH)

Okay. You want the truth? I'm not so perfect. My parents weren't June and Ward Cleaver. For fifty-something years I had not done the right thing at the right time in my father's eyes. Even when he was ninety-four he still buttoned up my winter coat and asked me if my underwear was warm enough; seven seconds later he admonished my lack of independence. Guilt was my mother's domain. "A son shouldn't visit his old mother once in a blue moon?" The first time she said this to me I was three years old. And my children used to make the Our Gang kids look like Smurfs. "It's mine!" "No, it's mine!" "I get to sit in the front this time!" "She got more than me!" "It's no fair!" "I'm telling!" One of them would tuck her porridge on the underside of the table and pat it until it was flat and petrified. Another would sit with her feet in the toilet and flush, screaming, "Whirlpool!" My son would make obscene noises in public places. The baby, a bully in her own right, would amuse herself in the kitchen, in a kitchen cupboard, in a roasting pan. With the lid on! The extent of their intellectual conversation at the dinner table was, "Who farted?" Oh, sure, they listened to me . . . after I would bellow threats I had no intention of carrying out.

My wife and I never exactly had a Ken and Barbie relationship. Good morning! often became an argument. We spent our leisure time deciding which clothes lying on the floor beside the overturned baskets were clean and which were dirty. And what of our love life? Suffice it to say we referred periodically to our four kids as the most effective method of birth control.

As for our wide range of friends, if they were not discussing financial worries, loaded diapers, or cheesecake recipes, then they were getting a divorce.

So where does that leave me? How do I describe myself?

I am confused.

Not a light-headed, scatter-brained confused like deciding (with a nasal giggle and a vacant expression) if I should become a bleached blond (my hair *is* blond—was blond—what's left of it—though not bleached). Not an intellectual, respected confused like debating a well-planned, well-formed, well-spoken opinion. Not even a spiritual, reverent confused as a philosopher of time, space, and non-existence.

No, I am confused in a big way, a big melodramatic way. Surrendering to a pang of histrionics I can verbalize this overwhelming state of confusion thusly: Oy!

I need answers to the questions life poses. I need the keys to the doors that block my way to a happy and successful life. I need to know the secrets of the universe and more. Is this too much to ask?

But I *don't* have the answers, the keys, the knowledge.

I am confused, about everything.

I am confused about people, places, and things. Nouns confuse me. Pronouns baffle me more. I am at a total loss for words (verbs and adjectives included) when called upon to answer any of life's questions.

After much deliberation (about seventeen seconds worth) I decided that my confusion is merely an offspring of Fear and the Unknown. I am afraid of everyone and everything. I am afraid of not being liked, of not having the right answers, of not being perfect, of not doing the right thing, of not knowing what will happen tomorrow, of choices, of life, and especially of death. All unknown. All scare me. I am afraid of the Unknown and this makes me confused.

But the Unknown is, after all, unknown. How can I be afraid of something I know nothing about? That is an unknown, too. It is also neurotic (so I am told—by an Unknown!) Perhaps I am afraid of being neurotic. Now I'm really confused!

Although I knew my parents always loved me, I was afraid of them or, more correctly, I was afraid of being confused when I was with them. Of being wrong in their eyes. And I *was* always wrong or inadequate in their eyes. I had to be or else I would have disappointed them. "What have we done wrong?" They would ask. "We try to be good parents. We just don't see where we went wrong!" My parents were confused and afraid, too. Maybe it's genetic.

Then, of course, there is Guilt—the infamous brother to confusion—who inhabits my mind more often than I care to acknowledge. I feel guilty throughout much of my day. Sometimes, though, I don't feel guilty at all. Then I feel guilty about not feeling guilty. At that point I can't take it anymore. Confusion takes over.

When I am not all that ridden with Guilt (thrashing myself incessantly with regretful assertions of 'what should have been'), I become possessed with Guilt's twin: Worry (thrashing myself incessantly with anxious interrogatives commencing with 'What if . . . ?'). Cousin Anger steps in quickly when the others are at rest. If memory serves correctly, Anger was raised by Fear and the Unknown. Her parents disappeared so long ago I can't quite recall their names. Sometimes she is merely a mischief-maker but more often she is tyrannical. Immobility is the granddaughter of Fear and the Unknown. She is the family favourite and because of her frail, pathetic condition everyone dotes on her. Immobility is much preferred than Self-Pity, her Aunt Resentment's little boy. He is just a spoiled, egotistical brat but everyone puts up with him because Auntie Resentment is so domineering. There are more relatives—too many to list—but good grief! I sound as if I am inhabited by a family of mutant parasites! I can't believe I actually put this in print. I'm very Embarrassed (third eldest child of Fear and the Unknown).

If you are anything like me you've probably spent much of your time asking, "What the hell is wrong with me?" or "What kind of person am I?" Me, I am a passionate person. I loathe with desperation; I rage quietly; I love with unyielding caution; I procrastinate with uncompromising perseverance; I sally forth with great lassitude; I fear (did I already mention?) vehemently and religiously; I blush in (w)impish delight even in my own thoughts even in private! I take pride in my well-developed state of boredom; I have an overwhelming fondness for my reluctance, indecision, temerity, defense mechanisms, and all the other things that make me the fun person I am.

Charlie Brown is my mentor.

I also spend a great deal of time wishing. Not willing to recognize that fine line between fantasy and reality, I engaged, throughout my formative years, in practices of nose-twitching, heavy blinking, ear-wiggling and just plain wishing. To make objects (and people) appear or disappear. To be able to fly. To read minds. To make people behave the way I wanted them to behave. To have power. Control. Today my wishes are somewhat modified. I wish I could be blissfully ignorant or uncommonly wise or brilliantly intelligent or hysterically funny, or dazzling and glamorous, or seductive and sexy, or noble and honourable, or happy and innocent.

I cry at Frank Capra movies. Does that count for anything?

I wish I were profound. Everything I say or think sounds dumb to me. My thoughts are so disjointed that every time I think I am on to something—say, the solution to some great philosophical paradox—I end up blanking out or thinking of purple elephants.

Sometimes I get so mad I wish, as in days gone by, I had the power to blow up the world real good with a twitch of my nose. Other times I am so possessed by a presence of overwhelming compassion and benevolence that I wish I had the power to become a saviour of mankind. Or else I get a craving for Chinese food.

Why? I go through life asking "Why?" Why am I the way I am? Why can't I be more like the person I wish I could be? Why is it so bloody important for me to prove my worth to every scum that slithers over the face of the Earth? Why do I feel it essential to be loved by every lousy shithead that passes my way? Why do I want every stranger I see to be my best friend? Why do I resent every Tom, Dick and Mary for not being as interested by me as I am (or think I am) by them (him . . . her . . . it)?

Why do fools fall in lo-ove?

Often I feel that if I succeed in anything, excel to the limit in life, it's that I am an accomplished failure. And I flagellate myself with the utmost determination. I must be an anal retentive. But that's okay. I have to get my jollies from somewhere!

Some people dream about faraway places; others dream of wealth and good fortune; still others dream of love and satisfying relationships. Me, I dream of psychoses. I mean, wouldn't it be heaven to slip away into my own little world of persecution, debasing myself to my heart's content, purging me from myself and becoming someone I'm not, perhaps several someones I'm not?

As an accomplished failure, however, I bet I wouldn't even make a good psychotic. It figures. I'll probably be reincarnated as a squid. My tentacles will become knotted and tangled and all the other squids will laugh at me or ignore me.

Why am I telling you all this, you ask? Don't ask—I'll tell you: I just wanted to reaffirm the fact that maybe I am not so perfect. Oddly enough, that makes me, by definition, human (of all things!).

But before I become too morose I had better get back to:

THE POINT OF THIS BOOK

I always thought my calling was to impart wisdom and knowledge in living a rich and fulfilling life. After all, isn't *every*one trying to find meaning, purpose, and happiness in his/her life? Or is it just me? Sometimes I think that I am the only one in the universe with issues. Nevertheless I was determined to seek out answers, so I started at the local bookstore. I discovered hundreds upon hundreds of books in the self-help, well-being, personal growth and psychology categories. I scanned the internet and got several million hits on these subjects in 0.03 seconds. It was very discouraging. What purpose could it possibly serve to write a book on a subject that has been written about seventy-two trillion times? Why bother? (an annoyingly repetitive theme in my life).

Anyway, I checked out many of these websites and read several of these books. What I discovered was that there is no such thing as *original thought*. More importantly, it seemed that *I* did not possess a single original thought. Every unique, interesting, entertaining, or informative idea that I ever had was all said before!

I was too depressed to write a book about overcoming depression. Too overwhelmed to author a manuscript about managing anxiety. Too emotionally depleted to pen a treatise about the virtues of the pursuit of happiness.

After spending several days and weeks staring with contempt at the blank screen on my computer, I realized I still felt a strong pull to completing my opus in spite of everything. So I read and re-read articles, columns, books, and blogs. What was it about the subject of self-help that made it so compelling? And so disappointing?

I began to believe that most of us are looking for some answers to life's questions, be it the old standard, "What is the meaning of life?" to "Why am I feeling depressed?" to "Am I going to get lucky tonight?" Obviously some of these questions are easier to answer than others. Perhaps those answers that dissolve into air when we reach out for them are the answers I should set out to explore. Yes, yes, it was painfully clear that zillions of people probably far more qualified than I have written books, given lectures, performed experiments, and engaged in therapies on this very subject: How do I overcome obstacles? Or, how can I live a successful and happy life? In other words, how do I help myself? What are the answers? The problem is that, when all is said and done, the answers found in those books, lectures, experiments, and therapies also dissipate into the air as merely more unattainable answers. Have you ever left a seminar or put down a compelling book on self-help, exclaiming, "Wow! Cool! Groovy, man! Awesome!" only to stop dead in your tracks a few hours later, wondering what all the fuss was about? Or asking, "Now what?" Or deciding, "Nah, that'll never work. Forget it. I can't be bothered. What a waste of time *that* was!"? The question was rhetorical. If you can't answer 'yes' you are not of this planet and you don't need this book.

But back to my research. These books, many of which were best-sellers, all had similar information to the point of repetition and redundancy. Moreover, they all offered platitudes (for example, "Have a positive attitude and you can turn your life around!"), cute expressions (for example, "When life gives you lemons, make lemonade!"), and, above all, gimmicks (for example, "The ABC's of a Successful Life" and "Dream Catcher—Grab Onto Your Dreams and Live Them!"). I wanted to line up these authors and smack them upside the head! The more I researched, the more I found myself drowning in a sea of metaphors! With a lifebuoy of right thinking, we'll cruise back to this point shortly.

Meanwhile, I needed to give consideration to <u>the driving force behind my desire to write a book</u> about helping oneself. Did I want to help others? Or was I seeking therapy for myself? Or both?

<u>What would be the premise for this book?</u> To suggest that everyone lacks self-esteem, confidence, and clear-thinking is both inaccurate and presumptuous. To speak on behalf of the rest of the world is rude, ingratiating, and egotistical. Still, such words and phrases as "personal growth, self-help, empowerment, learning, development, creation, betterment, enhancement, and well-being" all resonated with me.

<u>What would be my objective in writing this book?</u> Much to my dismay, I discovered I am not omnipotent, magical, sagacious, all-knowing, or even, at times, coherent.

<u>What would I have to offer to those inclined to read this book?</u> I have limited life experience, little imagination (save delusions), and cloudy perceptions.

So I decided to throw in the towel. And I thought, "Throwing in the towel" is a silly metaphor. But then, what isn't a metaphor? *Life* is a metaphor!

I started piecing together all of these thoughts:

What if I write this book to help others? AND

What if I write this book as therapy for myself? AND

What if my premise is that life is about growing, developing, learning, creating, bettering, enhancing, empowering, self-helping and being well? AND

What if my objective in writing this book is to convey ideas that are not omnipotent, magical, sagacious, or all-knowing but, instead, human? AND

What if I offer my limited experience, what little imagination I have and my cloudy perceptions? AND

What if I peppered my prose and practice exercises with metaphors? AND

What if?

What?

It was an affirmative response to my own rhetoric that prompted my quest—a journey, as it were (I hate that expression 'as it were')—for the ideal guide to self-help based on *me*. Self-centred little me!

The kind of self-help referred to here evolves from the identification of a trinity in the psyche (sounds painful): thoughts, feelings, and behaviour. These are the very elements which shape who I am. Due to circumstances, events, and influences, my thinking sometimes becomes irrational or, at best, blurred. My emotions may sour and create a tendency for me to focus on 'malevolent' feelings. I may act out on those feelings, behaving in inappropriate ways.

How I *measure* what behaviour is good or bad, which emotions are positive or negative, which thoughts are rational or just plain nuts, is a fundamental prerequisite for me to make desired changes. To create, develop, and maintain a belief system, a moral code, a list of personal values is therefore crucial.

Consequently, the purpose of my rambling is to provide myself with avenues for clear thinking, to lend focus to managing difficult, unwanted emotions, and to uncover ideas for monitoring and changing inappropriate behaviours. The overall objective is to remove obstacles that have been blocking the way to a more productive and meaningful way of life.

My next task was to establish a suitable title for my book. Believing the title should embody the essence of the book (what a concept!) I began with a working title of:

Life Is a Metaphor. Maybe. Too gimmicky?

The Definitive Self-Help Workbook. But, I wondered, does it encompass the true purpose of this book? Am I setting my expectations too high? Can self-help be definitive? Will this be a workbook? Do I want to make this pursuit into work? Then I thought that maybe a simpler title would be better:

Oy! Oy? Too simple. Too whiney.

Confessions of a Self-Help Junkie. Too technical.

Rewiring, Reinvention, Resourcefulness, Resilience. The four 'R's'—ugh!

A Pessimist's Guide to Positive Living. Too confusing.

My Journey Through Life. Boring!

A Lived Experience. Whose isn't?

Aspiring to Mediocrity. Perhaps an apt description of me but not the point of this book.

Making the Most Out of Life. Am I saying life is generally crap?

Into the Light. Sounds like a near-death experience or a Shirley MacLaine epic. What else?

Integrity.

Muddle.

Flipside.

Focus.

Muddle, Flipside, Focus.

A Liberated Life.

Clean Slate.

Reinventing Myself.

Vibrations.

I Say I'm Awed; She Says I'm Odd.

Beano for the Brain.

I could have gone on forever but I needed something for the book cover and the copyright, so I went back to the beginning of my title search and selected *Life Is a Metaphor.* If this doesn't work for you, you can choose any one of the above.

Next, I needed to determine a format for my book.

<u>Part I</u> is the Starting Point of my journey—the Primal Kvetch. This is the Darkness. L'Inferno. Captivity. It is the beginnings of my life and ruminations about myself, encompassing notions on my thoughts, feelings and behaviours—the stuff life is made of.

<u>Part II</u> is my Journey Without—the Quest. This is the Gray Fog. Purgatorio. Probation. Here I seek out the answers to the questions of my life through an exploration of external sources.

<u>Part III</u> is my Journey Within—the Find. This is the Light. Paradiso. Liberation. It is a return to my thoughts, feelings, and behaviours, but through a transcendent approach, a paradigm shift, a revelation. Following each section in Part III is a little something you might want to try.

Also included in each section are all kinds of metaphors I found myself using in my journey of self-discovery.

Essentially, this was the journey that has helped me and is still helping me to screw my head on a little more tightly. Ultimately, this approach, applied to *your* journey, may be of some value to you as it was to me.

So here it is. I share with you now (perfect person that I am):

LIFE IS A METAPHOR

PART I

THE STARTING POINT

THE PRIMAL KVETCH

THE DARKNESS

L'INFERNO

CAPTIVITY

The Starting Point of my journey was in a small bungalow in a banal, middle-class Toronto suburb a zillion years ago. I was sitting in the middle of the living room floor surrounded by toys, books, and a TV (a focal point in my life). It was a boring Sunday afternoon. My mother was yelling at me from the kitchen to find something constructive to do like clean my room. My father was sitting next to me asleep in the chair that faced the television. My older sister, all of nine years old, was yakking incessantly on the phone to her friends.

Suddenly a wave of anxiety overcame me. I tossed my teddy bear aside, rose to my feet, and with outstretched arms, I cried out in desperation, "Is this all there is?!" I knew immediately something had to be done. I had my future to consider. I was not about to allow something as trivial as the meaning of life to eat away at me until I was nothing more than a shell of a man before my fifth birthday!

So, at the tender age of four, I began a review of my Starting Point, the place I was at, the events and circumstances, and the associated thoughts, feelings and behaviours that made me the miserable little wretch I was. This review lasted fifty years. I think I now finally know my Starting Point, beginning with a chronology of circumstance.

I made a grand entrance into this world—I stopped the Santa Claus parade. My father was at work so my aunt and uncle sped along the streets of Toronto to get my mother to the hospital, located along the parade route on University Avenue. My uncle screamed at my mother, "Cross your legs!" for fear that my birth would mess up his new 1954 Buick. They got the police to stop the floats to let them pass through to the hospital. To the disappointment of the angry mob of spectators on that frosty November afternoon, I was born.

I was a scrawny, wiry, sickly child who measured his milestones in life by illness, injury, and dire circumstances. This made me feel important, loved, and happy.

I had the chicken pox at one month old, scoliosis diagnosed at one year, and a tonsillectomy at age four. At thirteen, I had corrective eye surgery. I also suffered with various respiratory illnesses including asthma, pneumonia, and pleurisy. Continuing into adulthood, I developed myriad other illnesses and debilitating diseases.

I was delighted.

My parents were doting, and I always felt loved, even though my father, forty-one years older than I, worked twelve hours a day and was always too tired to play ball with me, and was too old-fashioned to have a meaningful conversation with me because "only sissies talk about their feelings". My mother was a smart, funny and loving woman who also happened to be manic-depressive (as bipolar was known in those days). She was in hospitals for treatment more than she was at home. From the age of eight, I would take care of her at home while she lay in bed in agony with severe headaches, as I stole glances out the window at my neighbourhood friends outside playing. Or else I was visiting her in hospitals with barred windows and naked light bulbs. On many occasions, she was reeling from electro-convulsive shock treatments or was stupefied into submission by the smorgasbord of tranquilizers and anti-depressants prescribed to her.

I was elated.

My only sibling was a typical older sister whom I love very much . . . back then, however, not so much. When she wasn't on the phone with her friends, she was threatening to tell my parents that I was watching TV instead of studying or she was blackmailing me if I didn't do her favours. Much of the time, she was begging me for reassurance that my mother's illness was *only* mental and not physical. Once I confirmed this, she was off with her friends again, leaving me to my own devices and holding the bag.

I was overjoyed.

School was a struggle for me. Just because I knew my times tables and could spell polysyllabic words in grade two, I was accelerated in grades three, four, and five, completing them in two years. This left me bewildered and socially inept. At ten years old in grade seven, I was beaten up by some schoolmates and teased mercilessly by others, some of whom were three or four years older than I was.

I was ecstatic.

I married my sweetheart after a two-year teenage courtship. We declared our love and discussed our dreams for the future. Now, decades later with four grown children and a grandchild, we are still very much married. Mostly she ignores me, nags me, or tells me all the things I do which are wrong.

I am enthralled.

I had secured employment in the field of Social Services for the City which I held for thirty-three years until my retirement. I am now at home with my wife, complaining about my health, worrying for my future, and constantly looking around for something to keep me busy. My wife is not pleased.

But I am enraptured.

Our four beautiful kids are the lights of my life. My wife and I cared for them through the ups and downs of family life and I worry about them every minute of every day, even now that they are adults. My son was hit by a car when he was fourteen and sustained a severe head injury. I have three daughters, one who overcame OCD, anorexia, and anxiety, one who was a rebel in her teens, and one who fought a battle with depression and trychotillomania (hair pulling) and won. All of my children insisted on learning about life the hard way despite my attempts at teaching them and helping them. But this paragraph doesn't belong here. My success stories are found in Part III.

These were some of the circumstances of my life to date. I am sharing them to give context to the thoughts, feelings, and behaviours that I developed over the years with which you, lucky reader, are now to become acquainted.

THOUGHTS

In order to examine thoughts, I believed it was necessary to understand two basic elements:

1) What is a thought?
2) Where does a thought come from?

So I started simply with a dictionary definition:

Thought (n): the act of thinking; an idea. Guess what I found when I looked up the definition of 'idea'? A thought. Naturally! So my thought on thoughts was that this is bullshit.

I explored some more and got much more than I bargained for, and each answer elicited more questions, leading me into the fields of physical science, neuropsychology, linguistics, spirituality, and philosophy. Here is some of what I found about *thought*:

- *An organization of electro-chemical impulses in the brain.* Do I have to become a card-carrying member of this organization?
- *An internal response to internal or external stimuli.* What could the internal stimuli that trigger imagination or creativity possibly be? A stomach cramp?
- *A mathematical computation which occurs above the level of consciousness.* What if you're lousy at math?
- *Depends on the type of thought: reflective, reactive/responsive, connective, deductive, intuitive, idle, directed, psychic, interpretive, perceptive, etc.* Huh?

- *There is no such thing as individual thought . . . We all tap into a pool of infinite cosmic thought.* Where did this pool of cosmic thought come from and how do we tap into it? Does this mean you know what I'm thinking (God forbid!)?
- *We do not actively think; thoughts pass through us and we simply become aware of them.* So now I'm a ghost?

All of this research was fascinating but it was taking me in directions I did not want to go, at least for the purpose of this book. And I still did not understand what a thought was or where it came from. Besides, I think all this thinking about thoughts was giving me a headache.

In an effort to stay focused, I decided that, as a review of my starting point, I was not going to worry so much about what thought is or where it comes from but would, instead, focus on the kinds of thoughts one has and their impact on living and well-being. More specifically, what were *my* thoughts and how did they shape *my* life?

Here are some of them. This is by no means a complete list but I believe they do show where I was coming from . . .

WHO AM I?

(What I think about myself)

"I just retired from a successful thirty-three-year career in Social Services.
Not bad, considering I'm **anti**-social*!"*

I am stupid. I am fat. I am ugly. I am lazy. I am incapable. I am unlikable. I am inadequate. I am sick. I am boring. I am worthless.

And so it goes, on and on.

Labels.

My mother used to sew labels on my summer camp clothes that read "ROTTEN LAZY BRAT" for easy identification.

Adjectives.

Adjectives are the prettiest part of any language and open up a whole world of imagination. Strange that, like thorns on a rose, they can have a painful aspect to them as well. Adjectives are lethal weapons. They provoke arguments. They initiate wars. They are instrumental in battles. More significantly, adjectives can be the cause, effect, and justification for suicide.

Labels are adjectives.

Labels describe who you are. I know who I am. I am a stupid, fat, incapable, unlikable, inadequate, sickly, worthless, lazy bore.

It says so right here on the back of my shirt collar.

IDENTITY CRISIS
(Seeking my identity)

*"A young man walked into a dermatologist's office and said, 'Can you help me?
I think I'm a moth.' The dermatologist said, 'You don't need a dermatologist.
You need a psychiatrist.' 'Yes, I know,' said the man. The dermatologist asked,
'So then why did you come in* here?' *The man replied, 'The light was on.'"*

At the risk of sounding like an amnesiac, I have often asked myself,
"Who am I?" I never allowed myself the chance to get to know me and
consequently was never able to answer the "Who am I?" question to my
satisfaction. Oh, deep down I indulged in an assortment of fantasies like
we all do (don't we?), of who I am.

- What I do (or did), my profession: Now retired, I was a Social
  Services supervisor for the City
- What I would like to do or be: I would like to be a writer, I
  would like to be smart, I would like to be famous
- What my relationships are: I am a father, a husband, a son, a
  brother, a relative, a friend, an acquaintance, an employee, a
  student, etc.
- What I have accomplished:???
- How I would like to see myself: I would like to see myself
  as a good person, useful, important, kind, virtuous, honest,
  honourable, sincere, blah, blah, blah . . .

But those fantasies always maintained a faded, translucent quality
that never quite took form. Ideas were never fully developed, goals were

never clearly defined. And so I remained in this hazy state of limbo for much of my life.

Could a reality check help me figure out who I am? Well, I am one of several billion people on this planet; I am a microspeck in the cosmos; I am a figment of someone else's imagination (dumb son-of-a-bitch! That someone else is either a masochist or has the world's worst imagination!).

Heavy sigh.

I never learned how to define myself and consequently never really knew who I was.

THE PHYSICAL ME

(Dealing with who I am physically)

"I was trying to write a joke about penis size but every time I come up short."

I do not like my body. I think it is rather grotesque. I am unequivocally the baldest, fattest, ugliest man in the whole wide world, even when I was a kid (except I had hair on my head; except I was skinny; except I wasn't a man when I was a kid). I have the crookedest face, the yellowiest teeth, the smallest endowment, and the bumpiest cranium. I concede that I am a superlative specimen of Homo Sapiens. Not all my attributes are God-given; some of my hideous corpus is self-made: chewed-at fingers, portly paunch, stooped posture and the like (nothing less than an ostentatious demonstration of my passive-aggressive psyche). But everything must be put in perspective, mustn't it? The body is only a host, after all. My body is not the real me; it *contains* the real me. When I secrete body fluids I am not making a statement. My body is my body and has a life of its own (doesn't it?).

I particularly do not like my body when it misbehaves and causes pain. I have a very low pain threshold. Often, when in pain, I make a bargain with God (usually in a whining, pleading voice), "Please, God, make the pain go away and I promise to be a good husband, father, son (depending on with whom I have argued most recently). The rule is usually one promise per favour. I will never offer to be a good husband *and* a good son in exchange for help with just one pain or just one unpleasant occurrence. By the time I recover or by the time the bad experience has disappeared I have already broken my promise. Hastily I tell myself that I didn't really make a promise because perhaps there is no God, or that the promise was actually invalid because there is a good scientific or psychological explanation. Hence no more pain *and* a clear conscience. But I would rather not have had the pain in the first place, if the truth be known. Physical discomfort definitely reduces emotional pain to mere self-indulgence.

To wit I raise my Maalox cocktail and hurl it at the mirror in honour of the physical me.

WHY BOTHER?

(Finding a sense of purpose)

———◦◦◦◦◦◦◦———

"Everyone has a purpose in life. Mine is watching television."

"My mother told me that my sole purpose in life is to serve as a warning to others."

———◦◦◦◦◦◦◦———

One of my favourite pastimes is writing, however, more often than not I am stricken with writer's block. Everything I want to say has already been said one way or another anyway so why bother? "Why bother?" seems to sufficiently answer most of my problem questions. Rhetoric is my life.

There were so many things I wanted to do with my life (on good days) and still do. But we all end up dead anyway, so why bother?

My wife seems relatively content with her life. I hate her. She goes through the motions of filling her day with things that "have to be done". This was my father's notion of an ideal lifestyle. Except he didn't believe my wife was really doing anything that had to be done. My father insisted that she did nothing and what she did do she did wrong. This made him happy. He picked on me more; after all, I was his flesh and blood. I never did the right things at the right times. I would argue with him about this. And he would reply, "Fine, you don't want me to be a father, I won't be a father!" I would try to explain and he would accuse me of being a know-it-all who didn't know much about anything. "His heart! His Heart!" my mother would shout, whipping me into submission. I would always surrender to it all with a sigh: "Why bother?"

My wife can be quiet, remote, and withdrawn. She denies it and accuses me of being sarcastic, moody, and depressed. "What's wrong?" she asks, feigning concern in a most obvious manner. "Nothing," I answer in an extremely sarcastic, moody, and depressed tone of voice. Why bother?

Sometimes, out of frustration, I would pack my books away, or clean out the basement, or rearrange the furniture. Or I would go upstairs, throw myself on the bed, and exclaim in a well-rehearsed, melodramatic voice, "Why bother?"

I've always been searching for meaning in my life, a sense of purpose. At first I wanted to be an architect but my Lego blocks kept tumbling over.

Then, I thought my purpose was to be creative. I tried my hand at carpentry but I found out that I was not very handy. At six years old, I showed my father my handiwork, using the tool set which he bought me for my birthday. "Look at what I did!" I shouted with pride. The blood drained out of his face when he saw that I sawed the legs off our dining room chairs.

Next, I wanted to be an actor, bestowed with fame and riches, so I joined the drama club at school. But when the school bullies caught me at the stage door and beat the living crap (ew!) out of me, I suspected acting was not my purpose.

Well, maybe a singer. With my voice yet unchanged, my mother bragged to all her friends, "He sounds just like Julie Andrews!" As if that wasn't enough, one of my friends told me I was so off-key that everything I sang sounded like I had invented a whole new melody. Singing, therefore, was not in the cards for me.

Perhaps a scholar. Except I spent most of my studying time daydreaming or trying to figure out how to get out of studying and still pass the exam.

Later, I wanted to be a psychologist but I failed Statistics 333 three years in a row.

Raising four kids kept me too busy with life to think about its purpose, even if it was right under my nose.

Being in Social Services gave me a purpose of sorts—like having somewhere to go every day for thirty-three years—and there were fleeting moments when I did feel useful and that I may have made a difference in some small way. I would, however, not know since most of the time I was quagged and mired in paperwork, regulations, and office politics.

But was my career synonymous with a purpose? It wouldn't be until I retired that perhaps the meaning of my life might be found elsewhere. But where???

"Good morning," Anyone says to me.

"Why bother?" I reply. There is no other response.

GREAT EXPECTATIONS
(my unrealistic brain)

"I never make the same mistake twice,
mainly because I make such a variety of them."

I have great expectations for the world and its inhabitants, including myself.

I expect myself to be nothing less than perfect, a true success story, held in high esteem by everyone, and lead us all into Utopia. I am a goal-setter.

I expect the people around me to think, feel, and behave as I do. Those who are not my clones are expected to simply disappear.

I expect the world to be as I want it to be. As a realist I know there will be floods and famine, earthquakes and fire, poverty and disease. But I expect all of those things to be in someone else's backyard.

With such great expectations, I suppose I should also expect a rude awakening.

I've been told that if I set my expectations too high, I am inviting disappointment and failure. Yet if I lower the bar of expectations, I will be able to aspire only to mediocrity.

I've also been told to hope for the best but expect the worst. Why hope for the best if all I am expecting is the worst? If I hope for the worst then I will have, at the very least, met my expectations each and every time and, at the very best, exceeded them.

I think these are great expectations.

CHASING MY TAIL
(being a failure)

"I took a psychology course at university called 'Deviant Behaviour'. I failed every test but the professor gave me an A+ for practical application."

"I'll probably screw up again, so why bother?" Nine times out of ten I'd used this line to get out of following through on a task. You see, I've failed before so why take the risk? On that one occasion when I did attempt something, I reminded myself of those times when I did not succeed. Setting myself up for failure, I proceeded to fail and vow never to undertake another risk because "I'll probably screw up again, so why bother?"

I've been told that failure is a good thing, not something which one would actually strive for, but good nevertheless. It is something everyone has done at one time or another, so at least I'm not all alone in my world of failure. Nor should I deliberately avoid failure. Failure is nothing to be ashamed of. I've been told that, too. If it were, then everyone would be walking around with his tail between his legs all the time. Believe me, I keep checking.

So, I have tried to learn my lesson about failure. As the headmaster in the school of life, I have been taught that failure is sometimes a strict disciplinarian and other times a benevolent old gentleperson. Failure was supposed to have taught me to be humble, patient, more down-to-earth, more realistic, to do better, to improve, to behave appropriately, examine or change my world view, to persevere, to set goals, to make and implement decisions, to build and maintain character, to strive for excellence through determination, hard work, and effort, to grow, and to learn.

Failure may have been a good teacher, but I was a lousy student.

IF I HAD ONLY ONE WISH I WISH EVERY WISH I WISH WOULD COME TRUE

(Facing reality)

———∿∿∿∿∿∿∿———

*"I have a pretty good idea of who I am,
but I'm still not convinced it isn't some elaborate cruel joke."*

———∿∿∿∿∿∿∿———

I live for bizarre occurrences, inexplicable coincidences, unusual sightings, uplifting music, inspirational thoughts, awesome motivations, and compelling people.

I live in a dull neighbourhood; I have a monochromatic routine; I have had a typical and bland upbringing; I have but a handful of friends, each whose interactions with me seem pre-scripted and always predictable.

That's why I am a *Daydream Believer.*

If ever my expectations remain hidden in the recesses of fantasy, the resourceful me will call upon my ability "to wish" to see me through. I have wished myself in and out of some pretty weird situations, believe you me. "I wish I were rich," says I, and voila! I am rich. "If only she loved me; if only he understood," and suddenly she loves me; suddenly he understands. "Would that the weather behave as I dictate." So it written, so shall it be done! Usually, though, I must cover my ears or squeeze my eyelids shut to prevent the wish from dissipating. And I mustn't move. Or breathe.

I wish wishes would last longer.

HONESTLY!
(Trying to be honest with myself)

———⁓⁓⌾⌾⌾⌾⌾⁓⁓———

"A man comes home from a night of drinking with the boys. As he stumbles through the front door of his house, his wife snaps at him, 'What's the big idea coming home half-drunk?' The man replies, 'I'm sorry, honey.
I ran out of money.'"

———⁓⁓⌾⌾⌾⌾⌾⁓⁓———

Being honest with and about myself was never a comprehensible notion. It rarely is to people who are consistently deluding themselves with falsehoods and untrue facts. The possibility of me having any "negative" or unpleasant characteristics was so unthinkable that I began to dabble in sessions of creative reality, calling upon my well-developed arsenal of resources: defense mechanisms. In time, I recognized myself, others, situations, and the world around me, as something real when in fact we were all products of my own creation. Wants and desires were tamed; goals and objectives were abandoned or altered or postponed or subdued. Sometimes I could come up with as many as eleven excuses for behaving in a particular way. I didn't take the program I actually wanted to take at school because the courses were boring; the program was designed to please my parents; the curriculum provided me with an impossible schedule; the teachers were known to be especially unfair; the program wouldn't provide me with the prestige I was seeking; the program couldn't possibly teach me more than I already know; it was too far to travel to get to the school. If I had been honest with myself, I would have admitted I was merely afraid I might not succeed at something I truly wanted. Consequently, I found the situation easier to deal with by lying to myself, not pursuing my goals and rationalizing my behaviour with some falsehoods and half-truths. Failure, making mistakes, and being rejected were unnecessary evils to me. If I could eliminate them through dishonesty—even to myself—why not?

HOW KIND OF YOU
(lack of consideration and respect)

*"When I fell and broke both my wrists, my wife didn't care. I told her, 'I could be lying in a ditch somewhere, bleeding, and all you'd say is, 'Why are you doing this to me?' She said, 'No, I wouldn't . . . but I **was** wondering if your insurance premiums are paid up.'"*

I was under the assumption that it was human nature to be considerate of others, polite, sensitive, thoughtful, kind, respectful, nurturing, and caring toward our fellow human beings.

Apparently this assumption may not be the case.

- A driver cuts you off and then slows down.
- You're playing a game of "Red Rover" and no one chooses you to be on their team.
- A colleague at work takes credit for something you've devoted your time and energy.
- A teacher picks on you when it's evident by the way you slump in your seat that you don't have the foggiest, but promptly ignores you when you grunt and wave and flap you hand frenetically.
- You do someone a kindness or a favour which is overlooked or berated.
- You entrust someone with a confidence which, within minutes, becomes a community concern.
- You spend a fortune on a ring for your spouse on the occasion of your wedding anniversary, only to hear her exclaim, "How nice, a toy from a Crackerjack box."

- You've worked hard all week, and your kids jump on your bed at five in the morning on your day off.
- Your parents pat you on the back for getting straight A's on your report card, and then offer a word of encouragement to do better next term.
- After fifty years with the company, you are given a pencil with your name engraved on it.
- Your girlfriend is reading your old love letters to her girlfriends, and they are on the floor rolling in hysterics.
- Someone with a three-foot head sits in front of you in an otherwise empty movie theatre.
- Your friends wait until you take your asthma puffers before lighting up.

Admittedly, I am not a statistician and I do not conduct scientific studies. I did, however, try an experiment to determine the frequency with which I encountered people who behaved in an inconsiderate manner. Over the course of two weeks, I experienced one hundred thirty-four such encounters, or an average of 9.5 per day. I am now very wary of assumptions.

WHEN WILL YOU BE READY TO HAVE DONE IT?

(Me? Impatient?)

———————

*"What do you **mean** you haven't got all day? How can you not have all day?"*

———————

"Come on, hurry up!"

"Are we there yet?"

"What took you so long?!"

Patience was never a virtue of mine. I am of the ilk who would arrive an hour early for the sheer pleasure of pointing a finger at those who show up on time in order to accuse them of being late.

Tardiness is a sin and waiting is a punishment. Those individuals who constantly pride themselves on being fashionably late are *un*fashionably rude in *my* book. I consider this to be a personal affront, even though I recognize that lateness knows no religious, ethnic, or socio-economic bounds. My sister always arrives on "Jewish time". A friend of mine from the Islands always shows up on "Jamaican time". If I attend a soiree (and I wonder why I'm not invited so much anymore), I always appear a pointe or sooner, much to the chagrin of the hostess in curlers and terrycloth. A delayed flight, anticipated test results, surprise parties, a doctor's waiting room all drive me to distraction! I cannot walk down a street with my wife at my side; I have to get behind her and push her. Standing in line for anything is forbidden. Five minutes in a room with any one of my in-laws and I'm already nudging my wife that we should make our escape.

I suppose at some point I shall inevitably be required to learn patience. Already I am at an age where time has become fleeting. I'm getting older, slowing down . . .

"Just a minute . . ."

"Hmmm . . . let me see . . ."

"Hey, wait up!"

CHASING AMBULANCES

(Injustice)

"Everything seems to be going well; obviously I have overlooked something."

"It's no fair!" my sister screamed at my parents after I was given a piece of my own birthday cake. "He always gets everything!"

In the name of justice, my piece of cake was immediately taken away and given to my sister. I was given a much smaller piece.

"That's better," she decreed, with a complacent grin.

"It's only fair," my parents capitulated.

I stared at my pittance of a dessert and pondered the injustice of it all, boiling inside until I erupted with an echo of, "It's no fair!"

My mother's face clouded with a philosophical front and exclaimed, "Whoever said life was fair?"

I guess she was right. Life wasn't fair and anyone who says it should be is living in la-la land. Broken promises, unrealized dreams, unfulfilled desires. This was more the stuff my life was made of.

YOU THINK *YOU* GOT PROBLEMS?!

(Being overwhelmed by problems)

A sign in my doctor's office: "I can please only one person per day. Today is not your day. Tomorrow isn't looking good either."

My wife hates the word 'problems'. In fact, she insists it doesn't exist. People have concerns or issues. In her brain, made of spaghetti, problems of any kind are negative, evil, and unmanageable. Concerns or issues she can work with.

Whatever the situation, no matter how large or small, my family would go into crisis mode, panicking about every single concern or issue. "Oh, no! Come look! A hangnail!" My parents would call my sister over and all of them would study my inflamed finger with shock and awe. A bruised knee would incite my grandparents to join in the congregation—their eyes would bore down on me, one eye full of sympathy, the other full of accusation and suspicion. A failing grade would set them all into a tailspin, not knowing whether to share the misery that had befallen them with the rest of the world or whether to keep their shame to themselves.

I learned some lessons as I wandered down the paths of my life, collecting problems—yes, problems—and putting them in my pocket. I realized that my problems became incorporated into the very essence of my life, to the point where I could not imagine what my life would be like without them. I suppose I was hoping for the sympathy and attention I received for my problems when I was younger. Besides, who would I be without my problems? How would I identify myself without them? What would I do with my life without problems to solve? How could I live without obstacles to overcome? Who would I be without great suffering and oppression?

I frequently checked my pockets to make sure my problems were still there. After all, there was a comforting sense of security knowing my pockets were full, knowing what it meant and knowing what to expect, even if it was all to my detriment. I spent a significant amount of time sharing my problematic stories with others, pulling my problems out of my pockets if only to hear piteous exclamations or commiserations. I was proud of my pocketful of problems; they made me feel special for having them, made me feel pleased with how heavy they felt, satisfied with how long I was able to hold onto them, rewarded by their novelty, even fulfilled by being able to put up with them.

I remember walking down the street, my pocketful of problems filled and swollen, when I passed by a little old lady toting a huge, bulging satchel over her bent shoulder. She looked at my stuffed pockets and emptied her satchel on the sidewalk right in front of me.

"Sonny," she said, "you think *you* got problems?!"

I'M DYING TO TELL YOU . . .

(Ruminating on death and dying)

———————

"I intend to live forever. So far so good."

"Live each day like it's your last; one day you'll be right!"

———————

I've always been scared to death of Death.

When I was just a little nubbin I used to lie awake at night and pretend to be dead, systematically shutting off my senses. I'd close my eyes, imagining I couldn't hear anything, lying still and holding my breath. Before turning blue I would envision maggots and beetles crawling in through my eye sockets and out through my nostrils and gaping mouth. In just moments, I'd scare myself silly and gasp for air. Sometimes I would pretend to be dead in a passive-aggressive attempt to 'show them', as in, "Oh, yeah? Well, I'll show *you!*"

I did not know anyone personally who had died until I was eighteen. My eighty-four-year-old grandfather had a massive heart attack and died. As I got older more people I knew passed away. The notion of Death produced a wild race of many emotions (including a fear of scythes), although being scared to death (ironically) won hands down every time.

Is it the pain associated with dying? The illness or the injury itself? Is it the concept of no longer being a life participant while the rest of the world carries on? Is it not knowing when it will happen? At a party? On the toilet? At work? During sex? On vacation? While driving? Morning, noon or night? After a lengthy illness? After a car crash? At what age: infancy, senility, or somewhere in between? Is it the thought of an afterlife or the possibility of no afterlife? I mean, a white light is all very well and good, but can it be endured for eternity? Maybe it can if the only other option is a black nothingness. Or a world of angels and devils playing tricks on one another.

Perhaps it is the fact that knowing Death is inevitable, waiting there for me, rattling in sync with the tick-tocking of the kitchen clock.

Of late I have taken to ardently following the daily obituaries just to make sure I didn't make the list.

Maybe I'm not only scared to death of Death. Maybe I'm also scared to death of Life.

FACT OR OPINION?

(What is truth?)

———∿∘୧୧∘∿———

"You see those people over there? I know what they're talking about.
They're saying that I'm paranoid."

———∿∘୧୧∘∿———

"I got ninety-nine per cent on my history test," Elizabeth boasted. "Did you pass?"

"I hate you, you big-eared fairy!" my sister exclaimed.

"You'll never amount to anything," my gym teacher counselled.

My father sighed with exasperation. "Why can't you do the right things at the right times?"

"You're wrong," my employer stated. "My way is better."

Across the street a group of kids were whispering and pointing at me and laughing.

"The moon is made of green cheese," asserted the man behind the bars of the asylum window.

They were right, of course, all of them. I was convinced their opinions were, in fact, facts. The meaning of perception eluded me. Consequently I *was* stupid, ugly, useless, inadequate, incompetent, and naive. And that's a fact.

IF A TREE FALLS IN THE FOREST . . .

(What is really real and what am I perceiving to be real?)

"Truth is stranger than fiction; fiction has to make sense."

I remember a visit to the Art Gallery of Ontario quite vividly. There was an exhibit by some obscure artist (obscure, famous, did I know the difference?) over which a young preppie couple were gushing with praise.

"Note the timelessness, the spatial dimension!" squealed the young woman.

"The intentional lack of definition is striking!" exclaimed her fellow.

"I'm certain the lack of framing was intentional, too!"

"Obviously intentional. It's central to the theme!" I opined.

They turned to look at me and curled their lips in piteous contempt, then returned to the canvass.

``Look! Look in the corner! That white dot!" I shouted from behind them.

They gasped in unison.

"Insignificance!" she said.

"Desolation!" he said.

"Cosmic oneness!" they said.

"Lint!" I said, and reached between them to pick off the fluff ball.

They looked at each other fleetingly and hurried off. Too bad they didn't stick around to watch the gallery curator remove the black canvass to reveal a pastoral painting in oils.

I tried to make sense of it. Is reality defined by the way in which our senses perceive it? Or is it something beyond our senses? It seems that often the individual perception one experiences is compatible with the perception of others. Grass is green, roses smell pretty, and a slap upside the head hurts. Our perceptions are modified by a number of variables and perhaps an assortment of combinations of these variables: mood, attitude, health, environmental influences, past experiences, interference from others, acquired knowledge, experience of the current reality, etc. A bouquet of flowers may be perceived as a pretty, fragrant object by one person, a kind gesture by another person, a funeral by still another, a sneezing attack by yet another.

Conveying one's perceptions seems to create a-whole-nother set of issues, a whole new kettle of wax, ball of fish. How perceptions are communicated takes into account not only the variables but also the communication of the perception, including who, what, how, when, where, why, *and* all the previously mentioned variables. No wonder life is filled with misperceptions! Actually, I believe the word "misperception" is a misnomer; it is an incompatible interpretation of the communication of the perception with which life is replete. There, that's better.

I told my sister she has a nice nose. She told me to go to hell.

It really is a nice nose: straight, narrow, aquiline, unblemished, and in proportion with the rest of her face. So, like, what's her problem, man?!

I decided to analyze the situation. I was in a good mood, almost giddy, but compassionate when I made the comment. My sister was always sensitive about her nose—why, I don't know. A nose is really no big deal to *me* as long as I can breathe through it and as long as it remains attached to the centre of my face. Essentially we did not perceive noses—at least, *her* nose—in the same way. And what were the communication issues? Well, we have rarely (if ever) exchanged compliments. I felt I wanted to kindle my affection for my sister by offering and innocuous yet sincere compliment. Oh, yes. We were at a family wedding surrounded by pretentious cousins who were aware of my sister's nose thing from when we were younger. And I guess I *was* a little tipsy from the wine, which may have made my voice a bit loud. And one cousin did make a sarcastic remark about the bride's wedding dress as being "nice"—the same word I used to describe my sister's nose. And my sister did have a cold which made her nose red and a bit swollen from blowing it all night.

Well there you go! Our interpretations of each of the communications of the perception were incompatible! No wonder she told me to go to hell.

Bitch!

(Analyze *that* one!)

Self-perception seems to work in much the same way and with the same variables. The outcome of a job interview will vary depending on whether you see yourself as one who is stimulated by new challenges or as one who is a failure at everything. I, of course, make it perfectly clear at an interview that I am a failure at everything. There is no misperception.

THANKFUL I'M NOT SOPHIE

(Making choices and implementing decisions)

———∿∿∘⟨⟩⟨⟩∿∘∘∿∿———

"I used to think I was indecisive. Now I'm not so sure."

"It's not that I can't decide; I'm just keeping my options flexible."

———∿∿∘⟨⟩⟨⟩∘∘∿∿———

"Well, Mr. President, do we go to war or not?"

"I wonder if I should become a general labourer or an accountant when I grow up? Maybe a rocket scientist!?"

"Hmm . . . should I wear briefs or boxers?"

We all have choices to make throughout our lifetime, each choice paving the way for some type of consequence.

"I *had* to! I had no choice!" I would tell myself.

Unlikely.

I always had a choice, with very few exceptions: the givens with which I was born (even with some of these there is choice), outside forces that are beyond the boundaries of my control, or being crazy (although some may debate this too is a choice).

Usually people say they had no choice to save face or to cover up an unpleasant consequence of the choice they made. I know I did.

'Selecting choices' is another way of saying 'making and implementing decisions'.

What often got me in trouble was how I made my decisions. I tended to make my decisions as a direct result of an emotional response. The problem is, feelings aren't too smart, clever, or wise, nor are they

Life Is a Metaphor

based on values or morals, therefore the decisions I made were often foolish or in conflict with my value system or both.

The guy who thinks with his little head rather than with his big head is not really thinking at all. He is just horny. If he makes a decision based on his state of arousal (an emotional response manifesting itself in a physical way) he risks the probability of suffering an unhappy consequence: rejection, guilt, disease, a bundle of joy, etc.

The young lady who decides to marry at age eighteen some guy she barely knows because she is insecure, or doesn't want to grow old alone, or is submitting to her parents' expectations, or peer pressure, or the desire to be taken care of, is making a major choice in life based on her feelings without giving consideration to what her brain has to say or what she really values in life. Trouble lies ahead.

And what about the little kid who wants to sing and dance his way through life only to be told by his parents he won't amount to anything and then enters a profession just to make them happy, sacrificing his lifelong dream and personal happiness, only to go through the motions day after dreary day, thinking "What if . . . ? What if . . . ?"

I'm just saying.

Some of us don't make decisions because the fear of the consequence is more powerful than the consequence itself. Others of us make hundreds of decisions but never implement them for the same reason. What I've experienced and learned is that not choosing is also a choice and has consequences of its own.

Choice had always been a mysterious phenomenon to me. When I was a young'un I used to wonder what would happen if each choice I made was different. The ways in which my life would have changed, even for the slightest alteration in even the most seemingly insignificant choice, is almost incomprehensible. Had I opted to wear my brand new silver satin turtleneck 'Lost in Space' shirt on my first day at school, I would have had some tortuous years ahead of me. Had I hesitated to assist a fellow camper who had fallen from the monkey bars, I might have missed out on a lifelong friendship. Had I decided not to go to a friend's birthday party I likely would not have met my wife, had four kids and my life would be totally different today. Had I chosen to leave for work five minutes later one stormy winter morning ten years ago, I would have been involved in a forty-six car pile-up and maybe not have survived. Had I selected the melba toast instead of the cappuccino cheesecake with praline topping and whipped cream for dessert, I might be in a preferred state of health today. The possibilities are endless.

The bottom line? Regardless of what or if I chose, a consequence was inevitable. In an effort to experience a pleasant or positive consequence, I needed to make an intelligent, value-based choice. But that was a lesson to be learned much later.

It's a choice.

RIGHT ON!

(Being right)

"My wife has confidence because she thinks she is always right. I have no confidence at all because I am too scared of being wrong."

"One good thing about being wrong is the joy it brings to others."

Growing up in a world where no one was interested in listening to my opinions was difficult, in my opinion. I remember some of my loud-mouthed relatives giving voice to their inane, sometimes insane, thoughts. Often the more they insisted their opinions were right, the louder their voices became which, in turn, fostered their belief in the 'rightness' of their opinions.

"*This* is how you do it!" Uncle Harry screamed at me when I let a customer leave the store without making a purchase. I was working for him as a summer salesman (a favour to my mother) in men's haberdashery. He chased the customer back into the store and sold him a billowy, clownish shirt along with a fedora three sizes too big. "It looks wonderful! A perfect fit!" Uncle Harry proclaimed. "I have been in this business thirty years and I know what I'm talking about!" He turned to me and said, "I'm right! Am I right? Huh? I'm *right*! Hmmph!" I nodded sheepishly, thinking the customer looked like an advertisement for a men's shelter, but what did I know? Uncle Harry was right. He told me so.

Once (and only once), I expressed my opinion to my Auntie Goldie that berating my father for giving me a hug was unkind and uncalled for. Once (and not only once) Auntie Goldie said, "Your father acts like an old woman. And you're an idiot! Listen, I've lived with him twice as long as you've been alive so I know what I'm talking about." My opinion made me an idiot and Auntie Goldie's opinion was right.

As I got older I decided that if I were to be heard I'd have to speak up, speak loudly, and insist that I'm right.

"Churchill is in northern Ontario!" I shouted affirmatively in a geographical debate with my friend Jean-Guy. "Uh-uh, it's in Manitoba." We went on like this for awhile, my voice getting louder and more aggressive, until he finally pulled out an atlas. Churchill was, indeed, in Manitoba.

I learned that there is a difference between fact and opinion, the latter being merely a point of view. In other words, an opinion is neither right nor wrong; it is just an opinion. I also learned that to be right, to insist on being right, to insist that an opinion could be right (or wrong, for that matter) was to insist on being a jerk.

Over the years I have come across a number of people who insist their opinion is the right one, the only one. What I didn't realize at the time was that this was more of a statement about them than about me. What was so wrong with having an opinion of my own, even if some people didn't think it was 'right'? Did it make me wrong? Inept? Stupid? Inferior? If I didn't agree that someone's opinion was right and s/he became angry or elusive or dismissive, wouldn't that make them arrogant? Argumentative? Narrow-minded? Unreasonable? If I insisted that my opinion was right, wouldn't that be turning away from possibilities, preventing myself from growing and learning? From expanding my knowledge and creativity?

Yup.

My wife was furious with me one day when I was cleaning the bathroom mirror. "You have to go from side to side, not up and down! You can't get the mirror clean your way!" I was about to argue with her (our favourite pastime) and tell her that wiping the cloth up and down the mirror will get it clean just as well as swiping it side to side. But I thought to myself, would I rather be right or be happy (and argument-free)? I kept quiet and wiped the mirror from side to side. It got the mirror equally clean (although I did have more to wipe with the residue dripping to the bottom of the mirror). "I told you so," she said, smiling smugly.

I am reminded: Happy wife, happy life.

I could have marketed the motto "Would you rather be right or happy?" but some TV guy beat me to it.

DEFREUDING MYSELF

(Focusing on problems too much)

"The advantage of having major depression is that you don't have to make your bed . . . because you're always lying in it."

There should be a law against too much self-analysis. Nothing major but at least a misdemeanour. A small fine and an electro-convulsive shock, perhaps. It's one thing not to assume responsibility for yourself, but quite another thing to accept blame for something that is not your fault. Often too much indulgence in self-analysis will lead to this and before too long you begin to believe that it's true.

I recall having studied a university course called *Deviant Behaviour*. With each new psychological illness discussed, I was convinced I had it. After all, I had all the symptoms: antisocial neurotic with obsessive-compulsive tendencies one day, cyclothymic paranoid schizophrenic the next. If I didn't have the symptoms at the time of the lecture I'd be sure to develop them by the following day.

I discovered it is important to be aware of who you are, of your thoughts, feelings and behaviour, but only in moderation. Analyzing your every thought, movement, feeling, and action can be criminal and, if carried to the extreme, lethal. Or it can make you want to write a self-help book.

FEELINGS

I was a cauldron of bubbling emotions, marinating in my own emotional juices, stewing in my own emotional pot of stew. All of those thoughts I had had elicited feelings, which led me to ponder:

1) What are feelings? And,
2) Where do feelings come from?

Back to researching, the dictionary defines a feeling as an emotional state of reaction. So what does the dictionary have to say about emotion? A feeling, of course! I was feeling frustrated!

Other descriptions? Feelings are:

- A release of chemicals in the brain in response to a thought and the brain's interpretation of those chemicals and what to do with them
- A divine intervention and a spiritual guide
- Designed to respond to our survival instinct
- Provide the affective component to motivation which directs behaviour
- Complex psycho-physiological experiences of an individual's state of mind (thought) based on biochemical (internal) and environmental (external) influences

Feelings can be perceived to have positive or negative attributes but, essentially, they just are.

Some feelings last only a few seconds and some last a lifetime.

Feelings can have varying degrees of intensity.

Feelings can be instinctual and intuitive (i.e. gut feelings) or based in awareness and realization (i.e. conscious feelings).

Feelings are the fulfillment, gain, or expansiveness (positive) or the unfulfillment, loss, or contractedness (negative) of a need, craving, or desire.

Feelings are an emotional barometer which measures our thoughts and helps us to set a course for our behaviour.

So I took all of these explanations and observations and threw them into my cauldron.

The next question that came to mind was: what can we do with a feeling when we have one? Well, we can express them or suppress them. We can hold onto them or let go of them. Regarding expression, there are some human physiological responses to what we feel, depending on the nature of the emotion. When we feel sadness, we might cry; when we feel love, we might embrace; when we feel anger, we might yell; when we feel pride, we might boast; when we feel lust, we might . . . well, you get the picture. Regarding suppression, this is akin to pushing down on or hiding a feeling so that the response to the feeling is withheld. Sometimes, it all just blows up in our face.

Both holding onto and letting go of a feeling can be beneficial or destructive, depending on the nature of the feeling and the resultant response or behaviour.

Eventually I needed to see if I would embrace my feelings and actually feel them, be in the moment with them without immediately acting on them. But more of that later.

So, what were my feelings with respect to my Starting Point? Glad you asked. Here are some of them . . .

PORTRAIT OF A TRULY MISERABLE PERSON
(Depression)

"Why did the depressed person cross the road? Who cares?"

*"My doctor just prescribed for me a dose of anti-depressants . . .
which I'm not happy about."*

"Depression is merely anger without enthusiasm."

There was a time a few decades back when I kept a record of my thoughts, feelings, and behaviour. Reflective of my starting point, the following is an excerpt of those records:

"December 31.

It's show time, folks!

My most bitter New Year's Eve ever! And I am obliged to feign polite repartee with my wife, my kids, perhaps a couple of friends. How exciting.

No pot to piss in; I'm a financial failure. Tried to paint the kitchen but did an A-1 shit job. I am so inadequate. No friends to speak of with whom I can or would want to spend New Year's Eve; I am an antisocial misfit. I am nothing . . . perhaps, at the very least, I have answered that haunting question: "But do we really exist?"

My wife calls me "Mister Depression Riding In From Hell". I would say that is an accurate description.

My world is becoming smaller and smaller. More fragmented. I cannot even think in complete sentences anymore. I cannot complete my thoughts. I cannot remember my thoughts and when I dare to utter one of my incomplete sentences, it is meaningless because I have lost my train of thought.

I open the blinds in the morning and close them at sunset. My world revolves around this activity. This is all that remains important. The rest is just filler.

I do not feel alive. I am a wretched member of the cast in Dante's Limbo. The world and its inhabitants change, and I remain, unchanging. There is movement and feeling and hope and faith but not where I am. The real hellish part is that my personal Limbo is surrounded by a soundproof room with a one-way mirror. I can look out onto the world and watch it go by but 'they' cannot look in. Nobody even knows I am here. Beyond the cackle are echoes of "Scream all you want and there is no one to hear!" On the outside, beyond the walls of my prison, time marches on and I cannot stop it. Or join it. Hope flickers dimly in these darkening days."

WONDERIN' WHERE THE LIONS ARE
(Fear)

———◦◦◦◦◦◦◦———

*"I have social anxiety and, believe me, it's not easy to deal with.
Even during sex I'm scared stiff!"*

———◦◦◦◦◦◦◦———

It is good to be afraid. Sometimes.

If a lion is chasing you down the street and you are not afraid, you have a problem.

If you think a lion might be chasing you down the street but there is actually no lion present, you also have a problem.

It is the latter neurotic fear which dominated my psyche. Not about lions, but in general. I was scared of everything, most of which was created by my ever-active imagination (although I didn't know it at the time).

If awards were given out for fear, I would be the recipient of the top three:

Third place goes to *me* for (drum roll) . . . Fear of the Ways of the World. I was both fascinated and fearful of natural disasters and was convinced that the next tornado, earthquake, volcano, or deluge was going to happen on the street where I lived. In the late sixties I was mortified at the thought of Canada being absorbed by the U.S.A. because I would be drafted into the army, sent far away from home, shot, stabbed, and blown to bits. I dreaded illness, injury, hospitals, bugs, heights, and depths. I was scared into numbness at the concept of death (a running theme, you may have gathered), wondering, at a tender age, how the world would survive without me and why life, as brief as it is, ever existed in the first place if only to be ended.

Second place goes to *me* for (drum roll) . . . Fear of Rejection. I always had a hard time developing relationships because, well, why would anybody want to be friends with *me*? I would not get involved yet longing to be involved, not disclose information about myself though eager to tell people all about me, not approach anyone but wanting to be approached. Had I participated, had I shared, and had I been assertive, I was convinced I would be shunned, ridiculed, and ostracized. So I didn't do anything. People thought I was a snob and was consequently not asked to join, not asked about, and not approached.

First place, highest honour in all of Neuroticland, goes to *me* for (drum roll) . . . Fear of Failure. I spent a lot of my time, while growing up, figuring out how to get out of doing things. I knew I would fail at whatever I tried and, consequently, I tried very little. I perceived failure to be a personal weakness which I would not take responsibility for; if I tried to do anything, anything at all, I believed people would think I was useless, inadequate, stupid, lazy, and nerdy. I would come up with an excuse for getting out of gym class usually by blowing my nose so hard it would bleed. I once refused to compete in an elementary school spelling contest (even though I was a spelling genius) by claiming to have amnesia, going so far as to bang my head on a table top. At university I sometimes skipped classes, including the ones I was really interested in, as a precaution; just in case I failed the course, I could justify it by not having attended the lectures. But . . . no fear!

I would certainly have failed as an investigator. Had I explored my issues with any degree of competence, I would have realized there was no hard evidence, nothing at all concrete upon which to base most of my fears.

Instead I found myself running from the lions.

BURSTING APPROPRIATELY
(Anger)

"A word of advice: never go to bed angry. Stay awake and plot your revenge."

I collected anger as a hobby. I was an anger addict. I went around all day long gathering bits of anger from here and there and at the end of the day when I was filled to bursting with anger, well, I burst! A sarcastic remark to my wife, a little guilt thrown (in return) at my folks.

If you must burst, it's always easier to burst in front of a loved one; you already know what they think of you (in most cases) and they are easy marks because you know (in most cases) which buttons to push. I would always burst in front of a loved one: it was quicker, safer, and easier than bursting in front of a stranger.

Being angry in front of a stranger made me mad. I didn't burst very well. The knot in my stomach would tighten, I would sweat like a pig, and my blood would boil like mercury rising in a thermometer. When I opened my mouth to speak, I would squeak. Or a relevant statement would get swallowed in an embarrassing gulp. Or I would lose my train of thought which, of course, made me all the angrier.

I never quite learned how to burst appropriately.

"RODERIGO, SAVE ME!"

(Hopelessness, helplessness, and vulnerability)

*"I had gall bladder surgery last year, and the scars on my belly
look like a happy face. It's not that I'm paranoid,
but even my stomach is mocking me!"*

Too often, I imagined myself in a silent movie cast in the dual role as victim and rescuer. There I am, a fair maiden tied to the railroad track, watching in horror as the big black locomotive chugs closer and closer. A sense of dread and hopelessness overcomes me. And there, stepping into the frame, I appear, the dashing young hero. I pull and tug at the binding rope but to no avail. I put up my hands to signal to the conductor to put on the brakes, but he toots the whistle to warn us off the track. Unable to rescue the maiden, I feel utterly helpless. Time for our close-ups, Mr. DeMille. But the only close-up is of the approaching train. "Cut!" I scream in unison, but the train pushes ever forward. No one can hear either of me; it is a silent movie, after all.

Hopeless victim. Helpless rescuer.

Maybe it was the myriad do's and don't's of childhood (it's so easy to blame the parents until *you* become one and your kids start blaming *you*). You catch your folks fighting but there is nothing you can do to fix it. You stick something up your nose and it won't come out—all you can do is cry. You want to stay up past your bedtime like all your friends but Mom and Pop say no. Or Pop says yes and Mom says no; they start fighting and make you feel helpless all over again.

These feelings of hopelessness and helplessness generally culminate in a prevailing sense of vulnerability which, as a child, is an adorable quality to exude (unless the child knows that s/he is being vulnerable in which case the vulnerability becomes both precocious and obnoxious). As an adult, however, being vulnerable is usually interpreted as being gutless and pathetic.

I, of course, was the exception to the rule. As a child, it was pointed out to me on several occasions that I was gutless and pathetic. Forever destined to watch the reruns of my silent movie.

WALLOWING
(Self-Pity)

———~~∿∽∾⟨∾∿~~———

*"For the holidays, I didn't know what gift to get my
kids . . . so I gave them each a neurosis."*

———~~∽∿∾⟨∾∿~~———

There was a purpose to being the King of Martyrdom, but the purpose
eludes me now. That is the tribulation of being King. King of Anything!
You become so adept at doing Kingly things or just being King that you
tend to lose sight of the initial reason for being or doing. Being the King
of Martyrdom is a wearisome task, denying yourself this, surrendering
that. Ensuring you out-martyr everyone who is trying to overthrow
you. And all for what? A few good minutes of wallowing, that's what.
Don't get me wrong; I enjoy a good wallow as much as the next fella.
But in the end, what's it all for? I self-deny and self-pity and self-deny
and self-pity, more and more, again and again, and then . . . bang!
I wallow. When it's over I just feel like rolling over and smoking a
cigarette . . . hardly becoming for a King. After wallowing I feel so dirty
and cheap. There is only one thing I can do to redeem myself: self-deny
and self-pity once again.

You dare to question the motives of a King (I suppose I should
address the issue of delusions of grandeur)?

HOW DOES PAUL ANKA KNOW *ME?*
(Loneliness)

"I'm so lonely that I sometimes go to the airport and yell,
"Bomb!" just to get frisked."

"I know I'm at the top of the world . . . because it's lonely at the top."

"I'm just a lonely boy . . ."

There I was sitting in the living room with my nose pressed up against the window pane watching all my friends, the rest of the neighbourhood kids playing road hockey, tag, dodge ball. My mom was lying in bed with depression and a migraine and my dad asked me to keep an eye on her while he was at work. How I despised my parents and resented my friends for my loneliness.

". . . Lonely and blue . . ."

There is a deep, penetrating pain which accompanies loneliness. A perpetual yearning. A feeling of not belonging and total isolation. It almost makes you want to sing a torch song: "Wanting You", or "My Man". Or it makes you want to sing the blues, something to do with misery and the muddy Mississippi. Or maybe a country and western tune: "My Heart Is As Broke As My '52 Chevy And That Ain't No Joke".

". . . I'm all alone . . ."

For years I could not differentiate between being alone and being lonely. It made sense to me that if you were alone you were lonely. I hated being alone. But I also hated being in the company of others, especially at parties or large gatherings. I felt alone in my anonymity. I envied the life of the party. I would stand in the corner by myself. Or I would run away. Which made me feel even more lonely. I finally realized that in order to like being alone I would have to learn to enjoy my own company. Running away didn't help because, as the saying goes, wherever I went there I was. Being alone was being without others.

". . . With nothing to do."

Loneliness begat depression, boredom, apathy, self-pity and a heavy, pervasive sadness that completed the cycle which was my loneliness. Being lonely was being alone inside myself.

Yet, how lonely could I really have been with a song written about me?

MICROCOSMIC ME
(Feeling insignificant)

*"The label on my bottle of cough syrup says that it will make my coughs 'more productive'. If only it could make **me** more productive."*

Dramatis Personae: me and anyone else
Scene: anywhere

ANYONE: (looking everywhere but at me) So how have you been?

ME: Oh, I'm—

ANYONE: Good! Well, I've been so busy lately. First there's work. Fifty-hour weeks. Then there are the kids. And I've just begun night classes. And the dog has diarrhea. And the divorce. And so much more. But first tell me all about *you*.

ME: Well, I—

ANYONE: Oh, that's wonderful! Did you hear about Alice and Ralph? He sure has nerve. Mind you if I were married to her, who knows? I might have done the same thing. Wouldn't you?

ME: I didn't—

ANYONE: Well of course you didn't! Who did? But that's the fun of it all. The challenge. The secrets. Me, I have no secrets. Busy with work and the kids and school and everything else it's no wonder I have no secrets. My life is an open book. But tell me all about *you*.

ME: To begin with—

ANYONE: Oh, what time is it? If I don't make it to the bank I'm in big trouble! I tell you, these bills keep pouring in, more and more, every day. It's been non-stop since the divorce . . . No! I don't want to talk about it! Never mind that at the end I'm left with absolutely nothing!

ME: I'm sorry you—

ANYONE: Sorry?! He doesn't know what sorry is! Wait until I'm back in court. Then that creep will pay. Through the nose! Speaking of which I had the worst nose bleed yesterday. I guess I'll have to go to the doctor . . . Life . . . what's it all about?

ME: I've asked myself that very same—

ANYONE: Hmm . . . I wonder if there will be a full moon tonight?

ON BEING INVISIBLE

(Feeling invisible)

"Some days I feel like a pigeon but most days I feel like the statue."

When I was twelve I remember wrapping myself in toilet paper. No one ever paid attention to me or took me seriously. I thought I was invisible and this would be the only way people would know I existed. Unfortunately, they didn't think I existed. They thought I was some kind of lunatic. I knew for sure I was invisible at age fourteen when I tried out a new "Knock knock" joke and nobody bothered to ask who was there. Aside from being teased occasionally, I went unnoticed, ignored, talked over, and forgotten. My mother once told me the story of the time I was two years old. I could have endured serious injuries when I was placed in my car seat on the roof of the car while my folks loaded groceries into the back seat. It wasn't until the engine started that my mother remembered I was still on top of the car. I also remember, in later years, being pushed aside by some people, deserted by others. Today, as an adult, I could make faces, rude noises, or walk down the street naked and wouldn't matter. I could draw a masterpiece, philosophize like Plato, or solve the mysteries of the universe and it still wouldn't matter.

I am invisible.

GOOD GRIEF!
(Grief)

"And now a word about the dear departed.
I was devastated at age twenty-five when I lost my poor . . . hair!"

Oh, how I mourned the loss of Humpty Dumpty! I remember watching that black-and-white cartoon, the jovial Mr. Dumpty perched high on a wall, laughing with delight one moment and then—splat! I shrieked in horror at the incident; then I sobbed uncontrollably when I realized how ineffectual all the King's horses and all the King's men really were: they couldn't put him back together again! I fell into despair. I felt abandoned, heartbroken, helpless! He was a good egg.

I carried grief with me throughout my life, watching childhood friends move out of the neighbourhood, experiencing my youth slip away, mad with remorse and melancholy at the changing dynamics of my family after my son's accident, inconsolable at the illnesses and numb with the deaths of my mother and father.

In each of these incidents all I could think of was how much I hurt. Why me? Won't anybody help me? Make the pain go away!

To this day, I still have a tearful eye as I swallow my omelette.

THAT'S MY BOY!
(Pride)

⸺⁂⸻⁂⸻

"I always try to be modest . . . and I'm damn proud of it!"

⸺⁂⸻⁂⸻

Feeling proud was always very confusing to me. On one hand, it was considered a cardinal sin, and on the other hand, my parents would occasionally say, "I'm proud of you, son" as if it were a good thing. Did my folks *want* me to sin?

There were times where I ruminated about a painting I had done well, a test I had aced, a ball I could bat beyond the infield (beyond my toes, actually), that fact that I could cross my legs in yoga fashion and walk across the room whilst balanced upon my knees. I felt good about these accomplishments. I felt proud. Would I be condemned to eternal damnation?

Some years down the line I came to understand what the problem was: dwelling on the feeling, immersing myself in pride, basking in the moment and the many moments that followed, coupled with getting others to notice and acknowledge my accomplishments, created a little monster within myself—cocky, arrogant, boastful, haughty, judgmental, self-righteous, self-absorbed, patronizing, overbearing, stuck-up, and generally obnoxious. This led to alienation and more isolation. I was not who or how or where I wanted to be. I needed to change . . . somehow.

No more peacock feathers for *me*, I thought, as I preened in front of the bathroom mirror.

"WANTIN' AIN'T GETTIN'"
(Lust)

"I don't have as much stamina as I used to.
The only way I get to be a dirty old man is by forgetting to use soap."

I was a little kleptomaniac, all but three years old, being pushed about in the shopping cart and grabbing things off the shelf. "Mine!" I declared, reaching over and taking hold of cookies, Mr. Clean, a can of tuna, an eggplant, and a package of Trojans.

A few years later, adolescence overcame me and, in my prurient pursuits, I saw something shapely, imagined illicit interludes, and fantasized with frenetic frustration, all the while declaring, "Mine!"

It was what I did not have that I thought I wanted. Yet whenever I attained any of it I never felt satisfied or even enjoyed what I did have, thereby always wanting more and more.

Wanting is tantamount to not having. My problem was that I was focusing on what I didn't have and the struggle I felt in getting what I didn't have that kept me driven, fixated, obsessed, and compelled. Moreover, I realized I rarely wanted what I could have and had and burning desire for what was beyond my grasp.

PRESENT OF MIND
(Guilt and Worry)

"I'm shy from head to toe. Even my bladder suffers from social anxiety!"

"A clear conscience is usually a sign of a bad memory."

I have spent much of my time in two non-existent worlds: the past and the future. Both are like walking in quicksand; the 'should have been's' and the 'what if's' swallow you up if you stay too long. The former is the domain of Guilt, which roams the land of Regrets. "I should have done something." "I shouldn't have said those terrible things." "I should have known better." Dwelling on the past had been my claim to fame and my claim to Guilt.

The latter world of the future gives birth to Worry. "What if I don't pass my exam?" "What if they got into an accident?" "What if it rains tomorrow?"

Sometimes my anxiety level was so high because of guilt or worry that I would have a panic attack (a modern-day term which replaces the traditional technical term, *freak-out*).

At any rate, with tomorrow yet to come and yesterday alive in memory, who had time to deal with today?

"TRUST ME, BABY!"
(Mistrust, Insincerity, and Betrayal)

———∿∿∿∿∿∿———

"I always try to be sincere . . . even if I don't mean it."

———∿∿∿∿∿∿———

My rule is that the last person in the world I would trust is someone who says, "Trust me." He probably has a yellow plaid sport coat and a gallon of product in his hair.

Trusting someone speaks volumes to that relationship which is why trust is such an important character trait.

It is not the act of trust that creates difficulties, but knowing what and whom to trust and the motive for trusting that person.

Sometimes an individual is entrusted to personal or private information. Other times someone is entrusted to take action on one's behalf. Either way, one's vulnerability is deliberately exposed, surrendering oneself to his or her mercy. This is why it is necessary to match what is being entrusted with the right person while fully understanding why this is being done. If the wrong person is chosen, the stage is set for insincerity, betrayal, embarrassment, and danger; if trust is given for the wrong reasons, there will likely be disappointment, frustration, anger, rejection, or failure.

I remember having completed my portion of a grade ten social studies assignment. The balance of the work was to have been completed by my project partner and handed in. She assured me she would do her part and I trusted her. The following week we got back the results: a big fat F. Not only did she not complete her portion of the assignment, but she failed to hand in my work as well. When I confronted her she merely shrugged with indifference.

I remember entrusting my kids to a babysitter of good repute for a couple of hours while my wife and I went to a movie. Pulling up in the driveway on our return, we heard howls and sobs coming from the house. My infant daughter was lying on the floor, her face red and knotted from the tears and the pain. It happened that the sitter was changing the baby's diaper and somehow managed to allow her to roll off the change table and fall to the floor. I discovered this had occurred more than an hour prior to our return. Not only did the babysitter ignore our question of why she did nothing when the baby fell, but was outraged at the fact that we did not tip her.

I remember as a randy teenager expressing my interest in someone to a person whom I thought was a trustworthy friend. Not more than a day after I shared this information, clearly in confidence, the object of my affection approached me to say, "Ew, you're gross! Don't ever come near me again!" Not only was my confidence betrayed but my thoughts and feelings were obviously embellished upon and distorted by my so-called friend.

I remember, when I was young and foolish (now I'm old and foolish), telling an acquaintance a family secret so he would like me and want to be my friend. After our first disagreement about something or other, the friend let the cat out of the bag in front of my other friends; this ended my relationship with that person. There was a double lesson to be learned from this one because not only was I betrayed, but I was also a betrayer for having told this individual the family secret in the first place.

I'm not suggesting not trusting anyone with anything for any reason. That would likely lead to loneliness, alienation, suspicion, bitterness and a host of other thoughts, feelings and behaviours which would sour if not destroy relationships. But I learned that it is imperative that what, with whom, and why I was engaging in a trust is fully explored and understood before I acted on it.

I SEEM TO HAVE
LODGED MY FOOT IN MY THROAT

(Embarrassment and Shame)

"I think I have a foot fetish . . . I'm always putting it in my mouth."

As a natural blond, like most natural blonds, I do not have the capacity to conceal my sense of embarrassment or shame, from a sanguine crimson to the slightest hint of a sparkling rosé. There are few feelings worse than butterflies of embarrassment fluttering in the pit of my stomach, the hot flush of shame rising to my scarlet dome.

I've always been an easy mark, not only because of the tell-tale signs but also because of my special knack of putting my foot in my mouth at just the right moment.

"So, you like school?" my aunt once asked me.

"Don't be retarded," I replied, realizing as the words spilled off my lips that her eldest son was developmentally challenged.

In grade seven, everyone used to make faces at Mrs. Langstroth's back whenever she was writing on the blackboard. I should have listened to my mother when she espoused, "Don't make faces; it'll stick." Well, it stuck and I was sent to the principal's office.

I am constantly checking to make sure my fly isn't open, an act which is, in and of itself, an embarrassment.

I have cursed other drivers for their poor driving habits, only to go through a stop sign moments later. I have been called upon by others for comment on issues that were a hundred miles away from where my mind was.

Trying to fit in with a group of jokesters by the water cooler, I asked in a convivial tone of voice, "How many people in group therapy does it take to change a lightbulb? . . . Just one, but he really has to want to change!" I wasn't looking for hysterics; a chuckle, a smile, even a nod would have sufficed. But their faces dropped instead. "I've been in therapy seven years!" exclaimed one and hurried away. "My husband will never change. I'm thinking of leaving him!" said another and began to sob into her water cup. The third looked at me with steely eyes and said, "Alright! I have trouble changing lightbulbs. Are you happy now?"

Have you ever had a sigmoidoscopy? Got caught in a lie? Said something regretful? Foolish? Let one rip in the middle of a Beethoven concert? Ever scratch yourself in unmentionable places while waiting your turn for a job interview only to turn around and find what would have been your future boss standing right there? Ever walk into a wall? A closet? A change room full of naked floor-hockey players?

Oops!

Been there. Done that.

And just when it seemed that there was nothing left in this world that could embarrass me any longer, my father had called me at work, on speaker phone, to inquire if I was still having problems moving my bowels.

I fell off my chair and split my pants.

IT DIDN'T SEEM TO BOTHER HOUDINI!

(Frustration)

———⁓∿∘☙❧☙⚬∘∿⁓———

*"There **can't** be a crisis today! My schedule is already full!"*

———⁓∿∘☙❧☙⚬∘∿⁓———

The first time I heard of Harry Houdini I knew we were kindred souls linked for eternity by deeply-rooted feelings of frustration. The difference between us was that Houdini turned his frustrations into a career as an escape artist and I turned my frustrations inward and let them fester for the longest time.

As with most 'emotion' words, the dictionary tends to describe frustration in terms of its outcomes (which is a very frustrating thing). Webster defines frustration as: "the act of turning into nothing; confusion; confoundment; disappointment." None of these definitions adequately describe the blood-boiling, fist-clenching, rage-to-helplessness that is frustration.

Frustration is a cause-and-effect feeling where the cause is an act of effort towards a goal and the effect is no result or, at best, poor results. Frustration is:

- Trying to make a point to someone who won't listen to what you have to say.
- Trying to fix something small and delicate with your big, clumsy fingers.
- Trying to catch the attention of a snobby waiter in a snobby restaurant.
- Trying to meet the deadline in two minutes with twenty-two pages to go.

- Trying to appeal to a higher being without any sign of acknowledgement.

Every situation has the potential to elicit feelings of frustration. In my life experience I have been able to exact that potential in almost every situation.

Good ol' Houdini.

He mastered the skill of slipping out of the straitjacket.

I mastered the skill of slipping *into* it.

COLOUR ME GREEN

(Jealousy, Envy)

───◦◦◦◦───

"I met this pretty girl who was all teary-eyed. She said,
'My boyfriend is young and handsome.'
'Good for him,' I said.
'He's real smart . . . he's a doctor.'
'Good for him.'
'He's got a great sense of humour and a full head of hair.'
'Good for him.'
'He's filthy rich.'
'So why are you crying?'
'He got hit by a bus.'
'Good for him.'"

───◦◦◦◦───

It was nap time in kindergarten. We were all neatly laid out on our floor mats, stomachs satisfied with their contents of cookies and apple juice. Most of my classmates had drifted into unconsciousness, but in my last seconds of awareness, my eye caught some activity beneath the flutter of my lids. The kindergarten teacher, Mrs. Yuen, was blithely thrusting at Brian a second round of cookies and juice. My eyes popped open with indignation. In a righteous tirade for fairness, I exclaimed, "It's no fair!" I riled my peers, made Brian feel self-conscious, and caused my teacher to feel uncomfortable. I involved my parents and the principal, too. Finally I was told that Brian needed the extra juice and cookies because of his diabetes.

It wasn't so much my embarrassment that bothered me; it was having to admit that I was jealous that was unbearable.

It can be such a petty, niggling feeling, jealousy. And you detest yourself for it afterward.

Envy involves not only wanting something that somebody else has, but also holding that person in contempt for having it: good looks, wealth, a healthy relationship, courage, spiritual well-being, a better job, being the teacher's pet, food, a harmonious family life; it doesn't matter if it is unfair, inequitable, immoral, or unjust. You're still jealous.

There's no payoff for feeling jealous. If you are depressed, you can take your meds. If you are angry or frustrated, you can act out to the point of catharsis. If you are scared, you can become immobilized or you can seek a safe haven. The only thing you can do for jealousy is to become unjealous. And that's no fun.

And for all of you who claim not to have a jealous bone in your body, I hate you!

BEHAVIOUR

Checking the internet to find a definition of behaviour led me to the conclusion that most sources agreed that behaviour is an action or reaction to an internal or external stimulus. Figuring out where behaviour comes from led me to numerous debates of nature versus nurture, genetics versus environment. I wasn't interested, for the purpose of this book, so I thought hard about what behaviour meant to me.

Behaviour is a complicated word with an even more complicated meaning. Behaviour is often synonymous with action, usually acting on a thought, often fuelled by a feeling. It is a response to something. Inaction, though, is also a behaviour.

Behaving is usually thought of as a socially or culturally acceptable way of being, whereas misbehaving is often regarded as unacceptable, frequently associated with immature, childish, or naughty behaviour.

Behaviour may also occur as a result of or acting on a need, want, or desire. If you need food, want a new car, or desire sex, you will likely behave in a specific way that will satisfy the need, want, or desire.

Some behaviour is instinctual, such as putting your hands in front of your face if there is a sudden motion directed toward you, or experiential, such as stretching your limbs after sitting in one position for a long period of time, or a combination of instinctual and experiential, such as holding your breath or gagging when encountering a bad smell. Some behaviour can be quick and impulsive; some behaviour can be slow and painfully detailed; some behaviour can be rational and other behaviour can be bizarre. Unlike thoughts and feelings, though, behaviour doesn't seem to just pop out of nowhere.

While pondering some of the behaviours that I exhibited at my Starting Point and the years that followed, there are a few observations of note:

- My behaviour can certainly be seen in terms of doing or acting, acting as a result of ways of being, and acting on a need, want, or desire.
- It seems that an action is just that: an action. Recognizing that there are consequences to my actions and knowing what those consequences are were what really mattered.
- Understanding the value, moral, or judgment attributed to my actions (either by myself, by those who surrounded me, or by society at large) was also an important consideration.
- There were rules, regulations, and a code of conduct to be followed.

Ultimately, my behaviour shaped my life. Here's how:

MORALITY SQUAD

(Being told how to behave)

"I'm taking a mindfulness meditation class. The teacher told me to practise focusing on my breathing. So now I practise every time I dial a wrong number."

How is it that everybody knew what was good for me or what was bad for me, what was right for me or what was wrong for me—except me? Eating spinach to grow disfigured forearms was good for me; chocolate bars which tasted infinitely better than spinach, despite the acne, was bad for me. 'Pure thoughts' were right; masturbation was wrong. Respecting all adults, even the ignorant, misinformed or cruel ones, was the proper thing to do; being a noisy kid with bad table manners was deviant. What did I know when everyone else knew better? There were rules without exception that had to be followed. Doing what you were told resulted in the absence of punishment as the reward. But if you strayed there'd be hell to pay! Be a well-paid professional, not a tradesman. Go to this university, not that one. Get married and have children or everyone will think you're a loser. Pay attention, don't daydream! If you don't do the right thing you're not a good person.

And Guilt oozed out like roaches from the woodwork.

FROZEN TAG
(Being immobilized)

"My father's motto was always, 'Think positive!' I told him, 'Dad, I'm a loser!'
'Think positive!' he reprimanded. 'Okay,' I said, 'I'm positive I'm a loser!'"

I had developed quite a skill at being immobilized by certain thoughts and feelings. A deer in the headlights, my emotions (fear, embarrassment, anger, depression and the like) often rendered me catatonic. I was the sort who would erringly walk into a closet at a dinner party and stay there for hours, hoping no one would notice. I would have rather watched my meal crawl off my plate at a restaurant than say something to a waiter. If a person of authority, stature, or status even so much as glanced in my direction, I would dissolve into a melee of sweat and grin.

There were two childhood games at which I excelled: *Frozen Tag* and *Statue*. Unfortunately, I retained these skills into adulthood.

I'M JANE; WHAT'S YOUR'S?
(Being passive-aggressive)

"The last time I went snorkelling, a school of fluorescent fish swam up my bathing trunks. I don't know what kind of lesson the school of fish were trying to learn, but I came out of the experience positively glowing!"

A recurrent theme in my life is the constant oscillation from the good little boy, a product of the crinoline and ducktail generation, to the evil little man, a product of the 'me' and 'screw you' generation. I can't count the number of times I was told to be a martyr, a sacrifice, a whipping boy, all for the sake of respectability. I learned that this was what good little boys do, from relatives, friends, clergy, teachers—everyone! Having sacrificed and feeling none the better for it and certainly no more respected, the pitchfork on one shoulder pierced the halo on the other, and I rebelled. I was too meek to harm anyone (for which I am grateful), but I found ways of fighting back with most of the seven deadly sins. After all, I convinced myself, there is no such thing as altruism. Everybody does a good deed or says a kind word for *something* in return. Even if it's only to make him/herself feel good about it. Being mean and selfish, however, proved to be as unrewarding as being kind and generous.

Consequently, I managed, over a period of time, to blend my two personalities, like Eve White and Eve Black in 'The Three Faces of Eve'. The problem was that my 'Jane' turned out to be a passive-aggressive malcontent.

So I became a world champion at sulking. "I'll show *you!*" says I with folded arms, heels dug in, and a bright, shiny smile on my face.

DO AS I SAY, NOT AS I DO

(Being a hypocrite)

*** *"I don't believe in stealing . . . I just take what should be mine."* ***

You know you are a hypocrite when:

- You tell your children that junk food is bad for your health and Special Sauce is dripping down from the corner of your mouth.
- You whisper to your best friend, "Promise me you won't tell a soul what I told you about my best friend Suzie because I promised Suzie I wouldn't tell a soul!"
- You agree with your blind date that beauty is in the eye of the beholder but you are saying to yourself, "I wish I were a *blind* date!"
- You tell your boss, with all the bravado and nonchalance you can muster, "I think it's *great* that Smith got the promotion. It doesn't bother *me!*"
- You holler at your kid, "Stop screaming at your sister!"
- You impart words of wisdom to your brood, "You've got to get out there and *participate* in life! Go on now, and pass me the remote on your way out."

I realized I was a hypocrite every time my behaviour did not mesh with my thoughts and feelings. If I had a belief, feeling, moral, or value that was important to me, but that I couldn't be bothered to act upon, or if I was too scared to do anything about, I could really feel my hypocrisy. Or if it was an issue that I didn't *not* really give a damn about but I still spoke as though I supported it (perhaps due to peer pressure, society's expectations, or my determination to *belong*), my hypocrisy reared its ugly head. Or if I really believed in something but thought it was too risky, or took up too much of my time, energy, and effort to behave as I should, hypocrisy possessed me. Being caught in the act of hypocrisy often resulted in my shame, denial, lies, and sometimes even more hypocrisy.

So do as I say, not as I do.

SAD SACK, BORN LOSER, BAD LUCK SHLEPROCK: I GOT 'EM ALL BEAT

(Being a victim)

*** *"I'm so pathetic. Whenever I took my kids out trick-or-treating for Hallowe'en, they would ask me to* **put on** *the gorilla mask so I wouldn't embarrass them."* ***

"Why does this always happen to *me*?" I recall saying throughout most of my life, and in all sorts of situations: enduring a lecture from my father, being hit in the head with a snowball, getting stuck in traffic, hating my job, and on and on. I was a perennial victim.

Things happened to me. Bad things. Frequently!

It took a long time for me to realize that there were several problems with seeing myself as a victim:

- Even when I wasn't really I victim (which was never, really) I could pretend to be one, or convince myself that I was one. Chances were that I really wasn't a victim, since I usually had control over many of my circumstances or, at least, how I dealt with them; it's not as though I was ever a real victim of, say, crime or a political upheaval where most elements of control were taken away.
- Once I reaped the benefits of being a victim, it was hard to let go of it. There were lots and lots of negative payoffs for being a victim, especially all the attention, pity, and offers of help I got.

- More often than not, seeing myself as a victim usually prevented me from facing my challenges effectively, since I was more focused on being a victim than doing anything about it.
- I began to reinforce my fears and worries which, in turn, allowed me to indulge in bouts of self-pity, whining, and complaining.
- It was easier not to take responsibility by telling everybody that I was a victim. I could be helpless and ignorant, hiding behind my victim label and using it as an excuse for doing or not doing all sorts of things.

My son was the victim of a car accident in which he sustained severe head injuries. After a long healing process and understanding his new limitations, he was faced with the decision to see himself as a head injury victim for the rest of his life, or get past it and continue to move forward. Fortunately, he chose the latter—a lesson I desperately needed to learn. In fact, he rose above his injury with his wonderful sense of humour. When he woke from a week-long coma and tried to speak, I feared the worst. He pointed to the scar and staples in his head and declared, "Dad, I'm a numbskull." With tears of joy and relief, I told him he needed this injury like a hole in the head. He said, "Dad, I *have* a hole in my head."

At that point, I knew I needed to get over my pitiable self-pity and get on with my life.

THE WORM SONG
(Wanting to be accepted)

"To me, the most important thing you can do is build character. Mine's Goofy."

"The worms crawl in, the worms crawl out; they eat your guts
and they spit them out.
If ever you see a worm go by, remember that you'll be the
next to die . . .
Nobody likes me, everybody hates me. Gonna be fed to the
worms.
Big fat juicy worms, long slim slimy worms, itsy bitsy creepy
crawly worms."

I was always uncomfortable in the company of worms, mostly because I knew that nobody liked me and everybody hated me. It was an undisputed fact of life. My parents ignored me or yelled at me all the time. My sister teased me incessantly. Friends were scarce. Sometimes I would give a cherished toy or a piece of gum to a 'friend' if only she or he would play with me. She or he would take my toy or my gum, laugh in my face, and walk away. Occasionally I would help set the table or clean my room, and smile to my parents that "see what a good boy I am!" smile. In exchange for this, I received criticism or nothing at all. Other times I would deliberately misbehave (sulk, lie, throw tantrums, or break things) if only my existence would be acknowledged. For this, I was inevitably scolded and punished.

Consequently, I dreaded rainy days when the worms came out.

THAT WAS GRATIFYING!
(Wanting instant gratification)

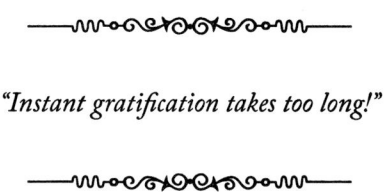

"Instant gratification takes too long!"

There is not much to say here: "I want it all and I want it now."

That was my motto during my first few decades of life. I couldn't be bothered to wait or to exercise patience. Who cared about savouring the here and now or experiencing the journey? And so I sought shortcuts, small alleyways through the long and winding roads of life.

Although I wanted instant gratification, my behaviour was tempered by guilt, fear, shame, and unabashed laziness. Sometimes all at once. And so my want was instantly ungratified.

"I WANNA BE LOVED BY YOU"
(Wanting approval)

"My biggest fear in the world is standing in front of a crowd and nobody is laughing at my jokes. My jokes are so bad, even the voices in my head aren't laughing."

Seeking approval was, for me, a full-time vocation. I had always strived to be the good little boy. Beyond the age (whenever *that* is) when it was no longer acceptable to do so, I found myself asking—nay, begging—those around me to love me and accept me. But a strange thing happened. I found myself not behaving like me but like the person from whom I was seeking approval, so that if I was at all liked, it was not the real me that was being liked. On those rare occasions that I was myself, I was convinced of insincerity or ulterior motives. Talk about tangled webs! But, still, I remained the good little boy.

TAKING CONTROL
IS A REMOTE POSSIBILITY
(Wanting control)

"'Knock knock.'
'Who's there?'
'Control Freak. Now you say 'Control Freak who?'"

I am an extremely low-tech individual. I am fascinated yet bewildered by modern technological advances. The one invention with which I am comfortable—cannot do without, in fact—is the television remote control. Spending hours pushing buttons to switch channels, or adjust the volume, or power on and off is sheer delight. Taking the remote away from my wife and controlling the remote is even more exciting.

There is something intoxicating about being in control. It gives the illusion of being powerful, all-knowing, and larger-than-life. Whenever I need to prove my point, demonstrate my authority, show that I'm right, or have my own way, I exercise control.

And how do I do this? Sometimes I'll yell, or talk over someone. Or blame. Or accuse. Or abdicate responsibility. Or manipulate. Or argue. Or get in your face. Or demand.

Or else I'll pull out my remote and click away.

LIFE IN A MINEFIELD
(Wanting security)

"I told my doctor all about my insecurities . . . so he tightened my restraints."

I've always loved a good disaster: the ravages of war; a volcanic eruption with the slow inevitable advance of a molten flow of lava; the seismic quaking of the earth as the ground begins to crack and crumble; a force-five tornado complete with pounding hailstones, whipping winds, and flying cows; a blossoming mushroom cloud illuminated by a flash of blinding light.

What I loved about these disasters was the overwhelming sense of awe without being physically impaired by them.

In short, I've always wanted a sense of security.

Life had always been like that for me: a battle for survival where everyone was the enemy. I would skulk through the shadows, wary of people, fearful of making decisions, or taking risks, avoiding confrontation and, forever expecting that next disaster in order to seek safety from it.

I would spend time building a fortress with thick, impenetrable walls and high parapets, steel inflexible girders, deep, dark storm cellars, and vaulted bomb shelters.

Yes, I've always loved a good disaster.

I'M SPECIAL
(Wanting separation/individuality)

—————ⵡ•◦◖ⵜⵔ•ⵔ◖ⵜ◖◦•ⵡ—————

"My mother told me, 'Always remember: you are unique . . .
just like everyone else."

—————ⵡ•◦◖ⵜⵔ◦ⵔ◖ⵜ◖◦•ⵡ—————

"You're . . . *special*," my mother said.

I didn't like the way she said it.

But I did like to be special, different, and unique. I spent much of my time as a kid trying to develop and assert my individuality.

I began by renaming myself—twenty-six names, in fact, each beginning with a different letter of the alphabet. I introduced myself with all twenty-six names all in rapid succession all the time. I was told to shut up.

So I tried doing different things: bending my thumbs to my wrists, crossing my eyes and rolling them around, wrapping my legs around my neck. I was told to stop it.

Next, I took a shot at singing (in an off-key falsetto), performing absurd one-man, one-act plays; I even took lessons in tap-jazz-ballet-folk dancing. I was told to sit down and behave myself.

I wore weird hats. I spoke with strange accents and in strange, made-up tongues. I proposed bizarre ideas. I was told where to go.

I just wanted to be different, extraordinary, stand out from the crowd.

"Why can't you be more like your sister?" my mother pleaded.

"Because I'm . . . special," I replied.

"... I BELONG TO YOU!"

(Wanting to belong)

"They told me that I was an idiot for thinking I was a social outcast, and they said my village misses me very much."

As much as I wanted to be myself, I also had an intense desire to belong.

Not realizing these two needs were diametrically opposed to each other, I found it difficult to understand why I would always be the last to be chosen for the team, why the girls would point and giggle, and why I would stand at a party, awkward and alone, in a corner away from everyone else.

Why couldn't anyone see that I just wanted to belong?

As time went on, my own identity began to dissipate and merge with others. I didn't just become a part of their group; I became them themselves! Yet, wanting so much to be one with others, I always felt alone and separated and longing more than ever to belong.

MY LINES OF DEFENSE ARE CROOKED
(Defense mechanisms)

"I suppose I watched so much TV as a kid to avoid social situations. I especially liked TV commercial songs and I would sing them all the time. Do you remember the jingle for Almond Joy Candy Bars?*—you know, 'Sometimes I feel like a nut; sometimes I don't.'? I remember thinking, 'Is this jingle telling me I have a mood disorder?'"*

My wife hates things that are crooked or on angles. She always feels compelled to straighten them. She runs around all day long, straightening and fixing pictures I have mounted, clocks I have hung, and boxes I have stacked.

She tries to straighten me out, too. My behaviour, that is.

My lines of defense have always been askew, and she gets frustrated because they are just not tangible enough for her to get hold of.

I had always prided myself on the degree of proficiency with which I had cultivated my defense mechanisms. I exercised them at every opportunity.

My favourite was repression. When in doubt, repress it! Repress everything! Won't remember. No worries. Just shove it away in the unlit corners of my mind. Works like a charm (now, of course, I can't repress anything, which enables me to write all this!). I kept my repression ship-shape because, without it, all my other defense mechanisms would have been out of whack.

Denial was a strong defense of mine, somewhat immature but effective nevertheless. If I denied the problem, it would simply cease to exist. "*I* didn't do it!" "What ball through what window?" "I just don't see the problem." "Everything is just fine."

Equally immature was identification. I would turn myself into a zombie-like creature, replacing myself with the soul of a hero, or the person I most admired, or the person I most envied, or the person I most wanted to be friends with.

Avoidance was my most used defense mechanism. If I avoided a situation, I was convinced it would go away. I avoided difficult people, unwanted events and, at times, I avoided important parts of my life.

Compensation was a talent, like juggling. I filled my stomach to replace the emptiness of love I felt in my heart. I became friends with movie and television characters to balance my lonely life devoid of pals. I took a job helping others to make up for my inertia at helping myself.

Projection came easily to me. Placing the responsibility for my own tribulations upon the shoulders of others was as simple as pointing a finger at them.

Displacement was fun. Although I never kicked the cat, I once threw a dinette set down a flight of stairs. It was an evil dinette set, what can I say?

Reaction formation was one of my stronger lines of defense, as it must be for most passive-aggressive personalities. I could go an entire day with one of those earlobe-to-earlobe grins while hating the world and its inhabitants.

Rationalization was an ever-developing defense, a rather sophisticated and increasingly dominant part of my psyche. From the philosophical perspective that everything must have a reason, an explanation, and a justification, I assigned a 'reason' to every thought, feeling and behaviour I ever had.

At times I would be working all my defense mechanisms at once, throwing everything helter-skelter. It's little wonder that my lines of defense were crooked.

FAULTY BEHAVIOUR
(Blame)

———∿∾◦◖◗◦∽◦◦∿———

"The secret of success is knowing who to blame for your failures."

"I didn't say it was your fault; I said I was going to blame you."

———∿∾◦◖◗◦∽◦◦∿———

My ever-loving sister pointed her index finger at me and shouted, *"He did it! It's *his* fault!"*

She was referring to the broken plate and globs of food scattered over the kitchen floor, which *she* pushed off the edge of the table in protest of her cooked cauliflower.

My parents turned to me, disapprovingly. I was more cooked than the cauliflower.

That's when I learned how to blame. (Thanks, Sis!)

Blaming is a time-worn tactic used as an avoidance of potentially negative consequences. It can be deployed in almost any circumstance, from "Honey, she *made* me have an affair with her!" to "No, General, sir. It wasn't me this time that caused the disaster; it was Johnston. He always pushes my buttons."

The blame itself can be true or it can be false, usually the latter for those who have the urge to blame.

Rationale for the accusation is frequently a ruse, an elaborate cover-up on the part of the accuser. More often than not the finger-pointer will incorporate 'always' and 'never' in his accusation to justify the blame. "It's *your* fault we don't get along. You're *always* criticizing me. You *never* listen to what I have to say . . . no . . . I don't want to hear it!"

The consequences that one is trying to avoid by blaming are significant. In fact, the more dire the consequences, the more overt or elaborate the blame. "*Me?!*" "It wasn't *my* fault I didn't hand in the assignment. I was mugged on the way home last night; my wallet and my essay were taken. And the little I could salvage, the dog ate!"

Placing blame is usually a remedial step in a much larger underlying problem: not accepting responsibility.

BLAME IT ON ME
(Assuming responsibility)

—wwwooooooooooo—

*"My daughter has Obsessive Compulsive Disorder and it's all my fault.
I always told her, 'Practice makes perfect.'"*

—wwwooooooooooo—

Why, I lament, did I assume responsibility for everyone but myself?

When everyone around me would fall to pieces all over the place, I would appoint myself chief custodian. For some insane reason, I consciously took on the responsibility of solving everyone's problems, including mankind's. A friend with a marital problem, a parent with a health problem, an employee with an emotional problem, the world with an economic problem—all mine to solve!

Conversely, when it was *my* marriage in question, *my* health, *my* emotions, and *my* financial dilemma, everyone but me was responsible. It was my wife's fault our marriage wasn't blissful all the time; it was God's fault my health wasn't what it should have been; it was my friend's and/or my parents' fault that I was an emotional mess, and it was the economy's fault that I was drowning in financial disaster. Whew! With lifelong catastrophes such as those, I'm glad *I* was not responsible for any of it. Besides, I was too busy solving other people's problems to deal with my own. And toting such a weary load was a full-time job.

Confidentially (so don't tell anyone), I had grown to resent all those people who drained the lifeblood out of me via my heroic problem-solving efforts. Just once, I would have liked to see them wrestle with their own problems. It reminds me of a sappy line I heard on TV about how everybody touches everyone else's life in so many ways and that even if you personally find no meaning in your own life perhaps you—albeit unwittingly—have given meaning to someone else in his/her life which, as a result, implies your own meaningful existence. I think the person on TV (in a night time drama) was telling this to a potential roof-jumper with a terminal illness. At the end of the long-winded speech the jumper jumped anyway. And I thought, Good for him! Then I felt guilty for thinking such a cruel thought.

No matter how much you do for someone you never get the appreciation or satisfaction out of the hard work you put into taking on responsibility for others. In the end they are probably going to do for themselves what they want anyway.

WHINING FOR FUN AND PROFIT
(Complaining)

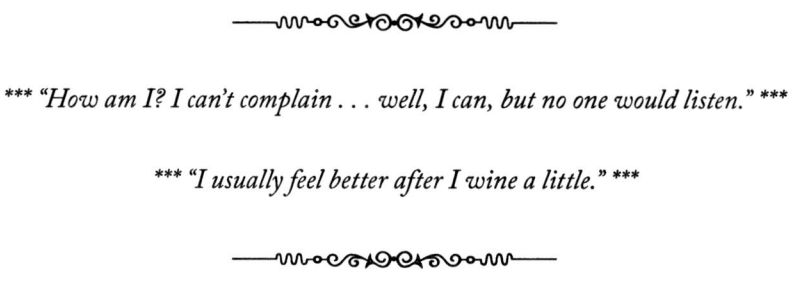

*** *"How am I? I can't complain . . . well, I can, but no one would listen."* ***

*** *"I usually feel better after I wine a little."* ***

One of my favourite pastimes growing up was complaining. I would 'kvetch' about everything; in fact, the whinier my voice the better. And like most of my shameful behaviour, I was a *champion* complainer, a proud and devoted one. Even though I despised any competition in this area, I knew how to really put my game on.

"I can't do it. It's too hard!" I would complain about my math homework.

"I can't eat it," I whined, pushing the broccoli aside. "My stomach hurts!" Then I would shove a chocolate bar down my throat when my parents weren't looking.

"I don't want to go outside today and play during recess," I would grumble to my teacher. It's too cold out!"

Complaining was so satisfying, at first: I got out of doing things I didn't want to do; it gave me all the attention I longed for; it gave me the opportunity to blame other people and things.

Later in life I realized that most people responded to my complaints with annoyance and disgust. Or they would ignore me. Or, like the boy who cried "*Wolf!*", my complaints (even the legitimate ones) were no longer taken seriously or nobody would believe them.

Come to think of it, there really isn't anything to profit from by complaining.

MAKING CHANGE
(Taking Risk)

"Change is inevitable . . . except from vending machines!"

I had always dreaded change of any kind. Carrots invariably had to be eaten before the fish sticks. I would never deviate from this. Underwear always went on first. I would sweat myself into a state of frazzle on the first and final day of each school year. And woe! the day a friend would move from the neighbourhood—intolerable!

The drive toward the illusion of safety and comfort had been my prime objective for as long as I can remember, although I never quite defined it as a goal in these terms. Do nothing, resist change, overlook, and ignore was my motto. It was safe and, in a world in which I thought cared nothing for me, it felt good to feel safe. Developing habits was my means to an end, the end being safety and comfort. As a result, no risk was worth taking without an unconditional guarantee that I would be safe and comfortable. So, I was in the habit of saying no to opportunity, ignoring good advice, overlooking my mistakes, and generally feeling miserable. I had fallen into the habit role!

As I grew older (an inevitable change in its own right) I began to realize that some change is not only essential, but preferable. I saw people who were unhappy in relationships or disheartened at work that only change would remedy. I noticed people who were dissatisfied with what they had (or didn't have), distraught with financial difficulties, or discouraged with the state of the world. Me, too!

It was then that I knew what had to be done. I had to make change.

And I did make change the very next morning. I put my underwear on last. Well, my underwear may not have been in the right place but my heart was.

Recognizing the need for change and making appropriate change are quite separate matters. If you give someone a quarter for two dimes, you will likely be disappointed with the change.

MY PET GRUDGE

(Holding a grudge)

"Holding a grudge is letting someone live rent-free in your head."

"If you can't forgive and forget, pick one."

"I never hold a grudge for more than a decade or two."

*"A lawyer was reading out the will of a rich man to
the people mentioned in the will.
'To you, my loving wife Mary, who stood by me in tough times,
as well as good, I leave you the house and $2 million.'
The lawyer continued, 'To my daughter Jennnifer, who looked after me in sickness
and kept the business going, I leave you the yacht, the business, and $1 million.'
The lawyer concluded, 'And, to my cousin Charlie, who hated me, argued with
me, and thought that I would never mention you in my will—
well you are wrong. Hi, Charlie!'"*

I had a pet grudge. It was my best friend. It was warm and cuddly. I gave it a home. I used to take my pet grudge with me everywhere I went. I would feed and nurture that grudge until it got big and fat and satisfied.

Sometimes it would fade and die. I did not get sad, though. I knew that before too long a new pet grudge would come along. It always did, every time a seedling of anger was planted. Then I would have a new friend, a new pet grudge all over again.

I loved every pet grudge I ever had. If anyone had anything to say about my pet grudge I would dig my heels in and defend it.

Sometimes, I did get sad when my pet grudge would die, but only if I was the one who made it die. Sometimes I killed my own pet grudge! If I gave forgiveness, it would get sick and die. If I thought of why my grudge was alive, or if it was worth having as a pet, it would wither and die. If I tried to talk with someone about my pet grudge, it would bristle and die. If I starved my pet grudge, if I did not give it its daily supply of anger, it would shrivel up and die. If I did not give my pet grudge lots of love and attention, it would die.

Taking care of my pet grudge was hard work, and it took up most of my time. Having a pet grudge was a lot of responsibility!

Neil Katz

THE SCARLETT O'HARA SYNDROME
(Procrastination)

*"Procrastination has its good side . . .
you always have something to do tomorrow."*

"I'm going to stop procrastinating . . . once I get around to it."

Amazing how we all think we shall live forever, at least those of us in pre-mid- or post-life crisis. Life is eternal; life is the natural state. When I wake up every morning I expect the world to be there and I expect to be in it. I do not expect to be dead (although if I were dead would I know the difference?). Therefore I do not feel compelled to wake up every morning to thank God that I am alive for yet another day (except for some days, when I wake up, look to the heavens, and say "*Thanks a lot!*"). Somehow I cannot face the fact that there may not be a tomorrow for me. That is as abstract to me as my wildest fantasy. Tomorrow I must go to work, go to the dentist, clean the house, fight with my wife, argue with my parents, and yell at the kids. There must, therefore, be a tomorrow.

Confident that there will always be a tomorrow, there is no practical reason for me to do anything today. I am the world's second worst procrastinator. The world's worst procrastinator was the guy who thought up that poster slogan: "Today is the first day of the rest of your life."

My confusion rests in the fact that, although I never expect to die, I have a lingering fear of Death. Many of those to whom I have spoken on the subject assured me that their fears do not concern death, but aging. Age doesn't bother *me*. After all, I was twelve when I went through *my*

96

mid-life crisis . . . these are my bonus years. What scares me to death is Death: the imminent cessation of aging. My grandmother was one hundred three years old (give or take) when she died; she spent most of her waking hours (about four per day) complaining that she had lived too long. Shortly before she passed away, my mother said she felt like dying not due to any physical or mental ailment, but as a sensation; she was very matter-of-fact about it. My father was constantly proclaiming he had but a couple of good years left, and he told me on my thirteenth birthday, "You're a man now. Go purchase a cemetery plot." My sister reflected on aging in front of a mirror, camouflaging her thoughts behind hairdresser gossip. She told me that if she refused to think of death, it simply wouldn't happen. My kids scare me: they ask questions about life, aging, and death all the time . . . each a chip off the very old block.

Aging doesn't bother me. I see getting old as a goal to strive for. It's an accomplishment. If I achieve nothing else in my life, at least I can say that I got old. I'm here and I did it. The physical deterioration of the body bothers me. Maybe that's why I complain so much now; I'm trying to get it out of my system so I won't be one of those miserable old whiners thirty-something years from now. The mental deterioration scares me more. I wonder what the connection is between my soul and the mental me? If I go loony-tunes, you know, talking to pictures on the wall, dressing in six layers of clothing, asking the garbage collectors for a lift overseas . . . if I go a bit peculiar, will I still be me? Will I know the difference? Or care?

But aging doesn't bother me (have I convinced you yet?). What if I don't make it to 'old'? What if I choke on a burp next year? What if I drown myself in a wet dream when I'm sixty? I cross the street wondering which car will run interference with my life. I read the newspapers searching for the next report on a natural or unnatural disaster which will affect me for sure this time. I watch soap operas on T.V. and wonder how many fatal diseases will befall *me*. An earache becomes cancerous; heart*burn* becomes heart *attack*. I listen to people of the previous generation talk of their friends and siblings dropping dead like flies. I think of my parents, now both deceased, and me stepping up to the edge of the precipice.

No doubt about it, getting old will be my crowning glory.

Feeling the way I do now about aging and death, how could I, in all good conscience, contemplate procrastinating for even another minute?

I don't know. I'll think about that tomorrow.

AN EYE FOR A TOOTH

(Do unto others . . .)

—————ᴡᴡᴏᴄᴇ₁ᴏᴏᴋᴏᴏᴏᴡ—————

*"I recently became a grandfather. Just think: a whole
new generation for me to screw up."*

—————ᴡᴡᴏᴄᴇ₁ᴏᴄᴋᴏᴏᴏᴡ—————

The first time I went to a flea market, I was both curious and apprehensive. Earlier in the day at Hebrew school, we had been discussing a reference in the Bible: "an eye for an eye, a tooth for a tooth". Being not much of a Biblical scholar and paying too little attention, I imagined the expression related to some kind of barter and exchange. I spent the entire afternoon at the flea market searching for a stall displaying eyeballs and teeth.

Of course I now realize that, although somewhat negative and punitive in nature, the literal interpretation is a lesson to be learned in the fairness of maiming.

Similar behavioural tutelage, also Biblical in nature but more humane, is the notion of "Do unto others as you would have them do unto you". For example, if you want people to treat you with kindness, then you must treat them with kindness first.

I learned that we are constantly teaching people how to treat us, even if the lesson we are teaching is not in our own best interest and even if we are unaware we are teaching it. If you are a parent who is not demonstrating behaviour that garners respect, and you are not showing respect for your children to model, it is probable that they will not respect you. If you want your boss to trust you with more responsibility, then teach your boss by behaving in a way that will encourage trust and responsibility.

Neil Katz

I should also note that even if you do unto others, it does not automatically mean that they will do unto you. The consequences of doing unto others may be a million miles away from where your teachings were headed, and perhaps through no lack of effort on your part.

All we can do is figure out how we want to be treated, and treat others like that.

An eye for a tooth.

TAKE *THAT*!

(being aggressive; acting out)

"We all have our special talents. As a kid I wasn't so good at throwing a ball, but I was a star at throwing a tantrum."

We were six-year-old playmates but we weren't playing anymore that day. Ellen got me good and mad. She took my toy and said it was her's, refusing to return it.

So I slapped her on the back.

Her mother came running out of the house and yelled at me that I shouldn't be hitting girls, especially in delicate places. Even if Ellen was only six and undeveloped enough not to have delicate places, you would think her mother would know the difference between her own daughter's frontside and backside!

When Ellen's mother threatened to tell my parents, I wanted to swat *her* on the back. But, of course, she was older and stronger and bigger.

So I tore out her prize rose bushes.

I spent the rest of the summer replanting and tending Ellen's mother's garden.

And I never hit a girl in a delicate place again. I did, however, break Lynnie's hairband and twirl Marilyn around by the ponytail. I got into trouble for both.

John and Ken cornered me after school, grade seven, and beat the crap out of me, punching and kicking and burning me with their cigarettes. I'm not sure why; maybe because I was ten years old, skinny and showed as an easy target. They got the strap for it. Then they threatened me for snitching. I snitched on them for their threat and they got the strap again, as well as a suspension (which they thought was great because it was a day off from school).

My sister once got mad at me and threw a forty-pound dictionary at me. It landed on her foot and she broke a toe. I was eleven when I got mad at my dog. I lifted her on top of the refrigerator and made her sit there for five minutes. When I carried her down, she peed on my head. You can always count on a dire consequence as a result of acting out.

LYING AS AN ART FORM
(Lying)

—⁓⁓◦◦⟨⟩⟨⟩◦⟨⟩◦◦⁓⁓—

"I don't lie. I just provide an alternative reality."

"The following sentence is a lie: The preceding sentence is the truth."

—⁓⁓◦◦⟨⟩⟨⟩◦⟨⟩◦◦⁓⁓—

Some people see lying as a crime punishable by death or worse.

"I didn't do it!" asserts the man with the smoking gun in his hand.

Well, maybe in *that* situation.

"What a lovely dress!" exclaims the woman to the hostess, who is wearing a maroon monstrosity with a big yellow rose sash.

"These are all the receipts I have," you say to the taxman, while slipping little pieces of paper discreetly into your undershorts. "The rest were destroyed in a fire."

Often these are the very people who self-righteously decry liars because honesty is the best policy.

Some people see lying as no big whoop: A fib. A little white one. Harmless. As long as it can be justified, it really isn't lying, so they think.

"This house is a real charmer," says the real estate agent. What he is really saying is: Pay no attention to the cracked foundation or the sagging support beams. "Cute as a button." Meaning: small and cramped. "Priced to sell." The house has been listed forever and the vendor is desperate. The justification? "A person has to make a living, right?"

"So what if I defrauded the government? Governments have more money than they know what to do with. Besides, my kids gotta eat!"

"No, I didn't see the stop sign, officer. Was there a stop sign? Oh . . . well, I have terrible cramps and I was trying to make it in time to the bathroom."

Some people see lying as a sport, trying to compete and even outdo one another.

"I just got over a cold."

"I just got over the flu."

"Well, I just got over pneumonia!"

"Oh, yeah? Well, I just returned from the dead!"

Lying is so versatile a behaviour that one can even attempt to outdo oneself. Have you ever told a story, embellishing just a little more with each recantation until your final product resembles nothing of the original?

Sometimes people lie as a matter of necessity.

"Of course I'm washing my hands, Mom. What else would I be doing in the bathroom for forty-five minutes?"

Some people think that by omitting information they really aren't lying.

"Well, sweetheart, I never said I *wasn't* having an affair!"

Common sense tells us that the origins of lying are set in our childhood when we receive positive reinforcement as a result of a lie we have told.

"Honestly, Mom! I swear! She hit me first!" It was a boldfaced lie, of course. I had hit *her* first, but I was afraid of being punished. Except for some short-lived guilt and fear of discovery, I felt great.

Lying is therefore a cover-up designed for our protection. To thwart punishment, to save us from embarrassment, to enable us to obtain or benefit from something we otherwise would not have, to self-aggrandize, or to prevent us from having to face the truth.

As with any type of risky behaviour, there are always consequences: getting caught, fear, guilt, embarrassment, punishment—the very essence from what our lies were supposed to protect us in the first place.

Some people think that even if they lie just once, it was just the one time, and it won't happen again because basically they are honest people. Too soon do they learn that one lie often begets another and another, growing in frequency and magnitude until it takes on a life of its own.

Pants on fire!

RESOLUTION REVOLUTION
(Making decisions)

———— ∿∽◦⊙⊶⊙⊷⊙∽◦∿ ————

"From now on I resolve to make better bad decisions."

———— ∿∽◦⊙⊶⊙⊷∽◦∿ ————

Making resolutions is a fairly easy concept to grasp. You simply state what you intend to do and then you do it. I began making resolutions when I realized Father Time wasn't really an old man in a diaper, tossing an inflated beach ball. In those days, my intentions were quite honourable, even if they were a trifle unrealistic: to be the richest, most powerful person in the galaxy; to blow away every school bully who had ever been mean to me; to be a model child to my parents and admired by all, starting tomorrow after I apologize for biting my sister; to become a movie star or a child prodigy of some sort before the spring thaw.

I was furious with myself when not a single resolution came to pass.

Several New Years's later, I decided to try my hand once again at making resolutions and adding them to next year's list. Ultimately, I resolved to adhere to only those resolutions which I knew I would break by 12:01 a.m. New Year's Day. I also resolved to break only those resolutions that would result in the most amount of guilt (will I ever be able to survive without Guilt?).

In search of the definitive self-help approach, I had, one year many years ago, undertaken to list my resolutions and identify the outcomes of each. Here are the results:

1. I resolve to be happy even if it makes me miserable. Outcome: I am more miserable than ever (and loving every minute of it). Life is hard.

2. I resolve to be alive, even if it kills me. Outcome: I am alive, barely.

3. I resolve to be productive, even if it bores me to death. Outcome: I am still totally useless.

4. I resolve to be nauseatingly sweet and kind to my wife. Outcome: This was considered to be an unnatural act, punishable by law.

5. I resolve not to be depressed (a whole new me!). Outcome: Fat chance. See first resolution.

6. I resolve to be a social being for a change. A social dog, as my friend Moo would call it. Outcome: I am neither social nor a dog. One or the other would be nice. Instead I am an outcast, a loner, and an in-between. I try to be sociable. I really do try. Can I help it if the rest of the world is bat droppings?

7. I resolve to be somewhat creative. Outcome: I have transformed into a species of plant life—that's creative!

8. I resolve to stop complaining. Oy! Outcome: Get real! Complaining is my life!

9. I resolve to be the healthiest, hunkiest human specimen this side of Pluto. Outcome: a croaking piece of fungus is neither healthy nor hunky, not even on Pluto.

10. I resolve to finish projects. Outcome: too difficult for a plant, especially a complaining piece of fungus.

11. I resolve to take a "new fuck you stand". Outcome: my parents *and* my wife washed my mouth out with soap over this one.

12. I resolve to discover the meaning of life and spread the word to all mankind. Outcome: silly me! Everyone already knows *that* one!

Consequently, last year has just been discounted entirely.

In retrospect all my intentions were well-meant. I recognized that I wanted to be something better than I was before. A noble goal. What I didn't take into account was:

a) Which of these resolutions were within my own control, and
b) Were any of these resolutions within the realm of realistic expectations, and
c) What was my plan of action for completing or maintaining each of these resolutions?

Resolutions themselves are nothing more than empty promises. They sound good when you make them. You are held in high esteem by making such honourable pronouncements. But I discovered that unless resolutions (decisions) are within your control, realistic, and carefully thought out, they are meaningless. And the consequences (outcomes) are usually not so great.

The worst possible scenario, with respect to resolutions, one which I have personally experienced, goes something like this: you have just broken your resolution, say, to be the nicest person in the world. You suspect it may be a tad unrealistic and not entirely within your control but, hey, it sounds good. Not that you have the slightest idea of how to go about ensuring you will be the nicest person in the world. When Monday comes, nine thirty-six a.m., inevitably somebody does something that pisses you off. By nine thirty-eight a.m., you are cursing your finest swear words. By nine forty a.m., you realize you were unable to keep your resolution. So you tell yourself, okay, I just didn't give myself enough time. I'll start next month. That way, I can swear my face off for the rest of this month and get it out of my system. But next month you find yourself cursing again. Not to be disillusioned! New Year's Day is just two hundred seventy-four days away. You'll be nice *then*! You'll have a clean slate beginning on the first day of a brand new year. That way you can kick the cat, slam the door in the face of charity canvassers, and curse to your heart's content until December 31st. But, alas! When this past year is safely tucked away in whichever metaphoric container you may choose, and you bring your resolutions out of mothballs, it is only a matter of time before there is a blot on the new slate. And all that will be recorded in the annals of your personal history is a milestone of insignificance.

You may then, as do I, happily declare, "See? I told you I was a failure!"

FORKS AND KNIVES
(gossip/evil language)

———⟶∿∘◦⟨↔◦⟩◦∘∿———

*** *"I never repeat gossip . . . so listen carefully the first time."* ***

———∿∘◦⟨↔◦⟩◦∘∿———

"Hey, did you hear about _____?"

   "What a jerk _____ is! Guess what he did *this* time?"

   "I know a secret about _____."

   Sometimes, having a conscience is a pain in the ass. More succinctly but less eloquently, behaving in an unconscionable manner gives me a cringing, twisty, uncomfortable sensation in one of the lower quadrants of my abdominal cavity. This sensation, the same one that arises whenever I engaged in any behaviour incongruent with my morals and values, was acutely apparent whenever I indulged in gossip or waggled my evil tongue. The feeling I got was so profound that it was almost a religious experience, and not the good kind.

   In fact, according to some religious teachings, speaking, writing, behaving or communicating in a disparaging way about a fellow human being is not only forbidden, it creates a distance from the good that exists in the world, and it also severs any possibility of attachment from the World to Come.

   In more fact, speaking badly about another person is viewed as the equivalent to murder, adultery, and idol worship. And! All three!

   I was so screwed!

   And here's what I discovered:

   Whether you speak negatively about someone directly to his face or gossip about him behind his back, and whether or not it registers on your moral compass, you're guilty of gossip. Coming up with a million reasons for gossiping, or being coerced, or even or retaliating against someone who gossiped about you does not permit you to gossip about someone. (Uh-uh.) Whether you are creating the information as you go or speaking the gospel truth, you are not immune to the consequences of gossiping. (No, no, no.) Whether gossiping is a once-in-a-while event or an ongoing habit, it doesn't allow you to absolve yourself from being a gossip. (Nope, no way.) Speaking negatively against someone is still speaking negatively against someone, regardless of how you speak negatively against someone. This includes speaking in a derogatory manner, being sarcastic, hurtful, hateful, resentful, causing embarrassment or humiliation, making up stories or telling lies, or disclosing information about someone that is not your place to disclose. It also includes saying nothing to someone who is gossiping or silently supporting the gossiper. (You'd better believe it!) Gossiping is often based on limited, inaccurate, or false information which is usually obtained by hearsay or by playing Broken Telephone. Gossiping, or speaking negatively about the lives of others, or defaming the character of others, is hateful, hurtful, mean-spirited, and unjust.

So why did I engage in gossip in the first place?

- I felt included, especially when others were doing it, too
- I was able to elevate myself in order to (ironically) feel better about myself (since I didn't know how to elevate myself by my own merit)
- I felt important; after all, I was the first to spread the news; it was my scoop
- I was able to be in control, and I was a force to be reckoned with
- I was able to establish, break, or strengthen alliances
- I was "helping" the other person
- I wanted to get revenge
- I wanted to prove a point

- It helped me to avoid dealing with my own difficult and plentiful issues
- It gave me something to talk about, especially since I didn't have anything better to talk about
- It gave me a sense of belonging and inclusion
  I had gossiped for all these reasons.
  It is well-known that a forked tongue is a knife in the heart!
  I was so screwed!

PART I—SUMMARY

So this was my Starting Point, an ominous foray into my life's path, filled with oodles of negative thinking, dark emotions, and leaden, profoundly burdensome behaviour.

I had a colleague/friend from Newfoundland, smart, affable, and with a fully affected accent, who started most of his sentences with, "I don't means to be negative, but…"; he then let loose a run of negatives so full and extensive that I was sure he meant for them to all cancel out one another, resulting in a sentence that could be construed only as completely positive.

Sadly, that skill eludes me. It always has. I can remember being a negative, pessimistic entity as far back as age one-and-a-half. Most kids my age were learning to say "Mamma" and "bye-bye" and "mine!". My infantile phraseology included such gems as, "I can't!" and "Impossible!" and "Never in a million years!"

Negative thinking was not only what I did, it was who I was, how I defined myself, both as a child and also well into adulthood. Here are some of the skills I acquired from a very young age:

- I always figured that what I thought or how I felt or how I behaved, which was almost always negative, was accurate and based in fact; this was my reality.
- I perceived everything negatively and made predictions about how badly things would turn out, even when—especially when—I had no proof.

- No matter how good the going was, I would search for and dwell on a single negative detail (even if I had to invent it) and ruminate on that negative aspect, no matter what; in the process, I would ignore or discount all of the good stuff.

- I saw everything as all-or-nothing; if something didn't turn out perfect, which it never did, then obviously I was a total failure.

- Without checking my perception for truth and accuracy, I *knew* that others saw me, hated me, and reacted to me negatively because I *knew* what they were thinking and why. And I *knew* I was right.

- For me, even just *one* negative event confirmed that I was a loser; everything revolved around the emphatic words, 'never' and 'always'... I inserted them into my conversations with others whenever I could: "You always do this" and "You never do that", not a particularly popular way to interact.

- I would dismiss or ignore a positive experience by discounting its significance, and I would insist that it didn't matter or that it wasn't important (often accompanied with a pretty dorky explanation). This allowed me to suck the fun out of life and replace it with feelings of helplessness and hopelessness.

- I usually exaggerated the importance of my problems, and focused on my shortcomings, rarely acknowledging any positive or desirable qualities and situations.

- I was always telling myself that things should have turned out the way I had hoped or expected them to, whether or not those things were within my control.

- I practically grew a tail of negative labels which I attached to myself; it followed me wherever I went.

- I was responsible for undesirable outcomes in my life and in life in general—and I could find a way of making them *all* undesirable, even if they weren't entirely within my control, and even if I had little or nothing to do with them.

- "I'm a failure!" "I'm a loser!" "I'm no good!" "I can't do anything!" I reassured myself of these assertions daily, year after year, until the meaning of them became my nature and the assertions themselves became second nature.

It came as no surprise, then, that my feelings were also pretty negative and extremely unenjoyable. I was depressed, filled with fear and rage, left hopeless, helpless, and vulnerable most of the time. As a result, I immersed myself in self-pity and resentment, since nobody else cared a whit for how I was feeling. This, in turn, led to feelings of insignificance to the point of being practically invisible to the rest of the world. Consequently, I became mistrustful and jealous, thinking everyone was insincere and was betraying me at every turn. And so I became terribly lonely. I was grieving for having lost who I was, for my very essence. Even if I dabbled in feelings such as pride and lust (not that there was much to feel proud or lustful about, mind you), I was still fraught with such intense guilt and worry and shame and embarrassment. My anxiety level was through the roof. I was beyond frustration! Aargh!

Clearly, I was doing something wrong. I was not behaving appropriately. I knew this because everyone kept telling me so or telling me how I should behave. At first I was immobilized, usually communicating with passive aggression. Sometimes I acted out, even lied on occasion, gave resistance, blamed others, and even took on responsibility for things that weren't mine to take on. I complained about everything, I gossiped—usually for attention—to anyone who would listen. If I wasn't holding a grudge about one thing or another, I was finding ways of getting out of doing things, seeking revenge, and neither making nor implementing decisions that could have benefitted me. Even if I knew what was good for me (which I didn't), I would do the opposite and preach the opposite. But why? I just wanted to be accepted, to be approved of, to be validated. I just wanted to have some semblance of control in my life, of being safe and secure. I just wanted to express my individuality and, at the same time, to be a part of something, to belong. Unfortunately, I tried to accomplish all of this by using every defence mechanism known to mankind. But it wasn't working. Nothing was working. I was doing something wrong! And I had to fix it!

To do this I had to look at the world around me...

PART II

THE JOURNEY WITHOUT

THE QUEST

THE GRAY FOG

PURGATORIO

UNCERTAINTY AND WANDERING

A nifty if somewhat obvious double entendre: the Journey Without.

As noted several times in Part I, and as will be noted throughout the rest of this book, the key to any successful self-help book is a gimmick designed to unlock your doubts and inhibitions, and to inspire you to seek and find that blue bird, that pot of gold, that buried treasure, that silver lining, that Shangri-La. I am not above the use of such a gimmick and so, as you have seen and will see, this book is filled with metaphors enough to stimulate the hardiest of pyloric valves. I am humble enough, however, to admit that my examples and analogies are banal and unimaginative for even the dullest of human beings. Consequently, I welcome—nay, challenge—you to substitute your own more lucid, creative, and personally meaningful examples and analogies wherever possible. For this there is good reason, which will become apparent in due course.

Imagine, if you will, your own neighbourhood. You step into the starlit night, the same starlit night that encompasses lovely country roads or crazed neon streets. The tinny chirping of crickets, the blaring of taxi horns and ghetto blasters—it doesn't matter. You've wandered many, many times aimlessly through the maze of familiar streets in your neighbourhood but you have not found it. You know every nook and cranny, every doorway and alleyway but, still, it eludes you. The frustration and dissatisfaction become too much to bear. You must leave. You must break out.

Like Dorothy on the Yellow Brick Road you take your first step, toes tingling with an odd combination of anticipation and apprehension. You take that first step away from all that is familiar to you. Before too long, there is a fork in the road. A voice in the back of your mind echoes, "Some people do go both ways!" You peer into the distance down one road, then the other. You can see that each road contains more forks, more paths, some criss-crossing, some only running parallel, some doing a weird dimensional thing with spirals and twists and turns, like an out-of-control roller-coaster. In nightmarish terror, heart pounding, beads of sweat running off your brow, you shut your eyes tightly and choose one of the roads. You step forward. Slowly, you open your eyes. There's a signpost up ahead. A movie marquis: *starring Bob and Bing in: The Road to* . . . What? What?! You grab your head like it's in a vice and scream, "Stop! Stop, I can't stand it anymore! I'm drowning in a sea of amalgamated allegories! A mud puddle of metaphors! Make them go away!" But they won't go away. You must choose another from other forks in the road. But where will it lead? This road. This road to . . .

Like Dante's journey through Purgatory, I set out on my Journey Without by first exploring that which was accessible and familiar. So I began with the physical world around me, with scant criteria: Does this confuse me less? Does this provide me with the answers to that which I am seeking? Does this lead to or offer happiness, contentment, fulfilment? This road to . . .

THE ROAD
TO THE PHYSICAL

I began by easing on down the Road to the Physical, taking it slow partly because I did not know what to expect, and partly because I really was not sure what I was looking for: a safe haven, perhaps, or a special place; somewhere private where I could explore all the pleasures and excitement that hedonism had to offer; somewhere that I could envelop myself in all my senses and perceptions. Perhaps I could discover ways of enhancing and developing my senses and perceptions.

This was going to be great! I would sample all the different foods of the world with relish—well, maybe without *relish*! Experience tastes and flavours, all manner of exotica. I would wrap myself in silk and softness and Cottonelle. I would feel the butterfly kisses of a tropical breeze as it riffles through my imaginary hair while I gaze into the hypnotic emerald-azure sea. I would immerse myself in soothing, bubbling mineral waters, inhale intoxicating fragrances, maybe get a deep muscle tissue massage while having a feather lightly caress my skin. I would engage in all sorts of sex and all kinds of kinkiness. Most importantly, I would bask in the glow of good health and well-being.

Surly *this* is bliss. *This* is fulfilment. *This* is happiness . . .

LIVING IN A BUBBLE
(self-protection: shelter, clothing, safety, security)

—⟡———

*"I live in a beautiful house made of glass, and it's close to
everything . . . just a stone's throw away."*

—⟡———

I have never known homelessness. The fact that there might not always
be a roof over my head not once ever occurred to me as I was growing
up. Even while taking an evening stroll downtown, stepping over legs
outstretched from storefront doorways and under cardboard boxes, I
never entertained the notion of not having a place to live. Not that I
was holed up in a mansion with valets, maids, and butlers. I lived in
a modest suburban bungalow. But the only cold I knew came from an
open refrigerator. The only exposure I was exposed to was an odd little
man who literally hung out at the neighbourhood park.

Once I went camping, and I was not impressed. We had a tent;
we had the camping equipment. But the ground was damp, the night
noises distressing, the creepy crawlers unnerving, and the lack of private
bathroom facilities downright humiliating. No cable either.

Clothing is another type of protection, although the way some
people dress it's more like a crime. Through sheer temerity and dislike
of full-length mirrors, I have not aspired to nudity except in the shower
with a closed curtain and a locked door, where I can boogie with
the best of them. So I sport my anonymous apparel of shirt, pants,
underwear, socks and shoes. I now have a tendency to dress down to
dull as a result of my somewhat flamboyant finery in my early teen years.
My father worked in a men's clothing store and brought home some
pretty outrageous outfits. He would beam with pride at my brand new

embroidered slacks and Elvis shirt, exclaiming, "I'll bet no one in your whole school has clothes like *this*!" "No Dad," I would respond, "I'm the first." And the last. But my clothing did work as protection. It kept many people at arm's length.

My parents sheltered me from many of life's unwelcome intrusions. I never wonted for food, for a home, for clothing and, in a peculiar way, for love. I was never abused by them (unless guilt can be used as a form of abuse) and was always provided for. They gave me a sense of security. Then one day we had a break-in. Some neighbourhood thugs smashed the kitchen window to gain access, burgled, and took off with some jewellery and cash, leaving heaps of rubble in their wake. My sense of security was dented. Several years later my mother, and still later after that, my father died. My sense of security was demolished.

Same thing with my sense of safety. When I was ten I was beaten up at school and, many years after that, my son was injured in a motor vehicle accident.

So I concluded that no one is safe; nothing is secure. The best you can do is to minimize the vulnerability and constantly adjust your perceptions of self-protection. Am I worrying about where I am going to sleep tonight or am I worried about the square footage of my family room? How do I hide my frayed shirt collar versus how do I slim down to a 34 waist size to fit into that Armani suit? Do I reaffirm that people come and go in this world and nothing is forever? Decide upon the degree of caution you want to exercise. Shall I insist on making my child wear a helmet, or shall I forbid him ever to cross a street? Should I chance a relationship, or isolate myself, fearing a departure?

And what about the threat of nuclear warfare? he segued. Terrorist attacks? Earthquakes and floods? Civil Unrest? War? Collision-course asteroids? Environmental deterioration? Solar burnout?

Can we really ever protect ourselves? Unlikely. Eventually, illness and/or injury is/are inevitable.

Dum-de-dum-dum . . .

MURDER BY INGESTION
(consumption)

"Now that food has replaced my sex life, I can't even get into my own pants!"

Call me 'wimp'. Call me 'wuss'. Call me 'square', 'uncool', 'a drag'. I don't drink and I don't do drugs. I'm not preaching; it's just that drugs and alcohol aren't for me.

Drugs frighten me. In my quest for happiness, I have always shied away from drugs. As a kid it was my naivety that steered me clear. I knew drugs existed; I just never knew where people got them from and I was too embarrassed to ask. And the mere thought of administering drugs into my body: shudder! Pills were out; I could barely squeeze an aspirin down my esophagus. I'd probably choke to death before the pill could take effect. Too squeamish for needles; blood tests make me dizzy. With anything that was snortworthy, I'd most likely sneeze myself into a frenzy. As for smoking, I never learned to inhale (smoke, that is). But the thing that frightens me most is the inability to take charge when under the influence. The way I see it, happiness is something *you* control, not something that has control of *you*.

As more socially acceptable as alcohol may be, it's not my cup of tea. One drink gives me the excuse not to be me. Two drinks make my legs heavy and give me the excuse to be me while pretending that I'm not. Three drinks encourage me to chase people around the room. Four drinks make me cry 'til I laugh. Five drinks and I am blanketed in my own barf . . . not a pretty sight and not my idea of happiness.

For some perverse reason, however, food will give me a buzz. Despite my vows to be health-conscious, despite my commitment to animal rights and my commitment to vegetable rights, and despite my affirmation that my body is my temple, I am forever desecrating myself by ingesting anything that no longer moves and will fit into my mouth. The weirder the better: smoked eel in green sauce; grilled medallions of anything that once roamed the prairies; you-name-it dripping in dressings, sauces, or gravies; cakes, cookies, pies, or tortes of all shapes and gooiness. I pack it in until I'm good and sick. Then I make all sorts of promises between groans that carrot sticks for the rest of my life will be my penitence. Before too long, I am stepping out of the toilet, a smile on my face, anticipating with delight that next bite of pickled squid. Ahhhhh . . .

But is this happiness? Contentment? Self-satisfaction? The cycle of the digestive system suggests that all is for naught, save the stimulation of a few hyperactive tastebuds. Like an infatuation or a quickie, it may be a pleasurable experience but, by its very nature, you can't have a lasting relationship with food.

And so the quest continues . . .

SEX IS RUFFLED SHIRT

(sex)

*"Life is very confusing. I spent the first nine months trying to get
out of a vagina and the rest of my life trying to get back **in**!"*

My plain white shirt is a practical garment. It has a function; it serves
a purpose. My plain white shirt keeps me warm, modest, and covered.
If I sew a ruffle down the front of it and onto the cuffs, my plain white
shirt has different properties and new connotations: I am going to a
formal affair; I am a circus performer; I am a dandy. It all depends on
how my brain interprets a ruffled shirt.

Sex, in my opinion, begins as a plain white shirt. It is a physical act
that happens to feel good in order to instigate or initiate procreation.
The natural flaw (or bonus, depending on how you look at it) is that you
are not required to procreate in order to engage in sex. This allows us to
sew ruffles all over the place; that is, we have the ability to give different
properties and new connotations to sex. Our thoughts, opinions, morals,
values, and desires, are our ruffles. Hence the common theme that our
brains are the largest of our sex organs.

Just as living without a shirt (ruffled or otherwise) is uncommon,
chilly, and leaves us with a feeling that something is missing, so is living
without sex. It can be done, but who really wants to?

There are physical differences in the sexual anatomy of men and
women (for those of you who haven't noticed). There are also an apparent
number of psychological and emotional differences although some argue
that these differences are learned and some argue they are innate.

The power of sex is stupefying (ask any woman how men view sex). Whole cultures, civilizations, and entire lives have been based on sex, sexual practices, sexual orientation, sexual preferences and so on. It can be very confusing. Throw in the concepts of love, romance, and relationships and, well, some could say we have sewn one too many ruffles. Sex has become the focus and raison d'être of books, movies, plays, television programs, advertisements, magazines, and internet selections. Sex occupies our time and preoccupies our thoughts.

And underneath all the ruffles, what you have is a few seconds (multiple seconds, in some cases) of muscle contractions between the legs and a mess on your plain white shirt.

Neil Katz

PAGING DOCTOR FEEL-GOOD
(health/physical well-being)

"I went for a sleep study because of my insomnia and the doctor told me I have hyper-aroused neurons in my big ol' head. Now if only the **little** *head would get insomnia!"*

I decided, what with all the subliminal messages from television advertisements (which must all be true and meritorious or they wouldn't be allowed on public airwaves), that looking good, being fit, and feeling good embody the happiness I had been seeking. I wanted to have a six-pack instead of a one-pack; I wanted to grow strong bones twelve ways; I wanted to be "Yoptimal" and bathed in "Oil of Olay"; I wanted to exude the confidence that my deodorant stick promised to give me; I wanted to watch age lines disappear, reap the benefits of Preparation H, and lope in slow motion through fields of clover, feeling well-protected and fresh as a daisy by my panty-liner.

Purchasing a gym membership seemed like a good place to start. I did a sit-up once so I knew something about physical fitness. But when I saw all those treadmills, elliptical machines, and stationary bicycles, it seemed like an awful lot of work to go nowhere fast. The sounds of ritual grunts and the olfactory assault of stale sweat was not something I would look forward to at each visit. Moreover, I did not relish the thought of humiliating myself by straining to lift five-pound dumbbells while those around me would be flexing and kissing the bulge of their biceps, each the size of a small mountain. Also, paying money to move my body seemed rather foolhardy when I could move it on my own, any way I liked, outside the prison of a fitness club, and for free. My thumbs, in fact, got plenty of exercise with the TV remote, until I developed arthritis in them. So I bought a lanyard from which I dangled my gym membership card around my neck as an affirmation of my athletic prowess (more like an albatross), while secretly willing it to expire.

Having a gym membership was exhausting, so I decided to turn my attention from being fit to looking fit. Although nothing short of radical plastic surgery (and many of them all over the place) would really get me looking the way I thought I should look, I could not stomach the notion of subjecting myself to being sliced and diced and otherwise vivisected by some sadist surgeon who would probably take a world cruise on my pain and suffering. And there were so many body parts in need of repair that I didn't know where to begin. At random, I supposed I could start at the top and work my way down, starting with my shiny-domed noggin. There wasn't a whole lot I could do about its flat-backed, forehead-dented, misshapen quality, thanks to an impatient OBGYN and his forceps. I mean you can't exactly caulk it, or spackle it, or fill it in with wood putty. So I figured I could hide it under a crop of hair which I didn't possess. Having been bald since before my twenty-sixth birthday—genetics is nothing more than a cruel cosmic joke—a co-worker presented me with a gift. "Works better than Rogaine," he exclaimed. I unwrapped the gift to discover a bottle of bull semen. After my initial shock, disgust, and reluctance, I went home and dumped the bottle on my head. To make a long story short, I didn't grow hair but I did develop an insatiable desire to grunt at red capes. As for other alternatives, hair plugs would be too painful, toupees too sweaty, and comb-overs too pathetic. I decided that if I waited long enough, I could simply grow and style my nose and ear hair to distract from my lack of cranial hair.

As a kid I had these enormous appendages growing out of the sides of my head. Not only big but perpendicular as well. "We can get the doctor to pin those ears back," my mother considered. "Or surgically remove some of the excess cartilage," my aunt offered. I was terrified!

My sister told them to leave me alone, but she had an ulterior motive. Whenever she got mad at me—which was a daily occurrence—she would delight in telling me to "flap your ears and fly away to Africa with the other Dumbo elephants, you big-eared fairy!" Ultimately I was saved by the passage of time, which allowed my head to catch up with my ear size. Except now I had a big giant head to match my oversized ears.

I did have soulful blue eyes, even teeth, and a noble chin with which I was somewhat satisfied. Through karmic intervention somewhere in my thirtieth year of life, however, I contracted a virus which partially and permanently paralyzed the right side of my face. Consequently I developed a lopsided grin, my eye drips tears when I eat, and closes shut when I smile.

As I approached my middle years, I watched my spine curve into a number seven and I saw my belly go to pot. Nervously I chewed my fingers to bloody stumps as I once again cast my gaze into the looking glass. I witnessed my own metamorphosis into *old*: Wrinkles and skin tags and jowls! Oh, my! Age spots and turkey neck and cataracts! Oy, vey!

Where was this search for happiness and meaning—this Journey Without—taking me?!

I thought I could cover up all my flaws with nice clothes and accessories, ensuring I was always in vogue, in haute couture, and a la mode. Nehru jackets, sandals, and pookah necklaces in the sixties; bell bottoms, platform shoes, and gold chain ID bracelets in the seventies; preppie vests, yuppie suits, and multi-function watches in the eighties; and so on. The older I got and the more flaws I developed, the more outlandish the outfit. One day I returned home to my family, after a day of shopping, wearing a shiny black shirt with red embroidery on the cuffs and collar, fitted black denim pants, a pair of pointy red leather shoes, and a black bowler with a red plume.

"Ew, Dad, you're so embarrassing!" my daughters chimed.

"Is the circus in town?" my son queried.

"A new wardrobe to flit around in . . . how flamboyant," said my wife, somewhat less than enthusiastic or encouraging.

I went back to the mall the next day to exchange my outfit for a beige and gray potato sack.

Well, if I wasn't fit, and if I didn't look good, at least I could feel good, or so I thought. Every time I became resolute with the concept of feeling good, my body would betray me with some form of illness or another: hypertension, diabetes, pneumonia, stomach ailments, a rogue gall bladder, neuralgia, neuropathy, scoliosis, osteo-arthritis, spinal stenosis, fibromyalgia, costochondritis—the older I got, the longer the name of the illness. My doctor finally gave up and diagnosed me with Syndrome X: General Weirdness. I didn't realize until, one day, singing the children's song to my granddaughter "Head and shoulders, knees and toes, eyes, ears, mouth and nose" was simply a musical way of identifying my aches and pains.

I suppose I could have blamed my parents, considering I was genetically predisposed to unbalanced neurotransmitters, but that wouldn't make me feel better.

I hated taking medicine. Ingesting massive doses of antibiotics as a kid and pain medication as an adult was not how I envisioned the way to feel good.

As my assortment of "-ology" doctors recommended the use of opioids, steroids, cannabinoids, and even botox injections and dangerous surgery, I began to wonder what it was in the body that made one feel good in the first place.

Although fascinating, science was not a subject in which I was well-versed. So I decided to research (skim rather than delve) into the inner workings of the brain, namely the hormones, amino acids, neuropeptides, chemicals, and neurotransmitters responsible for feeling good.

First, though, I needed to determine what I *meant* by "feeling good". This includes (but is not limited to): feelings of euphoria or bliss, cravings, desire, increased goal orientation, attentive focus, sexual desire, trust, affection, sensuality, and sensitivity, feeling less depressed, more optimistic, and seeing people in a more positive light. Feeling good also includes relaxation and a better ability to sleep, reduction of pain, change in hunger cues (increased or decreased, depending on what was required), a sense of excitement, exhilaration, and even heightened orgasm.

In order to feel these good feelings, I learned that the body needs to release (or absorb) certain chemicals and hormones, such as dopamine, serotonin, melatonin, adrenaline, epinephrine, GABA, oxytocin, endorphins, pheromones, testosterone, estrogen, vasopressin, cortisol, phenylanaline, glutamine, tryptophan, thrypto-crypto-cyclo-globulo-lutenizing-andro-neutro-blah-blah-blah . . . you know, *stuff*.

A "normal" body is supposed to produce this stuff naturally. Since there is nothing natural about me (insert chorus from father and wife, "You're not natural", here), and therefore did not want to introduce anything artificial into my body to unnaturalize me even more (that is, drugs, prescription or otherwise), I needed to find a way to elicit, stimulate, manufacture, or squeeze out those chemicals and hormones.

I admit I did try vitamins, Andro-type products, and melatonin tablets from the health food store, but it didn't do much for me other than to give me the opportunity to keep neutraceutical companies in business.

Anyway, I had to view this whole feel-good notion from the perspective of a "normal" person. If my body were to behave the way it should, what would induce a release of afore-mentioned stuff?

I was drawn back to my ruminations of thoughts, feelings, and behaviour. First, I have at least five physical senses (that I am aware of). When I see a beautiful lush garden, I feel calm; a sudden loud noise may cause me to jump; a waft of freshly baked cookies might get my stomach growling; a deep muscle tissue massage might make me feel exhausted or refreshed or both. It's not so much the seeing, hearing, tasting, smelling or touching in itself that causes the chemical response but how the brain (the thought) interprets the messages received from the eyes, ears, nose, mouth, and skin. Doing something to stimulate the senses would likely initiate some kind of chemical reaction, so it was really a matter of discovering the right stimuli to effect a positive, desired response that would make me feel good.

The same cause-and-effect principle would hold true, I supposed, for emotions. Blind rage or abject fear would likely cause a rush of adrenaline. Moments of inspiration that create feelings of awe or joy might cause a feeling of euphoria or peacefulness. Amorous feelings would probably promote a spew of pheromones. Instigating a feeling therefore would create an internal chemical reaction.

And what about behaviour? Is it possible that the actions I take, what I do, and how I behave can, in turn, trigger a thought or spark a feeling, which would ignite a response in me? I uncovered (upon further research) that the following activities can stimulate such a response:

- Singing, whistling, laughing, humming
- Laughing, watching a comedy show
- Exercising, moving the body, dancing
- Listening to music
- Watching an emotionally charged movie or play
- Looking at certain colours, spending time outdoors, preferably in sunshine
- Gazing at the stars, a beautiful scene, or a pretty picture
- Massage, acupuncture, meditating, practising yoga, enjoying solitude
- Aromatherapy, smelling perfumes, or smelling freshly baked goods
- Engaging in sex/lovemaking

- Having a gourmet dinner, eating chocolate, or consuming spicy food
- Reading stories of inspiration, praying, expressing a belief
- Being in the company of positive and supportive people, or involved in community
- Holding an infant, taking care of a pet
- Creating something

So, what are the effects of these chemical reactions? Some are mood elevating, enhancing, and create a sense of euphoria. Others are excitatory, make you feel happy, alert, motivated, act as an antidepressant, control appetite, give energy, and enhance sexual arousal. Some may cause feelings of bliss and pleasure, control motor movements, and help you feel focused. Still others facilitate alertness, memory, sexual performance, and cause a release of growth hormone. Some may induce feelings of infatuation, or restrict transmission of pain, or reduce craving, or help to lift that depressive haze. Some can be found throughout central nervous system, and create an environment of anti-stress, anti-anxiety, anti-panic, and anti-pain. Others have been known to promote and improve sleep or, at least, allow rest and recuperation, increase self-esteem, regulate the body clock, and aid in diminishing anxiety and worry. Some can cause you to feel happy, loving and motivated. Others can help you to feel calm and in control.

If all of this is true, and I'm still debating myself about it, then there is definitely something to be said for the physical aspect of feeling good. Still, there seemed to be something missing from this entire exploration . . . the idea that life has meaning. What good is having a body full of happy chemicals if there is no substance, no deeper meaning or sense of fulfilment other than feeling good?

So onward I trudged on my Journey Without.

THE ROAD TO
THE INTELLECTUAL

Clearly, the Road to the Physical wasn't all it was cracked up to be; it didn't lead me to the happiness I was seeking. At best, there were a few fleeting moments of fun. At worst, it left me empty, hollow, and insubstantial.

Perhaps I needed to explore a different road. Maybe I needed to be more cerebral, to be a disembodied big giant head.

I began this leg of my Journey Without by stepping onto the bridge connecting the Road to the Physical to the Road to the Intellectual. On this bridge I would be able to explore the concepts of money or wealth, of fame and recognition, and of order, government and control, not only from their physical, practical aspects but also from an intellectual perspective. This would then lead me to the true Road to the Intellectual where I could explore at leisure, with my enormous noggin, all of the different and varied off-the-beaten-path ideas concerning who I am, what I am doing, where I am going, and with whom and how I am interacting. Also, there would be the well-trampled paths that would show me the way to happiness and fulfilment through education and knowledge, the philosophy and psychology of life, and through various forms of therapy.

Will seeking answers through these external intellectual resources help me find true happiness and the meaning of life? Let's see, shall we?

"KID, I'M GONNA MAKE YOU A STAR!"

(fame/recognition)

——∿∾⊶⊙⊷∾⊙∿——

"One of the good things about not being famous:
I have to do something really, really stupid to make the tabloids."

——∿∾⊶⊙⊷∾⊙∿——

Like being hurtled through a time portal in a really hoaky sci-fi movie from the sixties, I found myself tossed on the floor and dishevelled in the arena of fame. I decided to explore this venue for happiness because, after all, who doesn't strive for recognition? For his fifteen minutes?

The clock started ticking.

Like wealth, which often accompanies it, fame (or infamy) is fleeting and next to impossible to achieve. Some people stumble upon it, some are introduced to it through someone else, a few work towards it. More often, it is happenstance that casts its limelight on someone who, as fortune (or misfortune) would have it, just happened to be in the right (or wrong) place at the right (or wrong) time.

Being famous should have come easily to me, considering I spent most of my life seeking attention, usually by misbehaving or whining. It got me punished, not famous.

If you are seeking fame and if you are, at best, mediocre like me, you need to accomplish something of significance or, at least, do something with a unique flair, with panache, and with confidence. After all, you are competing with seven billion other people in the arena.

Ten minutes left on the clock.

So how does one really become famous? By possessing and demonstrating a talent: in the arts—singing, dancing writing, acting, painting; in science—a medical breakthrough, a new discovery, a different kind of law in quantum physics, or a different kind of physics altogether; in sports—the best defence, goalie, pitcher, sprinter, boxer, or golfer. By putting yourself in the public eye: politician, TV reality star, monarch, terrorist, news anchor, bank robber, or supermodel. By creating: architect, composer, or inventor. By doing something or being someone distinctive: winner of a slug-eating contest, having loads of money or owning tons of properties, or being ten feet tall with two heads and tree branches growing out of your nose.

Five minutes left and counting.

I racked my brain to figure out what my claim to fame would be. I have a singing voice like a bleating goat; I dance with three left feet; my innate ability to create, invent, design, and produce are exceeded only by my ability to sing and dance. Nobody would tune in to see my life unfold on television; they'd rather poke out their eyes. I could never deliberately show myself in a public forum since I'm afraid of my own shadow.

Two-minute warning!

Besides, there are already so many talented, creative, and unique people in this world who *aren't* famous. How would I stand a chance? And how would I know where, when, and with whom to be to create the chain reaction that would catapult me to fame?

Most importantly, does fame even result in happiness? When you see all the divorced Hollywood stars, the cracked out rockers, the broken, impoverished, and starving artists, the disgraced politicians, asylum-bound philosophers, and paparazzi-hounded newsmakers—

Time's up!

I looked around the arena of fame at the spectators who, in turn, were alternately looking inquisitively at me and in bewilderment at one another. After fifteen minutes they unanimously called out for the next act.

"IT'S A RICH MAN'S WORLD"
(money/wealth)

*** *"Whenever I pass by a bank I get withdrawal symptoms."* ***

*** *"I earn a seven-figure salary. Unfortunately,*
there's a decimal point involved." ***

Whoever said money is the root of all evil was probably a religious fanatic who was strapped for cash. In my opinion, money might not buy happiness, but I sure as hell wouldn't turn it down if I were offered some.

Clearly I'm not a rich dude. I am neither old money nor new money. Closer to no money. In fact, I am just an average Joe with the requisite amount of debt and a small desire to keep up with the Jones's. I had a steady paycheque—now a steady pension—which gives me enough to see the odd movie or go out to an occasional restaurant. I have a functional automobile and a modest home. I have food in the fridge and sufficient clothes to keep me from being naked and out of jail. That's it.

So does money make the world go 'round? Money in itself as a physical entity doesn't have much intrinsic value; it's just paper or metal. As a convenient tool to replace barter and exchange, money has its purpose. It is the *want* of money, though, that is in question, especially with respect to its relationship with happiness and fulfilment. If indeed money does not buy happiness per se, it can buy things you might want to have or it can buy time to do the things you've always wanted to do.

The difficulty, as studies have shown, is *acquiring* money can be a bummer because it's not always as easy as it sounds; also, having money can be unsatisfying because the more you have, the more you want. It turns out that once basic needs are met, having more money does not necessarily increase your happiness.

Also, with money comes responsibility. This includes determining how shrewdly the money is allocated (such as investments and diversified portfolios) or how wisely the money is spent (not squandered).

In addition to all of this, it has been said that the *manner* in which one acquires the money has more to do with the happiness factor—albeit short-term—than the actual possession of the money itself. The thrill of winning a lottery, the pride of having worked hard for the money, the gratitude for having received an inheritance, the anticipation and adrenaline rush from a slot machine pay-off… it all quickly dissipates over a relatively short period of time.

And I can prove it to you: Just give me some money and watch how fast I'll ask for more. Go ahead. Your donation will be our little experiment at proving this theory true. Really. Just hand it over. I've already spent it in my head. Give me the damn money!

It seems there is a fine line between desperation and happiness.

"ORDER IN THE COURT!"

(order and government; control and routine)

"All power corrupts; absolute power is pretty neat, though."

I read something somewhere once about a second or third law of something-or-other which states that everything in this world naturally attempts to move away from order to return to its original state of chaos. Yet most of us strive for order in our lives: order in our daily routine, order in our society, order in our relationships. We attempt to achieve order by planning and scheduling, by organizing, by government, by laws and their enforcement, order through democratic or autocratic means, order through control and manipulation, order by taming and disciplining, by queuing, by categorizing, and by putting things in their place.

I, for one, hate a messy desk. The less on it the better I function. The office of one of my colleagues looks like it is constantly hosting a ticker tape parade; I don't know how she manages. Crowds drive me nuts. The thought of a free-for-all lawless society scares me. I prefer a neat closet, a well-used day planner, and an orderly existence.

But if chaos is the natural state, why is my inclination to fight against nature?

My wife intimates I have a proclivity to being anal, which is probably why she calls me an asshole. She also says I'm not natural. Perhaps she is telling me I am anti-chaotic, valiantly trying to make some sense out of a non-sensible world. Which really is a compliment. I must remember to thank her next time she calls me an unnatural asshole.

Anyway, the question still remains unanswered: Am I fighting against nature by trying to put a little order into my world? Could this be, perhaps, why I always feel at odds, unhappy, unfulfilled? And is there anything I could *do* about it?

What I could *do* about it, thought I, in my infinite wisdom, is a little experiment. I could make a concerted effort to put aside my penchant for organizing. No more planning my days. No more scheduling or keeping appointments. Let the kids run amok, undisciplined. Mess up my desk. The room. The house. Break a few rules. Break a few laws! Run through the streets naked and free! . . .

Well, maybe not *that*. But I really did try to be less rigid, more spontaneous, less concerned about having my ducks in a row, more adventurous, less controlling, more in the moment, less uptight, more or less.

Still, and in spite of everything, I kept gravitating toward the unnatural state of order.

Order in the court! *Order in the court*?

The jury is still out on this one.

"AS TIME GOES BY" . . . "THE TIME OF YOUR LIFE" . . . "TIME IS MY FRIEND" . . .

(vocation/work, pastimes/leisure activities/hobbies: how I spend my time)

———⁓⁓⟋◦◠⟍⟋⊙⟍⟍⊙⟍⟍⊙⟍⟍———

"In just two days, tomorrow will be yesterday."

———⁓⁓⟋◦◠⟍⟋⊙⟍⟍⊙⟍⟍⟍⊙⟍⟍———

The next few stops on my Journey Without were, in fact, just one stop with several components to ponder. I wanted to take a look at my vocation/work life, my pastimes/leisure activities/hobbies, my daily needs, my involvement with current events, and so on. I soon realized that what I really wanted to examine was an element common to all of these areas: how do I spend my time?

First, what was my vocation? Was it a job or was it a career? Did it provide me with the rewards and fulfilment that a vocation ought to? Being involved in Social Services first as a case worker, then as a fraud investigator, and finally as a management person, from one day to the next, I reviewed files, completed reports, settled disputes, managed a large number of staff, ensured the clients were being serviced appropriately, controlled the office budget, and took care of the physical plant. In short, I was a paper pusher, a babysitter, and a janitor. On good days, I was shown appreciation by staff; on great days, the clients would express gratitude for the service they received. Ultimately, I did what was expected of me, but could I have done more? I got myself promoted, as was expected of me, but was this what I wanted? I don't know for sure, even though I spent thirty-three years of my life at it. I know I have always had a strong pull toward providing service to others. But maybe I should have been a goat-herder. Or a town crier. Or a spelunking master. How do you ever truly know how to spend your life?

When I wasn't working, I was always trying to find something to fill my time. Occasionally, I would write, draw, read, learn a new language, and, once in a while, travel; sometimes I would see a movie, or go out for dinner, or listen to old records. Mostly, I'd watch TV. Every single night after a hard day at work. And on weekends. Usually I'd just sit with a bag of chips and stare at the television screen, often oblivious to the content of what I was watching. But I had the sense I was indeed filling my time, not *ful*filling my time.

I spent ample time on personal hygiene and maintenance. But these always seemed, however necessary as they might be, real time-wasters. Before I found a passion for food as a form of art and entertainment, I would scarf down what I had to in order to keep alive and then get on with it. Then, having married the self-proclaimed world's greatest chef (with which I am in complete agreement), my perspective and my waistline began to change. But I tried to turn my food experience into something useful. When my kids were younger and my wife was honing her culinary skills, we used to create imaginative feasts, such as a jungle cruise dinner (river banks of mashed potatoes, with broccoli trees, and roast beef rafts floating down a muddy river of brown gravy). Or turkey men at war (slices of turkey breast, cut into shapes of duelling warriors, complete with cranberry sauce for blood). We would have themed dinners, like a Valentine's Day meal, where everything was shaped into hearts and dyed red with food colouring. Or a Hallowe'en dinner, where each course was a zombie-like and weird-textured delight. Then there were the more sophisticated international themed dinners, which would transport us to a Parisian cafe, or a Cajun/Creole Mardi Gras party, or an exotic Indonesian rijstaffel, or a New England clambake, or a romantic Venetian gondola dinner fit for an emperor. The more innovative the better. The more courses the better.

This would inevitably increase the time I spent in the powder room, flushing away the meal along with the time and effort it took to create and consume. A waste in every way.

I also considered sleep a waste of time. Why sleep when there was so much else to do?

Why sleep when there was so much to get excited about? I remember the night before my first day at school (from kindergarten to grade thirteen), lying awake all night long, and eager with anticipation, already dressed and ready to go. I remember travelling on the night train (many years later) through Europe with my wife, peering into the darkness beyond my reflection, fascinated by the treasures that might lie beyond. "What, you're afraid you're going to miss something?" my wife, a great advocate of sleep, asked me. "As a matter of fact, yes," I replied. She shook her head and went back to sleep. Then she punctuated her point the next day by sleeping through an entire canal boat tour of Amsterdam. Caught in one of life's little ironies, now that I'm older, whenever I *want* to get some sleep, I'm wide awake.

I would also get caught up in current events. Much time was spent watching television and reading newspapers about wars and disasters, signs of the times, celebrity silliness, articles on cats with two heads or a moose on the loose, documentaries, and what's happening magazines. As long as any of this had nothing to do with me and I didn't need to actually *do* anything about it, I was interested. It passed the time.

Now that I have retired and have all the time in the world (did somebody just snicker?), I struggle every day to figure out what to do with my time and wonder where all the time has gone. I am drawn to Jacques Brel's song, "The Old Folks"; I am constantly thinking of "the old, old silver clock, that's hanging on the wall, that waits for us all". In my search for happiness and fulfilment, have I spent my time wisely? Am I doing what I need to do to declare that my time is well-spent? How much time do I have left?

Does it matter?

THROUGH A LOOKING GLASS? REALLY?

(relationships)

"I'm such a lousy lover that when my wife is in the mood,
*she tells me to give her an **anti**-climax."*

"I had some words with my wife and she had some paragraphs with me . . .
it was actually more like consecutive sentences."

I stopped for a while on my Journey Without to take a look at the various relationships I have had or am having that impact me in my quest for a happy and rewarding existence (insert apprehensive yet quizzical happy face emoticon here).

As previously asserted, my sister had been a major influence in my formative years, so it is little wonder that I blame her for the arrested development of my ability to form relationships of any kind. You see, when I was six years old, my sister informed me that all human beings were born with limited access to words, that there was a cosmic vocabulary pool from which each family was allotted only so many words. The trouble was, in *my* family, my sister like to talk a lot, incessantly, all the time to each of her gazillion friends. Every day she used up our family's word supply so that when it came time for me to interact with anyone, there were no words left for me to engage in a conversation with anyone. Most people just thought I was developmentally challenged and left me alone.

I have worked hard to improve my relationship skills somewhat over the years—that lexicon of the universe is probably much bigger than she led me to believe—and yet making friends is still a foreboding enterprise.

Still, I recognize that humans were designed to be social; so, despite my monastic, hermit-like tendencies, I began to forge relationships outside my immediate family, parents and sister (of whom I was certain already had a low opinion of me), first with the neighbourhood kids, then schoolmates, dates (not of the tree variety), spouse, kids, work colleagues, and others along the way.

But have any of these relationships worked? Have any of them made me happy?

As noted in my Starting Point, there were a few (a *few*?!) aspects of my nature that pretty much sabotaged any relationship, in one form or another, I ever entered into. And yet this was a Journey *Without* . . . why was I thinking at all about *my* involvement when I was supposed to be reviewing external possibilities that contribute to my happiness or unhappiness? What about the other half, those with whom I was relating, those who pretended to like or to love me, those who had flirted with me, scorned me, taunted me, rejected me, abandoned me, teased me, and ignored me? After all, I wasn't having a relationship with *myself*; I was bringing others into the picture. What was *their* responsibility in all of this?

Suddenly a very strange thing happened on my Journey Without, a sort of schism, where there was a rip in the fabric of this external exploration, leaving a gaping hole. The hole was then quickly sealed over with a sort of mirror. When I looked into the mirror I unsurprisingly saw my reflection, but as I moved closer to the mirror and gazed more intently, I saw a whole other world, an *internal* world. But the looking glass prevented me from going through to that other world. My exploration of relationships would have to wait (more on relationships in the next section).

MEAT AND POTATOES IN MY SOUP

(philosophies and psychologies)

*** *"How many existentialists does it take to change a lightbulb? Two: one to screw it in and the other to observe how the lightbulb symbolizes an incandescent beacon of subjectivity in a netherworld of cosmic nothingness."* ***

*** *"I successfully went through therapy to overcome my neurotic unhappiness. Now I am **normally** unhappy."* ***

Next on my Journey Without, I sat down to the main course of the smorgasbord of my intellectual sojourn: the philosophy and psychology of happiness. I gobbled up and digested many of the ideologies, ethical theories, scientific inquiries, psychological considerations, and philosophical debates related to happiness and its pursuit.

Simply put, I decided to view happiness in two ways: as a state of mind (that is, the psychological aspect of happiness) and as a life of well-being (that is, the philosophy of happiness).

From the psychological standpoint, I needed to determine:

1. What are the positive emotions worth seeking?
2. How does satisfaction in life and pleasurable pursuits contribute to a happy state of mind?
3. What are the values placed on these considerations?

And from the philosophical perspective:

4. What is meant by "well-being"?

5. What are the philosophical theories of happiness?
6. What are the sources of happiness, that is, how does one seek and find happiness?
7. How is happiness measured?
8. Why pursue happiness in the first place?

There are, it appears, innumerable explanations, permutations, contradictions, and paradoxes, so many that my pursuit of happiness was making me extremely unhappy. With value judgments, subjective theories on hedonism, objective theories on hedonism, virtuous activity, confusing morals, ethics, variables, perceptions, changing perspectives, personal threshold of happiness, adaptability, genetics, and predisposition to happiness, what is happiness, really? Is being happy the same as living a happy life?

Here is what happiness could be:

- Experiencing positive feelings or good moods as well as having and maintaining a positive attitude
- Engaging in pleasant experiences and reaching pleasant states such as joy, peace, satiation, etc.
- Finding fulfilment to the best of one's ability, or striving to achieve or exceed one's potentiality
- Doing something that is good, beneficial, desirable, productive, and creative
- Anticipating or having memories of fulfilled pleasure/desire
- Engaging in and achieving day-to-day objectives, as well as achieving "big picture" objectives
- All or any combination of the above

Ultimately, how you define happiness will determine how you pursue it. There is the theory that tells us to get out there and seek happiness. There is also the theory that to be happy, one should not pursue happiness. In addition to this, there is the theory that presents a balance of these opposing ideas: don't make happiness the focus of every moment yet don't *never* give consideration to happiness. That's like saying: "Don't say anything negative or you'll summon on the *evil eye*. And don't say anything positive or you'll summon the *evil eye*."

So how do you know if you are happy? How do you measure it? Some attempts at measuring happiness involve: self-reports, group reports, normative comparisons (group and individual), targeted comparisons (such as cross-cultural, gender-specific, physiological, and socio-economical).

There is the theory that if you think you are happy, then you are happy. Then there is the counter-theory that states, because of all the variables affecting not only happiness itself but also its measure, there is a darn good chance that if you think you are happy, then you are probably kidding yourself. Or if you don't think about being happy, you probably are happy. Ultimately, however, because there are so many definitions, descriptions, and possibilities with respect to happiness, it's a safe bet it can't really be measured with any degree of accuracy.

Where, then, does happiness come from? Some of the main sources of happiness include:

- Having satisfying positive relationships
- Doing challenging and interesting activities
- Meeting basic needs
- Having a sense of meaning and purpose and achieving goals
- Having autonomy or having a sense of independence
- Having good governance
- Believing in a religion or a having a well-developed belief system
- Adhering to one's values and morals
- Having trust and being trusted; loving and being loved
- Being at peace

Other ideas to opine or food to digest:

1. Do the afore-mentioned sources cause happiness, or does being happy cause one to attain the so-called sources? Sort of like, what came first, the chicken or the egg?
2. Is it possible to be happy regardless of our physical and external conditions?
3. Do differing mental capabilities impact on the experience of happiness?
4. Where do morals fit in with respect to happiness? Or do they? Or should they?
5. What if being happy makes you act badly or what if acting badly makes you happy?
6. Is artificial happiness (for example, drug-induced happiness) still happiness?
7. Can you still have a good life even if you are not happy?
8. Would it be more sensible to examine only the *sources* of happiness, that is, what has made us happy in the past, in order to develop and enjoy future happiness?

Does your head hurt yet? At this point, mine sure did.

Anyway, having read some of the works, synopses, and biographies of several of the leading philosophers and psychologists of the ages and their take on happiness, I decided that, rather than adopt a particular view, I would create (since I have no original thought of my own) a composite outlook from many of these scholars. I could then adapt it and apply it to my life—at least, the views that were the most interesting, fun, and gave me that "yeah, wow, that makes sense!" revelation.

So I took a scoop of Aristotle, mixed it with a dollop of Locke, folded in some Buddha, added a pinch of Seligman, a tablespoon of Socrates, a dash of Epicurius and James, a little Diener, Csikszentmihalyi, and Mencius for seasoning, and added a whole bunch of Maslow and

Frankl. By doing so I came up with my psychological and philosophical soup of happiness; see if the combination of ingredients is palatable to you:

- The desire for happiness motivates everything one does; one's own experience (of pleasure and pain) determines the happiness outcome of any individual.
- Happiness is the exercise of virtue; it depends on acquiring a moral character where one demonstrates virtues such as courage, generosity, justice, friendship, and citizenship.
- All life is seen as craziness, and happiness in life is seeking a way out of this nutty existence through higher consciousness and mindfulness, that is, being totally involved with lived reality; happiness is attainable through knowing and doing the right things at the right times (sounds a lot like my father) and daily practice.
- There are three kinds of happiness: pleasure and gratification, the development and exercising of strengths and virtues, and meaning and purpose. These are attainable through thinking constructively about the past, gain optimism and hope for the future, and therefore gain greater happiness in the present. So if you time travel, do it for a reason. If there is the assumption that positive feelings cause happiness, then one can acquire these positive emotions by embracing six basic virtues: wisdom and knowledge, courage, love and humanity, justice, spirituality, and transcendence. Following practices that lead to these virtues will lead to a more meaningful life.
- One can learn to blend desires (e.g. physical pleasures and love of knowledge and virtue). Essentially, the idea is, like love and marriage, you can't have one without the other.
- Happiness is pleasure; all things are to be done for the sake of pleasant feelings associated with them. False beliefs produce

unnecessary pain. Happiness can be more readily attained in a society where we're all after the same rainbow's end.

- One must set realistic expectations about happiness since no one is all that happy all the time (if so, it would give pause to question one's sanity). Cause and effect needs to be taken into account. Rather than focus on doing, being, or having things to be happy, one should focus on being happy in order to do, to be, and to have things.

- Virtuous action and self-reflection lead to a state of joy and personal fulfilment. By cultivating the power of making moral choices, happiness can then be realized.

- Happiness requires making choices, requires active risk-taking, involves acting "as if" there is ultimate meaning in life and what we do, and often occurs when one questions one's purpose and meaning in life.

- Happiness is having clear goals, having immediate feedback to one's actions, establishing a balance between challenges and skills, becoming aware, not worrying about failure, not being self-conscious, and enjoying one's immediate experience.

The most flavourful and intense ingredients in my philosophical and psychological soup come from Viktor Frankl and Albert Maslow:

> Struggling and striving for a worthy goal and finding potential meaning is the primary motivational force in man. Without meaning, people fill the void with hedonistic pleasures, power, materialism, hatred, boredom, or neurotic obsessions and compulsions. There are three different courses of action in the pursuit of meaning: through deeds, the experience of values through some kind of medium (such as beauty through art or love through a relationship), or suffering. One must be responsible to life as well as seek out one's individuality through action (not through reflection) dictated by the demands of the day. Meaning is discerned

through creative values, through experiential values, and through attitudinal values. (Frankl)

Satisfying a "hierarchy of needs" helps to understand the motivation and the pursuit of happiness. Physiological needs (breathing, sleeping, eating, drinking, excreting, and sex) are biological and physical needs which, when unfulfilled, become a preoccupation. Following these are safety needs (physical, economic, social, vocational, and psychological). Then comes belongingness and love needs (such as being involved in community, human interaction, abundance of love). Esteem needs are next, which spring from being loved and embraced by families and communities. By acquiring a measure of self-esteem and confidence, it is then possible to be creative, to grow, and to be more generous to others. Finally, at the top of the hierarchy, is self-actualization, which is the desire and attainment of the fulfilment of one's potential. (Maslow)

By reflecting or referring to this assortment of philosophies and psychologies, by dipping the spoon in my soup, as it were, I could perhaps have a taste of this broth whenever I would be led off my path to pursue happiness.

Yet, as always, the more I questioned, the more questions I had until I couldn't digest another morsel of philosophy or psychology of happiness. I was stuffed!

THE MAGIC PILL

(education, courses, books, seminars, self-help resources)

———⌇⌇———

"I asked the salesperson in the bookstore where I would find the self-help section. She said, 'Sorry, sir, it would defeat the purpose."

———⌇⌇———

On the next part of my Journey Without, I was determined to find that elixir, that special potion, that magic pill that would transform everything into glowing happiness and perfection. I was convinced it was out there.

I hauled myself off to the bookstore on a weekly quest, hoping to find my magic pill or, since it wasn't a pharmacy, a book on how to get the magic pill.

I must admit I was taken aback by the rows and shelves and sections and categories of books devoted the topic of self-help, all proclaiming in one gimmicky form or another to know how, when, why, where, and what to do to get hold of that elusive magic pill. Each book was themed with a slightly different slant, but they all promised, albeit in an articulate, omniscient, and entertaining way, the same thing: everlasting happiness.

The magic pill!

After hours and days and years and even months of reading book after book, here is what I discovered:

- There is a "Secret", waiting to be revealed, that I already know even if I don't know it.

- I must "Look Out for Number One"—that's me. Tough luck for the rest of you.
- If I do "Sweat the Small Stuff", can't I just get a better deodorant?
- "Good Things Happen to Bad People"—no, wait—the other way around.
- There is "Life Before, Between, and After Life", so does any of it make a difference?
- All of my "Zones are Erroneous".
- Seekers of happiness are both "Idiots" and "Dummies"; I'm still on order for the Guidebooks but maybe the publishers are waiting for me to write them.
- Everything is dependent on knowing your numbers and letters, such as the 4 C's of what to do, the 5 D's of what not to do, and the 6 Z's of what and what not to do.
- Make a "Project" out of being "Happy"? Great, another unfinished project!
- I would like to "Win Friends and Influence People" but I don't know how to enter the contest. Besides, I'm more likely to lose friends and alienate people.
- "Why Is It Always About You?" Well, I was told to Look Out for #1!
- "Anxious 9 to 5". Yes, and Dolly Parton makes me nervous.
- "Get Out of Your Mind and Into Your Life". Too late, I'm already out of my mind.
- If "Men" and "Women" are from different planets, are intergalactic relationships next? What is happening to our universe? Could this be the Big Bang Theory?
- Okay, so "Now is Powerful", my "Parachute is Colourful", and we're all "Okay". Or, at least, Now my Parachute is Okay.
- "Effective People have Habits too? I have more than "Seven" and I'm not effective at all! So there!

- If "Life" is a series of "Games" and it's 'Twister', I'm *in*!
- Whenever I "Awaken the Giant Within", I only end up banging my head on the ceiling.
- If "I Was Born Rich", why is my wallet empty?
- "Self-Help: The Art of Auto-Eroticism"???

Anyway, after I got thoroughly discouraged at the thought of all these millions of authors all with knowledge of the Magic Pill and millions of readers who are so screwed up in millions of areas of their life, I briefly turned to vintage clips of Leo Buscaglia, love and hug guru of the seventies, for solace. Here is what he told me:

"Love is always open arms. If you close your arms about love, you will find that you are left holding only yourself."

"Don't hold on to anger, hurt or pain. They steal your energy and keep you from love."

"Find the person who will love you because of your differences and not in spite of them, and you have found a lover for life."

"The hardest battle you are ever going to have to fight is the battle to be just you."

"Don't walk in my head with your dirty feet."

"Those who think they know it all have no way of finding out they don't."

"Worry never robs tomorrow of its sorrow, it only saps today of its joy."

"You are the only you . . . You are the best you. You will always be the second best anyone else."

"Time has no meaning in itself unless we choose to give it significance."

"In the end, you have only you."

Satiated, I took a shower to rinse off the warm fuzziness of these quotes. Then I turned to the Internet to narrow down the most comprehensive and best self-help books of all time. I got 398,000,000 results, so I threw my computer out the window.

Maybe if I acquired information first-hand about the Magic Pill rather than just read about it, I could get to the end of my search for it that much more quickly. So I attended lectures, seminars, workshops and courses. I learned how to rewire my brain, live in my own dreamscape, say "no!" to anyone, discover my inner beauty, be myself, and that "change" starts with *me*. I also discovered there are lots of circles: power, drum, life, men's, women's, medicine, life, singing, hope, jerk(?!), giving, and guiding. Circles. No squares or other shapes. Finally, I learned that I can lead, follow, or get out of the way. I chose the latter. There are support groups, programs, services, personal growth groups, mental health associations, self-improvement centres, wellness clinics, encounter groups and retreats.

Not a Magic Pill in any of them.

DON'T DYS MY FUNCTION!

(therapies)

—⟡⟡⟡—

*** *"Neurotics build castles in the sky. Psychotics live in them. Therapists collect the rent."* ***

—⟡⟡⟡—

"I'm a nut, a nut, a nut, nut, NUT!

I'm a little acorn round, lying on the cold, cold ground.

Everybody steps on me. That is why I'm cracked, you see.

I'm a nut, a nut, a nut, nut, NUT!"

Call me crazy, but I was so intrigued with the concept of being crazy as the main impediment to seeking happiness and fulfilment on my Journey Without, that I decided to explore the realm of therapy as a means to my end. Never too ashamed or embarrassed to avert the stigma of mental illness, I researched therapy, but only—I repeat, ONLY—as a gathering of information for this tome and as a method for seeking meaning for my life (and a secret cry for help).

While growing up, I only heard of "being in therapy" in two contexts: as a mandatory treatment in psychiatric facilities or as a symbol of status for the nouveau riche. It never occurred to me that therapy might have other uses or benefits. I did have an inkling that it could be helpful to talk about my worries, shortcomings, fears, and general dysfunction with someone who would not ridicule or condemn me (although I did have visions of therapists around a water cooler laughing uproariously at my disclosures). I was fairly sure, though, that all therapists did was repeatedly ask, "Why do you think that is?" for a-hundred-and-fifty bucks a pop. How could they be worth their mettle if I had to provide the answers to my own queries? What a rip-off!

Still, I wanted to know more about it so I did some research (what else is new?). To my utter astonishment, my sense of loss and bewilderment increased ten-fold when I discovered there were dozens and dozens of types of therapy. How would I ever know which was the right one for me?

I found, on a very comprehensive and informative website called www.goodtherapy.org, a list of therapies, each linking to a synopsis of the therapy. There were over one hundred twenty types of therapy, covering everything from Anger Management to Neuro-Linguistic Programming to Mindfulness Based Cognitive Therapy to Psychodrama to Gestalt Therapy to Narrative Therapy to Logotherapy and on and on and on! I didn't know where to stop!

An intriguing type of therapy not mentioned above, but one which fits in with my overall theme here is one called Metaphor Therapy by Richard R. Kopp, PhD. This therapy uses both client's own metaphors as well as therapist metaphors to deal with, among other things, resistance both known and unknown to the client, by examining metaphoric language in order to change harmful thoughts and behaviours.

There are the more traditional therapies in addition to the various types of psychotherapy, such as chemotherapy, electroconvulsive shock therapy, lobotomies and other brain-tinkering surgeries. I have also come across some therapies that are radical, unusual, and controversial, such as "In Your Face Therapy" which employs a military tactic of screaming in one's face, "Clown Therapy", where you get to hide behind face paint and a red nerf-ball nose and misbehave, and "Get Over It! Therapy" where, whatever your issue, the therapist tells you to "get over it!" as a means to helping you overcome your troubling issues.

Even more bizarre or downright mind-boggling therapies used over the ages are the following:

- drilling a hole in the skull to let out the demons which create mental illness

- inducing a coma with an overdose of insulin to cure certain addictions
- spinning someone around extremely fast to cure mental illness by reducing brain congestion (doesn't do much for vertigo, though)
- placing magnets on strategic places on the body to get body fluids back to normal, thereby relieving the patient of mental dysfunction
- chemically inducing seizures which leave the patient feeling blissful and calm, even if a little spaced out
- drinking urine to cure a whole bunch of physical and mental illnesses; therapeutic benefits can also be achieved by having a nice, warm urine bath (at the very least, it is purported to give you smooth skin)
- exposing the entire body for just a few minutes to temperatures of minus 120 degrees Fahrenheit, shocking the body, and quickly releasing hormones that relieve pain and other physical ailments, as well as de-stressing
- letting go of physical and psychological trauma by recalling one's birth (possibly through regression therapy) and practising specific breathing exercises
- lying in an open grave or a casket or, preferably, both, for stress relief
- dancing, chanting, and laughing (albeit sometimes forced) in order to stimulate and combat stress and other mental health issues (an increasingly popular type of therapy); one group exercise (which I have also seen in a parlour game) involves placing one's head on another's stomach in a daisy chain and laughing in turn
- having the patient sit on a box filled with atmospheric disturbances, and then discharging them by having an orgasm which, in turn, will cure psychoneurosis.

It is important to note that any type of therapy can be used for good or for evil, that is, in a helpful, beneficial way or an unhelpful, even harmful way. Moreover, it is important to consider whom one chooses for a therapist, what and how they practise, the methods they employ, their knowledge and expertise, as well as mutual compatibility.

So, as you can see, having exhausted this thorough review of Therapy and its components, it is little wonder that I found myself just a little crazier for the effort.

THE ROAD
TO THE SPIRITUAL

Okay, so I discovered that I can't live by physical sensations alone and I can't live in my head. Something was still missing and something was still to be garnered on this Journey Without.

Even as I had approached adolescence, I entertained all sorts of esoteric epistemologies, the forerunner of which was the plaintive cry, "But do we really exist?!" I imagined that perhaps I didn't. Neither did anyone nor anything exist. In fact, I believed that I was a part of someone else's reality, existing only because this 'someone' dreamed me up and created a world in which I could exist but under his total control and caprice. I was somebody's figment!

I couldn't get my parents to buy into this, however; they still held me accountable whenever I managed to get into trouble, despite my pleas that it wasn't my fault since I didn't really exist in the first place. Once my mother gave me a whack on my bum and told me that I shouldn't really feel it since I didn't actually exist. I quickly abandoned this philosophy. Just as well. Being a figment is just too tentative and fleeting.

Still, I required some belief, something to hold onto, to rely upon during those times when my existence needed to be substantiated. Although I did formulate some rudimentary thoughts on God, probably out of fear of retribution just in case there *was* a God, religion was not something I was willing to accept. To me, religion was merely a string of meaningless rituals and utterances (prayers) invented by a bunch of people who were also fearful of retribution just in case there was a God.

As a child, I didn't particularly care why I existed—I was too busy playing, immersing myself in sensory stimuli and chocolate pudding.

As an adult, I desensitized myself to caring about the whys and wherefores of my existence with the mundane endeavours of daily routine. After all, why care about the reason for existence if you exist only to go to work and do laundry?

And then I was struck with an affliction in a traditional and stereotype fashion: mid-life! Instead of turning my attention to red sports cars and flirtatious, nubile women half my age like other Grecian Formula men, I regressed to the puerile ponderings of my adolescence. Only this time I was determined to find an answer. This is: The Road to the Spiritual . . .

KEEPING MY SPIRITS UP

(spirituality; metaphysics; dreams and symbology; magic;
chakras; karma; past lives and reincarnation; kabbalistic paths;
transformation and transcendence)

———— wwwwowwwww ————

"I didn't believe in reincarnation the last time, either."

"I don't believe in miracles . . . I rely on them."

———— wwwwwwwww ————

As a kid, I loved spirits. Ghosts, goblins, and ghouls were great fun. Hallowe'en was my favourite holiday. There was something intriguing and phantasmagorical about the world in which the spirits inhabited. Mostly, it was fun because I was blissfully ignorant about it. But it was exciting to conjure up spirits with interesting personalities, looking into a big crystal ball (actually, a big wineglass for lack of said ball) with a friend and predict each other's future; I was apparently destined to be a movie star astronaut monarch! Then I got a plastic Ouija board for one of my prepubescent birthdays, and I spent hours with my friends spinning yarns that wove together our spiritual imagination with our mortal coil. I revelled in TV shows like "I Dream of Jeannie" and "Bewitched". Isn't that both touching and pathetic? We would also conduct séances, open to all the neighbourhood kids, freaking them out with a well-rehearsed farcical script. I even went through a tarot card and astrology phase, where all the answers to our questions could be manipulated and swayed by the loose, vague interpretations of the placement of the cards or the celestial alignments.

In my teens, my inclinations inclined toward metaphysics and other supernatural phenomena. Feeling the power of omnipotence and omniscience, I would spend hours trying to bend spoons with my mind, or read the private, perverted thoughts of anyone I passed along the sidewalk. I would create and cast magic spells and incantations. Boogers and fingernail clippings substituted for eye of newt and toe of frog . . . maybe *that's* why they never worked. Also, I tried so hard to have visions of future events. My eyes would be squeezed shut in concentration; my parents thought it was constipation and I was forced to drink Metamucil for a week! I recall holding a deck of cards, one card at a time, against my forehead, hoping through the power of osmosis that I would be able to reveal the number and suit. I usually got three or four correct (even though I sometimes peeked), and I declared myself the world's most prolific psychic.

In my late teen years I became obsessed with dreams and symbology. Nowadays, I rarely remember a dream—they're so boring—but as my younger self, I would wake up in a cold sweat from having dreamt about terrifying purple shapes, about a melancholy recurrence of running slower and slower through a misty meadow, only on Thursdays, or about bewilderment at my friend's father who was an angry washing machine. I also set out on explorations, seeking great art with symbols, like an oil painting of Pegasus in flight up an escalator, or an ancient etching of a two-faced man, one face looking at angels with sadness, the other face observing characters of a less scrupulous demeanour with glee.

I never did drugs—I swear!

It took me quite some time to realize that my attraction to these weird and wonderful pastimes was really a desire to find meaning in all things, to both assign significance and to feel significant. This sense of meaning would be channelled through spirituality. I was, however, somewhat confused between spirituality and religion. Eventually, I decided that whether or not they were mutually exclusive, I would always consider spirituality a kind of connectedness with all living things and an awareness of purpose and meaning and inner peace—the very things I had been looking for.

And so, independent of their religious origins, I began to examine certain aspects of spiritual beliefs and observations to see how, on my Journey Without, these would fit in with my ideas and pursuit of meaning and happiness.

I liked the idea of having an afterlife, although I did not want to have to die to have one. It gave me comfort to think that I could live eternally in a state of enlightened bliss or, at least, be reincarnated to have another crack at doing something right in the next life if my current life wasn't so great. But what if I were reincarnated to a life that was less than what I already had? Or what if I were reincarnated as a lower life form—say, a flea or a dust mite? Or a tree? Or an inanimate object like a rock or a grain of sand and existed that way for millions of years? I came across some literature that said you can only be reincarnated in a better station than the life you last left for continued growth toward enlightenment . . . I really, really hope that's true. Otherwise, reincarnation would suck. So would the concept of no afterlife at all. Having completed the current life (which ends in death, almost always in some degree of pain and electrical brain neurons misfiring for the last time), there would be eternal nothingness.

Hand in hand with afterlife is the notion of karma or, if you will, cosmic consequences. If you do something bad now you will pay for it later in some way, shape, or form. If you do something good you will reap the rewards for your actions, usually in the next life. I must have been a real screw-up in my last life.

But what about my sense of spirituality in the here and now? Shouldn't I be more concerned with what is happening in *this* life than in the next one? Or the last one? What about the fact that I am here, now, in *this* life, and feeling like a wad of fecal matter: physically drained, emotionally imperilled, mentally numb, and spiritually depleted?

Some people had mentioned 'kundalini' and 'chakras' to me; I thought they were inviting me over for pasta and some weird kind of meatball. Turns out they were referring to the mind-body connection and the various energy centres. These centres govern the balance and well-being of different parts of the anatomy, as well as being associated with certain colours, elements, senses, symbols, and endocrine glands. All very artistic and scientific and difficult to debunk (my way of saying, in my usual optimistic manner, "That'll never work because . . ."), since it made sense and was quite appealing. Yes, very appealing, even though my ancestors would be rolling in their graves at the thought of my spiritual explorations not in keeping with my heritage.

So just as I was about to dive headlong into this sea of spiritual awakening, a voice from the miasma which surrounded me called out, beckoning me to enter the realm of the ten emanations of light and the mysterious matrix of the kabbalistic paths of enlightenment. Also through anatomical representation and the overlaid energy fields, and the various paths that connect these fields like electrically-charged wires, this vastly mystifying belief has associations with numbers and letters and symbols and colours and virtues and ethics and—most interestingly—thoughts, feelings, and behaviours. And, well, guess who got in over his head . . . again?

There was something to be said for spirituality but I couldn't quite discern what that something was. Maybe I needed to examine the origins of these fascinating, uplifting, and very confusing possibilities.

Maybe I needed to get me some of that old-time religion . . .

IF YOU BELIEVE, SAY "YES"!

(traditional religion)

———~~~∽⌒⊙⊙⌒∽~~~———

"Now that I'm older, I'm reading the Bible more often . . .
I'm cramming for the finals."

———~~~∽⌒⊙⊙⌒∽~~~———

With TV evangelism being so trendy, I decided I would attempt to turn my efforts to religion. Since the beginning of recorded history, man has turned to religion to seek solace, comfort, and answers to questions that are a blight on existence. So why not?

Religion is, after all, a set of beliefs, a series of rules, a code by which one lives. How confusing could that possibly be? Maybe I would restore some order to my superconfused mind.

I started my exploration of religion by reading the Good Book, of all things. Well, it *was* the most familiar and easily accessible material I could find. And it wasn't *too* horrifying to read once I got past the twentieth century translator attempting to provide ancient testimony in Middle English.

So the Bible was my first experience at this religion thing. Hell! You thought I was confused before? You should have seen me when I finished! Some of those commandments and laws were positively medieval!: condoning murder, encouraging slavery, reducing women to servile nothings, witnessing again and again that the 'chosen people' are forever doing evil in the sight of the Lord and the punishment they endure, knowing very well what they're in for. It's difficult to get into a story where the Hero is also the Antagonist.

One thing I did get out the Bible is the word 'smite' . . . it's such a cute, smurf-like word which can be translated as 'to do away with' or 'to tortuously and painfully wipe off the face of the earth'. 'Smitten': 'to be struck' or 'TO BE STRUCK!'. 'To be overwhelmed' or 'to be overpowered'. I smite, you smote, they were smitten (you naughty kitten). In the Bible, everyone is being smitten or doing the smiting, while a bunch of strange, old men with crooked sticks and cataracts (called Prophets) sit around, mumbling, "I told you so!" Where are the lessons the Bible is supposed to be teaching? Where are the explanations? The crib notes? This is an abomination, that is an abomination. Do as you are told or you will be smitten. I needed to spend hundreds of hours reading the Bible for *that*? I could have spent five minutes with my parents!

I abominate daily—sometimes twice a day.

So smite me.

I must be a very shallow person. The underlying messages and nuances, the inner meanings of the Bible escape me.

And what's with those burnt offerings? Some people call it dinner.

Busy beavers, these Biblical buckaroos. With all their smiting and abominating and offering, how do they still find time for begetting?

MANTRAS, CHAKRAS, AND A BOTTLE OF YOUR BEST SANGRIA

(comparative religions)

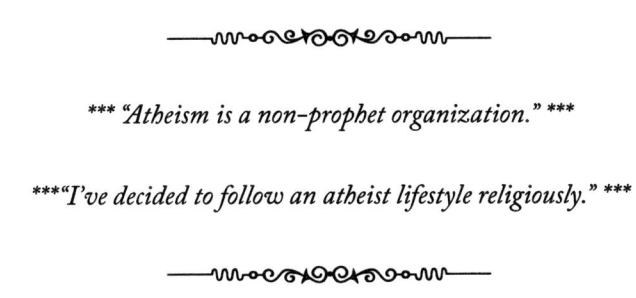

*** *"Atheism is a non-prophet organization."* ***

***"*I've decided to follow an atheist lifestyle religiously."* ***

But I transgress, er, I mean, I digress.

In order to give religion a chance, I knew I had to broaden my understanding of what religion is, what kinds of religions exist, what people believe, and what people practise within the framework of their religious beliefs. Off to the library I went.

First, I needed to define God, or gods, or the godhead, or no God, since there is so much controversy and emotion and sense of rightness when it comes to God and to God's existence.

It seems God cannot be defined; we can, of course, take a shot at creating a concept of God, based on our limited knowledge, experience, and perception. God could be an old man in a rocker with a long, white beard; a life force, a spirit, or the energy within us and around us. Perhaps God is a giant tortoise or a fire-breathing dragon, an oracle, a voice in a cave on a mountain, or a bunch of superior beings in the cosmos who toy with us inferior mortals just for sport. Or God could be our own fabrication of an omnipotent entity that we created out of fear, hope, and longing, to fill a void, to blame for evil in the world, to pray to for something better, to ask for things, to protect us, and to love us. Or just to be a cool dude (or dudette) for people to look up to. Or God could be nothing at all. Or everything.

171

Glad I cleared that up.

If religion is a set of beliefs, the laws that govern them, and the practices that support and demonstrate them, and if there exist, as it seems, dozens upon hundreds of religions and their variations (even some which now may be extinct but still with validity and merit), then I believe it is a worthwhile endeavour to examine if these beliefs are worthy of believing in or are even believable.

In my quest for true meaning and happiness in life, I decided to take a look at a few belief systems in this context, that is, is there an organized world religion whose beliefs about life's purpose and the human condition will unequivocally contribute to my personal well-being and happiness?

My first step was to secure a list of as many religions as I could find. Becoming overwhelmed as usual, I narrowed down the list and considered the number of adherents throughout the world, longevity and history, basic information regarding basic principles related to the purpose of people and life, the perspective on God (or no God, or various forms of god), the ideology of life (and, as it inevitably follows, the possibility of an afterlife), and religious practices as well.

This information was placed against my questionable ability to absorb, understand, and compare my findings. I came up with this:

- Judaism: believing in one God, obeying the Commandments, and living ethically; practices include: ritual circumcision, bar/bat mitzvahs, supporting community, regular prayer, going to Synagogue or Temple, celebrating historical holidays, keeping kosher; discussion of afterlife is shadowy and mystical, not the focus.
- Christianity: (with Divisions such as Catholicism, Protestantism, and Orthodox, and branches such as Episcopal, Unitarian, Anglican, etc.), believing in the Father, the Son, and the Holy Spirit; everyone is a sinner and therefore separated from God,

with salvation through faith in Christ and doing good; practices include: taking communion, baptism, Bible study, going to Church, confession, blessings, and celebrating holidays; afterlife includes belief in heaven, purgatory, and hell.

- Islam: (different offshoots, such as Sunni, Kurdish, Druze, Nation of Islam, etc.), believing in one God and that people must submit to the will of Allah to reach Paradise; practices include: attending mosque, adherence to the Five Pillars and the words of the Quran; the afterlife is in Paradise or Hell.

- Hinduism: believing in many gods/goddesses which, in totality, represent one Supreme Reality; purpose is to gain release from rebirth or, at least, have a better rebirth, and to live life according to one's Dharma (purpose); practices include: yoga, meditation, devotion to gods/goddesses, pilgrimages; afterlife is about reincarnation continuing until enlightenment.

- Buddhism: believing that nothing is permanent, that life's purpose is to avoid suffering and gain enlightenment and release from the cycle of rebirth (or a better rebirth) by gaining merit; practices include: meditation, mantras, afterlife concerns reincarnation (except that there is no surviving soul) until the attainment of enlightenment.

- Taoism: believing that opposites make up a unity (yin/yang), detachment and refraining from struggle, inner harmony, peace, and tranquility; practices include: tai-chi, acupuncture, and alchemy; the afterlife is a reversion to a state of non-being.

- Atheism: believing that there is no God, beliefs about the universe are based on the latest scientific findings, life is of great importance where only humans can help themselves and the rest of humanity; there are no specific practices; there is no belief in an afterlife.

- New Age: believing in a life force that pervades all things, and that mankind is on the cusp of a new age of awareness, heightened consciousness, international peace, and spiritual transformation; practices include: medicine, psychic abilities, angelic communication, channelling, amulets; unknown focus on afterlife.

Others on my list included: Mormonism, Wicca, Baha'i, Confucianism, Spiritualism, Hare Krishna, Satanism, Janism, Rastafari, Scientology, Mayan Religion, Shinto, even Chopra Centre for those Deepak fans, and dozens more, all with fascinating beliefs and practices.

Some of the more interesting practices in the various religions I have come across are: fortune-telling and other psychic activities, chants and prayers, mantras, chakras, and kabbalistic paths.

Rather than focus on the diverse beliefs and dissimilar practices, I found it incredibly profound and surprisingly reassuring that many of the basic religious beliefs (albeit some dark and terrifying) were about having and living a life of purpose and virtue, even if their beliefs were demonstrated through different practices. Generally, there also seemed to be a gravitational pull toward something greater than the human being, in one form or another, for humans to laud, praise, exult, submit, self-enlighten, discover, please, respect, or obey, whether or not there was an afterlife, in its various representations, to strive to attain. The more I learned, the more I was convinced that there was no *right* religion, only what seemed right for the individual and determined by the individual. Some people have established a composite religion by which they lead their life. And those that live with the fundamental interpretations of religious dogma to the detriment or destruction of others, I have chosen to renounce them. They don't make me happy.

So have I determined if I have found a sense of happiness or fulfilment though religion? I think that having any kind of belief which can be benevolent to mankind and can motivate, focus, and uplift, has merit. I have been thinking that if I want to become a happier person and more fulfilled, I need to become more religious. Or, if I want to become more religious I need to become happier and more fulfilled.

God knows!

Neil Katz

IF I HAVE ONLY ONE LIFE TO LIVE, LET ME LIVE IT AS A . . .

(being born into a religion)

"Life is very confusing. I don't know who to believe. My rabbi keeps telling me to follow the rituals; my therapist keeps telling me to stop the rituals . . ."

I am a Jew. You may or may not be a Jew, and that is okay. Being a Jew is a major part of my identity. It is second nature like an appendage. I know it is a part of me even though I'm not constantly aware of its presence. When I was little and other kids were opening their Christmas presents under their fancy trees with colourful balls and twinkling lights, I got to spin a dreidl, light the candles, and nosh on a little net packet of foil-covered chocolate coins for Chanukah. (Not fair!) I got to say my portion of the Bible with an embarrassing girly crackle in my changing adolescent voice when I became a man at age thirteen at my Bar Mitzvah. I got to play "Jewish Geography", our version of Six Degrees of Kevin Bacon, only kosher. At age ten, I got to be bullied and beaten for being a Jew.

I am a secular Jew. Some Orthodox Jews don't even consider me a Jew. Conservative Jews are not Orthodox, but religious enough to mock me. I go to the synagogue/temple on the occasional High Holy Day and once in a blue moon on the Sabbath, but only if I am dragged by my prayer shawl. I justify bringing non-kosher food into my home by eating it in the basement with newspaper covering the table and using plastic cutlery and paper plates. I, along with my family, celebrate our holidays by faithfully fasting or feasting as the occasion dictates, the latter only with a traditional kosher meal. Every year, in an effort to maintain tradition, we end the eight days of Passover's unleavened bread and other dietary restrictions with a good meal in a Chinese restaurant.

I was born a Conservative Jew. I could have been born into a family that was Catholic, Muslim, Buddhist, Atheist, Satanist, anything, really. But I was born a Jew. I was raised to believe in one omnipotent God but I have allowed myself to stray from some of the practices, like wearing a yarmulke (space beanie) and engaging in regular prayer, although when I was a kid I used to pray to God not to find out I hadn't been praying.

Some folk have an image in their mind of what a Jew is. For the record, I am blue-eyed, blond haired, and straight-nosed. I am not a doctor, lawyer, or banker (much to my mother's dismay). I don't own a big, furry hat (but I think they're kinda cool). I don't have long curly sideburns but I once shaved off half a beard just for the fun of it (not for religious purposes, as my boss at work supposed). Jews come in all shapes and sizes and manner of dress. And from all nations. It is neither in Jewish doctrine nor in Jewish practices to swindle, pinch pennies, or drink the blood of children.

Anyway, to me, being a Jew was confusing. There were not only the Orthodox, Conservative, and Reform Jews; there are now Egalitarians, Reconstructionists, and Jews for Jesus. There are Zionists. There are Kabbalists. Who knows what else? There are many must-reads for a Jew since we are all supposed to be perennial students, always educating ourselves in laws and commandments and ethical living. There is the Bible (the Five Books of Moses), the laws, the crib notes and explanations, the explanations of the explanations, the critiques of the explanations, and the rabbinical criticisms of the critiques. Not to mention the mystical writings which are to be read only if you understand all the other stuff, or if you are Madonna.

Consequently, my world view is coloured by the basic tenets of a religion in which I am not devout: I believe in morals and virtues, of living honourably and ethically, of living in a sense of community, and of living in a way that would move me closer to a God I am not even sure exists.

I am more "Jewish" than I am a Jew. You know, like "I'll be at your house around six-ish"? Sort of six. Jewish: sort of a Jew.

INQUISITION!
(undertaking a cause)

*"Some people try to understand the relationship between cause and effect; other people seek a cause **for** effect."*

In a feeble attempt to give my life some direction and meaning, I sought to undertake a cause.

I was ready.

From the distance, an infantry of knights in armour, swords on high, mounted on lofty steeds, gallop forward toward their cause, their crusade. They stop to get their bearings on the vast Spanish plain. The leader of the pack lifts his visor and squints in the blinding sunlight, searching for the enemy, the windmill, the village, the damsel in distress. I squint back at the leader and realize that the leader . . . is *me*! I begin to laugh at the image of me: a leader! Me: in heavy metal! I close my visor and wave my men onward toward the horizon, the horses kicking up a storm of dust behind them. I cough.

My first task was to decide which cause to undertake. I felt strongly, I told myself, about a number of issues that were au courant: breech of human rights, oppression of women, violence against baby seals, pollution of the environment, oil spills, ozone depletion, needs of charitable organizations, and world peace, to name a few.

It was difficult to find a cause that was well-suited to me. First, the choices were innumerable and I became overwhelmed. Two, I was too timid and inhibited to be an activist. And C, I just didn't seem to fit in. Women's groups informed me I had the wrong genitalia. Ozone groups shunned me when I indicated on my volunteer assessment form that I used spray deodorant. I told them I'd switch to roll-on, but they said in disdain that it was too late. The baby seal groups wanted to send me to the North Pole (or vicinity) in full battle regalia to poach the poachers, but I felt there was something inherently illegal about this. I could not envision myself de-oiling fish and fowl only to have them served up Kentucky-fried later on. I did not want to be 'outed' before I was even 'inned'. World peace organizations advertised for pacifists; they did not want passivists. Canvassing for donations, no matter how legitimate the foundation or how valid the disease, was nothing more than socially acceptable emotional blackmail. And I didn't require the slamming of doors in my face to sustain my fear of rejection, thank you very much.

Okay, let's regroup, people!

My first task was not to decide which cause to undertake; my first task was to determine why I wanted to undertake a cause. Well, a cause is a romantic notion. Noble. Something to take pride in. Something to rub other people's noses in. Something to immerse myself in. Something to busy myself in order to avoid doing what I really needed to be doing with my life.

Undertaking a cause would have had a disastrous effect at this point in my life.

I was not ready.

LIFE IS JUST A BOWL OF CLICHES

(words of inspiration)

"Trying to find inspiration is so uninspiring . . . first you have to have an aspiration. Then you have to give perspiration. From this you get rapid respiration. This is usually followed by exasperation. Hopefully, it won't result in expiration."

"I dream of a better tomorrow . . . where chickens can cross the road and not be questioned about their motives."

"Out of the frying pan saves nine."

"He who makes a silk purse from a sow's ear kills the cat."

I've got a million of 'em!

It was during my "Let's save humanity" phase. I remember a co-worker busily rummaging through her 'Book of Prayer and Daily Inspiration', when she turned to me and exclaimed, "A thought for the day: Happiness is the journey, not the destination." Suppressing an uncontrollable urge to respond to a message from my pyloric valve, I turned to another colleague who announced, with a deeper and far more moving profundity, "Life sucks." Him I could relate to.

Despite my own feelings which these statements elicited, a sense of calm and transcendent understanding overcame them, followed by a rejuvenation, a spanking fresh reaffirmation of life, whatever its treasures.

That was when I figured that all I really needed was a daily dose of Hallmark to see me through. I began rummaging through libraries, newspapers and bookstores for quotes and proverbs that I could use for my own daily affirmations. I put them on little slips of fortune cookie paper, tossed them in a bowl, and withdrew one per day.

They worked . . . sort of. On those occasions I was already feeling not too badly about my life. But the rest of the time when "life sucked", when I really needed those affirmations to work for me, to support and uplift me, all I was left with was a bowl of clichés.

PART II—SUMMARY

So? Is this the end of the road? Have I been successful on my Journey Without in uncovering those things that would ultimately lead to my true happiness?

I dunno. On one hand, as my life resume suggests, clearly I have demonstrated skills as a self-saboteur. I have excelled in non-excellence when it comes to ensuring my own happiness and I have promoted myself to Director of Mediocrity. On the other hand, I have the self-assurance of the lived experience of someone who knows what not to do, why not to think, and how not to feel. I have the requisite references as well to support this.

What, then, have I learned on this long and winding road?

The Road to the Physical has taught me that it is okay to satisfy my needs and desires; that there is a sense of reward for having taken measures to protect myself and my family from harm; that it is sensible to keep my body well-nourished and healthy; that it is preferred and encouraged (by me) to engage, unashamed, in some of the basic pleasures in life; that hedonistic desires may be enjoyed with temperance and not as an ultimate goal to happiness and fulfilment.

The Road to the Intellectual has revealed to me that I must continue to educate myself. As with the physical aspects of life, things like the accumulation of wealth and aspirations of fame may seem like exciting prospects but, really, they can be empty and unforgiving. As such, spending time in *any* manner—be it hobby or hard labour, satisfaction in attending to daily needs or being immersed in world events—offers happiness and meaning set by its inherent limitations. I have learned that if there is a 'magic pill' somewhere out there, its elusiveness entreaties me to abandon my pursuit; I must work on myself and not rely on external sources to make me happy. I discovered that some direction may be granted through an understanding of the psychology and philosophy of the very thing that I am seeking. Also, I realized that, if I require assistance, there is help; I am not expecting to function in isolation.

The Road to the Spiritual has led me to the knowledge that I can believe in anything I wish, by my own choosing. I can embrace spirituality; I can embrace religion; I can embrace both. Whether these embraces are sufficient to sustain happiness and a sense of meaning to my life still remains in question.

Nevertheless my Journey Without left me still with unanswered questions and a sense of incompleteness: a murkiness, a translucence. Could it be that I was losing sight of what I was after? Could it be I was actually seeking a transformation? If so, from what? Was I seeking transcendence? If so, to what? Well, this was, after all, only a Journey Without. I still needed to explore some uncharted territory: the Journey Within.

PART III

THE JOURNEY WITHIN

THE FIND

THE LIGHT

PARADISO

LIBERATION

At last! At last! I was beginning to see the light at the end of the tunnel. How, you may ask, did I get so far as to be able to see the light? The answers to this were right under my nose all the time, which kind of makes it sound as if I was born with my nose in the middle of my forehead. But this is what happens when you mix metaphors.

I gave a long, hard look at my Starting Point, my Journey Without, and those endless, difficult years during which I struggled with negative thoughts, unpleasant feelings, and unproductive behaviours. I arrived at the following observations and emerging themes.

In searching for the answers to the most pervasive self-help-type questions, I had poured through books of psychology, art, philosophy, religion, new age, and almost any other genre that exists out there. While some spewed out the usual platitudes of pop psych rhetoric, others left me scratching my head in perplexed bewilderment. Some provided beautiful imagery but with little practical application; others made me read and re-read the same sentences until there was nothing left to do but fall asleep.

One theme that continually emerged in almost all genres was the trinity. Things appear in three's, divided by three's, multiples of three's, and three's within three's: id, ego, and superego; proton, neutron, and electron; father, son, and holy ghost; physical, mental, and spiritual planes, etc.

As you've noticed in my ramblings, I'm no different. My focus is on thoughts, feelings and behaviour.

Continuing to muddle my metaphors, I looked at this whole notion of self-help from the point of view of a triple (three!) helix—well, maybe a hair braid:

- The first strand is thought (how you view the world)
- The second strand is feeling (how you react to thought)

- The third strand is behaviour (how you act in response to the thought or feeling)

To employ self-help practices, you can intercede at any one of these three (although the key focus is to behave in accordance with the thought rather than the feeling since, as we have established, feelings are void of morals and intelligent thought, whereas thought can be moral and intelligent . . . however many people's thinking is devoid of morals or intellect or both . . . I *do* ramble, don't I?). In this confusing metaphor of the triple helix (or hair braid), feeling is the strand that is the active ingredient, like the electron in the atom. It is energy and it just is: you feel what you feel. You cannot say, "Okay, I'm not going to feel this feeling", because you have already experienced the feeling. All you can do, as I discovered, is to suppress it, express it, or let it dissipate. You can, however, change the thought (and attitude) that produces the feeling and you can change the behaviours that are created by what you think and feel.

Another emerging theme in that which I have pondered is the duality of life: light and dark, good and bad, expansiveness and contractedness, positive and negative, forward and backward, up and down. Duality is a necessary component of life as it is that which maintains balance. So it is with thoughts, feelings, and behaviour. We have destructive thoughts and creative ideas; we have negative, reactive emotions and positive, motivational, inspirational feelings; we have negative, harmful behaviours and those that are positive and build character.

By its very definition, the coming together of our thoughts, feelings, and behaviour is integrity. It is the constant movement, vibrations within our triple helix (or rippling wave in the hair braid), which make us whole. We would not exist as entire, functional human beings if any or all of these components were removed or did not interact with the rest.

In the previous sections, I identified a number of thoughts, feelings, and behaviours that are on the dark side, bad, restrictive, down, and negative, as recapitulated in the following chart:

Thoughts	Feelings	Behaviours
labelling	depression	defense mechanisms
lacking identity	fear	wanting acceptance
poor body image	vulnerability	wanting approval
lacking sense of purpose	self-pity	wanting control
unreasonable expectations	loneliness	wanting security
failure	feeling insignificant	wanting individuality
being unrealistic	grief	wanting to belong
lack of consideration	pride	blaming
impatience	lust	not assuming responsibility
injustice	guilt and worry	being passive-aggressive
death	insincerity	dreading risk and change
inaccurate perceptions	embarrassment	holding a grudge
not making choices	jealousy	procrastinating
problems	frustration	acting out
incessant self-analysis	anger	seeking revenge
	feeing invisible	being a victim
		hypocrisy
		lying
		gossiping/language misuse

I stared at these lists for a long time until I realized that all of these thoughts, feelings, and behaviours had an opposite point of view (if duality counts for anything) which I had never before considered. It turns out that if I flip the coin, swing the pendulum, or otherwise spin the sphere to the bright side and examine the light, good, expansive, and positive aspects of thoughts, feelings, and behaviours, life actually has a whole new dimension.

What if I choose to focus on my abilities, my potential, and my *good* experiences, allow myself to feel *good* feelings, and do things that are *satisfying*? And what if I choose to seek clarity to this vision of *positive* undertakings?

What have I got to lose?

The moment I thought of my life in this way and began to ponder the possibilities, I began to get excited. This gave me the impetus to begin my Journey Within.

NOTE: Following each section of Part III is a little something you might want to try, some very basic exercises to help you focus a little more on the topic. At first glance, they seem to be obvious to the point of questioning their efficacy, but if you commit to them I assure you will find them to be particularly useful and insightful.

What have you got to lose?

THINKING GOOD THOUGHTS

My approach to thinking good thoughts was tentative if not downright confusing since I had rarely, up to this point, ever thought a *good* thought. My brain was rife with doom and gloom; I didn't really know anything else.

Still, I was determined to refocus on the opposite of all that I had previously thought in order to see, at the very least, if it would make any difference to the quality of my life.

First, I had to wake up and pay attention, smell the coffee, the roses, or, more in keeping with my penchant for melodrama, throw a bucket of cold water on myself. I had to wrench my head out of the fog of misery and despair. Slap myself upside the head. Stick a needle in my eye. I also needed to refrain from indulging in metaphors of self-abuse.

In other words, I had to explore the realm of awareness.

As well, I needed to rewire my attitude and my perceptions in a positive way.

I had to figure out a method to persevere, relying on thoughts I didn't yet know I possessed in order to assert my independence from negative thinking.

I had to stay focused on the here and now while reframing my thoughts to what was real, clear, untangled, and uncomplicated. To do this I had to ask myself some tough questions regarding evidence and intent of my thoughts. There were some thoughts of which I had to let go, even 'unlearn'. I had to understand what it meant to fail and to succeed, to comprehend the intrinsic qualities of human nature and of human relationships, to embrace the balance and vibrations of life.

Only then would I be really able to think good thoughts.

And so I dipped my toe into the swirling pool of my thoughts, trying hard not to squish my brain . . .

HUH? WHAT?

(awareness)

There was a time when I thought I was crazy, believe it or not (I'll bet you believe it by now!). As if I had a split personality. I had little voices in my head competing for attention. One voice was extremely critical, telling me all the things I do wrong, making fun of my attempts to do anything positive or worthwhile, putting me down. The second voice in my head was the supportive voice which told me I could do, be, or have whatever I put my mind to doing, being, or having. The third voice in my head gave expression to my gut instinct. The fourth voice in my head was the voice of reason, the logical one which gave sound advice based on logic. And there were other voices in there, too, some weak, some excruciatingly loud and obnoxious, all clamouring to be heard. I used to mock them, ignore them, shun them, or pray they would go away. None of that was particularly helpful. So I thought that if I paid attention to them, became more aware of them, I might learn something valuable. In my new-founded approach as I travelled along in my Journey Within, I knew right away that I needed to listen more to the voices that were in keeping with my inner strengths and being capable, creative, healthy, worthwhile, and in my best interests.

Furthermore I realized that I needed to be more aware of the world around me and in all aspects of my life. Up to now I functioned as an automaton, a robot, a zombie, going through the motions on auto pilot, led by repetitive thoughts (yes, mostly negative ones), by habit, by conditioning, by rote. I was managing to function, able to go from point A to point B but without being aware of how I got there. I *needed* to be aware. This was particularly poignant if I wanted to adopt the notion that happiness is the journey and not the destination. How much of life and opportunities to experience happiness must I have missed by not being aware? I needed to wake up, give my head a shake, and become aware of both my internal and external worlds.

A Little Something You Might Want to Try
Awareness #1

Use a watch alarm set for every half hour or carry a tape recorder, cell phone voice recorder, or a pen and notepad.

At various intervals (random or every half-hour, for example) stop and pay attention to what you were most recently thinking. Record it.

1. Which of your voices was speaking to you?
2. Was it negative?
3. Was it a judgment? An opinion? A fact?
4. What emotion did it express or conjure up?
5. What is the underlying message of this voice?
6. How could your supportive voice reword it?

A Little Something You Might Want to Try
Awareness #2

Go for a walk. Take note of everything your senses experience. Be mindful of your mind wandering; every time it does and you become aware of it, return to your senses. Ask yourself:

1. What am I seeing?
2. What am I hearing?
3. What am I smelling?
4. What am I tasting?
5. What am I touching?

A Little Something You Might Want to Try
Awareness #3

Pay attention to your body:

1. Sit in a chair in a quiet room, feet planted firmly on the floor. Relax.
2. Dim the lights or turn them off. Remove as many distractions as possible.
3. Start at the top of your head or at the bottom of your feet, paying attention to each body part, one part at a time. Spend a little bit of time with it before moving on to the next.
4. If or when you find your mind wandering or thinking about anything else other than that body part, let go of that thought and return to the body part.

A Little Something You Might Want to Try
Awareness #4

Engage in a conversation with someone. Make a concerted effort to pay attention only on what the other person is saying. Catch yourself thinking of other things, such as: planning a response, emotionally reacting, debating, judging, forming your own opinion before the other person has a chance to finish what s/he is saying, arguing, or replacing your own story with the basic components of the other person's concerns or ideas. Be aware of what the other person is saying, how they are saying it (tone, inflection, volume, emotion, etc.), and the body language.

THAT'S A "+"
(thinking positive thoughts)

My second discovery at the onset of my Journey Within was that I didn't need to be in recovery from a mental illness in order to improve the quality of my life (even though my wife has called me a mental case on more than one occasion). Many of the self-help books I had read were geared toward a recovery from bipolar disorder, clinical depression, chronic anxiety disorder, and so on. Although I have been anxious and depressed at various times throughout my life, I have never been diagnosed with a mental illness. And since my Journey Within is predicated on an approach opposite to how I regarded myself for the past several decades, I was determined not to continue to label myself at this point.

This in *not* to say that those who are suffering from mental health issues or are in recovery or have formal supports cannot share in my Journey Within. Indeed, everyone, I believe, can learn from others' experiences.

So my primary goal was to watch out for negative, self-effacing, self-deprecating thoughts which were constantly in my head to the point of total consumption. These thoughts could take on any change or form, from a subliminal, solitary message (Loser!), to a careful consideration (You're going to fail anyway!), to an elaborate image (Me, naked in a cage, a spotlight shining down on me, with passersby pointing and laughing).

Consequently, my first great task was to restructure my brain—daunting but doable. To begin, I had to catch these thoughts as they crept into my head by drawing them out from the recesses of my subconscious. Because these thoughts whipped across the universe of my mind at warp speed, it was difficult to grab onto them. With practice, however, I was able to initiate the process. My first attempt at being consciously aware of a negative thought occurred when I was walking on slippery patch of ice-covered sidewalk. I had an image of me, slipping and landing on my backside with a thud, thinking, "Of course!" No sooner had the image played out that I slipped, landed on my backside with a thud, and thought, "Of course!" Was this a wish fulfilment? Was I demonstrating a confirmation of my self-assertion of being a total moron? Was it a psychic déjà vu moment? Was it yet another example of my negative thought process?

Yes, yes, yes, and yes.

I sat for awhile on the shiny black ice, rubbing my sore left buttock and thinking, "I'm so happy!" I was able to single out a negative thought from my cosmic subconscious!

Well, it's a start.

A Little Something You Might Want to Try
Thinking Positive Thoughts #1

1. Trying to become more aware, stop yourself by holding up your hand and saying "STOP!" every time you find yourself saying anything negative or steering off-course from you want to go.
2. a) Which of your inner voices are speaking to you?
   b) Are they being compatible with your new approach?

A Little Something You Might Want to Try
Thinking Positive Thoughts #2

Put yourself in a positive frame of mind by trying one, some, or all of the following. Keep in mind that these are not one-time only exercises. They should continue to be done deliberately and regularly until they become incorporated into your life and into your day-to-day living:

1. Remember past experiences that were pleasant, successful, and/ or positive. Write down at least ten. Describe.
2. Stop yourself every time a negative thought creeps into your mind.
3. Be aware of using only positive words when thinking and talking for example, state: "I am able to . . ." or "It is possible . . ." or "I can . . .".
4. When embarking on a plan of action or when taking action on a goal, visualize a positive outcome. If a negative outcome materializes, try to understand why you are thinking this way and reword it in a positive way.
5. Pursue activities that elicit positive emotional responses, such as: reading words or stories of inspiration, watching movies that make you feel happy and motivated, listening to music that

you enjoy, and involving yourself in meaningful and/or awe-inspiring situations.

6. Associate with people who think positively (you know who they are) and limit the time you spend with those who tend to express themselves in a negative manner (you know who they are, too).

7. Engage in physical activity that makes you feel good, such as walking or hiking, swimming, or an enjoyable sport. Rather than just exercising, insert yourself into a setting that pleases you (for example, jog along a lakeshore or stroll down an interesting street rather than simply using a treadmill machine at a gym).

GIVING ATTITUDE
(attitude)

The third discovery, before reaching the nether regions of my Journey Within, was my *attitude* toward myself and my search inward. I realized that I had a choice regarding how I view myself, others, and the world around me. Up to now I had allowed circumstance to colour the way I viewed everything and it was a pretty dim view, I assure you. I once heard that your attitude is what you say when you talk to yourself. If the attitude resulted in thinking negative thoughts, feeling upset, or behaving badly, I could change it! I also realized my attitude had a direct impact on my expectations. I could choose to have a positive attitude and expect good outcomes instead of having a negative attitude and expect lousy outcomes. If I have a positive attitude and still I do not achieve my goals, I can continue hang onto my positive attitude while revising or setting new goals.

I also recognized that this was hard work. Considering I spent more than half a century criticizing myself at every opportunity and feeling pretty darn miserable for it, I had to keep plugging away, forcing myself to have a positive attitude no matter how unnatural it felt. There were, of course, little blips on my attitude radar, little thoughts that crept into my mind, expressed through that not-so-little voice that screamed, "Why bother?"

So, with a lot of effort and perseverance, I was determined to change my attitude. It was like a face-lift for my personality! With a positive attitude, it was more likely I would feel better about myself and behave in a more constructive and less self-destructive way. And so I was on my way to becoming one of those people whom I used to despise with their perky outlook and dung-eating grins... see? I slipped back to my old way of thinking. I told you it wasn't easy, but at least I caught myself! I guess my personality face-lift might need a little Botox now and then..

A Little Something You Might Want to Try
Attitude #1

Pay attention to your internal dialogue.

1. What are some of your usual thoughts, expressions or assertions, or comments? In other words, what are you telling yourself?
2. Are they giving you confidence and positive sense of well-being, or are they self-deprecating and contributing to low self-esteem?
3. If you are entertaining negative thoughts, can you see the restlessness, discord, irritability, dissatisfaction, and uncertainty in your thoughts? Can you detect the sense that something isn't right or isn't sitting well?
4. Do your thoughts often begin with: "I can't...", "What if...?", "I always...", "I never...", "I should..."?
5. Are you labelling yourself? What are the labels?
6. How can these negative thoughts be restated in a positive way?

A Little Something You Might Want to Try
Attitude #2

Try to promote a positive attitude by:

- Using meditation techniques
- Making appropriate preparations or plans for the next day (perhaps by using a journal or a day planner) to free your mind
- Undertaking activities that promote a calm, enjoyable, and positive atmosphere, such as taking a warm bath, having pleasant sensory stimuli (scented candles, comfortable clothing,

soothing natural sounds, relaxing music, soft lighting or no lighting, etc.)

- Getting sufficient, restful sleep, if possible
- Consuming substances that are natural, homeopathic, nutritional, and herbal
- Simplifying things; breaking them down into smaller, more manageable components
- Doing fun (but not dangerous) things without questioning or analyzing, even things you found enjoyable as a kid
- Learning something new
- Reading the following sections in this book as they can foster a positive attitude!

"I FEEL PRETTY!"

(positive self-talk)

My next discovery on my Journey Within was the realization that not every single moment of my life was filled with difficulties, illness, injury, adversity, trauma, chaos, stress, and misery. Again, with a little effort and a lot of awareness, I was able to identify hundreds of events, situations, occasions, and circumstances that were pleasant, calm, ordered, facile, and downright enjoyable.

Instead of carrying my troubles on my shoulders and always feeling the agonizing weight of the world, I was able to balance the world—light as a feather!—on the tip of my finger like an inflatable beach ball. I was Charlie Chaplin in "The Great Dictator"! Well, not a dictator, really. More like Gene Kelly in "Singin' In the Rain" but without the umbrella and the rain. No, wait! Maria in the dress shop in "West Side Story" singing about how pretty she feels. Well, perhaps I wouldn't be singing . . . especially about feeling pretty . . . and I wouldn't be in a dress shop.

Anyway, my point is that incorporating positive self-talk into my life began to nurture positive thoughts, feelings, and experiences.

A Little Something You Might Want to Try
Positive Self-Talk #1

Identify at least one (more, if you can) situation that was positive each day and write it down.

- Why was it positive?
- What was your internal dialogue about this thought?
- What are the positive words you used to describe the thought?

A Little Something You Might Want to Try
Positive Self-Talk #2

Every time you are passing judgement on others, on other things, on situations, and on yourself, try to find at least one thing you can find that you can state in a positive way. There will be *some*thing positive. Write it down. Keep an ongoing list to review periodically in order to make the practice of stating things in a positive way a habit.

MR. INVINCIBLE!

(knowing my strengths)

My approach, in this leg of my Journey Within, was to see myself in a new perspective: having inner strengths, and being capable, creative, valuable, healthy, etc., while trying to refrain from reverting to my old pattern of seeing myself as thinking, feeling, and behaving with difficulties, adversity, drama, chaos, and misery. Was this even possible?

So my next task was to identify what my strengths were.

The first inclination was to say to myself, "Come on, give me a break!" Asking me to reflect on my strengths and weaknesses was like being in a really bad job interview where they ask you to identify your strengths and weaknesses. I would usually tell them, with a shy smile, that my weaknesses are: being too much of a perfectionist, or being too punctual; my strength is: always wanting to do the best job I can. Then I would feel a bit of bile rising in my throat. Like I'm going to tell them at a job interview that I'm so anxious I'll probably screw up? Or that I think I'm an incompetent nincompoop? Or that I am their picture perfect employee? The best of the best?

Then, reluctantly letting go of my cynicism, I started to think of the strengths I really did possess. There were qualities and characteristics I had that I never before acknowledged. There were talents, abilities, proclivities, skills, and interests I had previously overlooked. Accomplishments and acquisition of knowledge I had previously ignored. I discovered I really did have strengths!

A Little Something You Might Want to Try
Knowing My Strengths

List your strengths, that is, those personal qualities or attributes or characteristics that you believe are positive and strong and make you glad that you possess them. They could be related to:

1. your culture/heritage
2. your community/environment
3. your talents, skills, or abilities
4. your interests,
5. your opinions,
6. your perceptions,
7. what others have told you about yourself, or
8. your experiences, accomplishments, knowledge, values, morals, or beliefs.

Keep this inventory and reflect on it as often as possible.

SELF-DECLARATION OF INDEPENDENCE

(taking responsibility for myself)

My next discovery, as I set out on my Journey Within, came as quite a surprise. Up to now, I was entrenched in avoidance, blaming, and not taking responsibility—it was my way of life.

It wasn't until I was willing to let go of my old way of thinking that I realized I am responsible for myself, how I think, what I feel, and the way I behave, regardless of any external influences.

I own me!

I even went so far as to write myself a statement of who I am predicated on the notion that I alone am responsible for my own thoughts, feelings, and behaviour. This is my:

Self-Declaration of Independence

I have chosen who I am. I take ownership of who I am. I am responsible for who I am. I am responsible for my thoughts, feelings, and behaviour. If I do not like what I experience, I can choose how I deal with it. If there is any part of me I do not like, I can change it. I can reinvent myself. I can embrace who I am. I have the freedom to decide who I want to be, what I want to have, and what I want to do. I can motivate myself at any time. I can immerse myself in awareness. I can choose my attitude and the way I see the world in my own unique way. I can let go of things not within my control. I can choose to learn from my failures as well as my successes. I am flexible and I am able to endure. I can wear my feelings of hope, courage, love, joy, humility, awe, acceptance and peace like a badge of honour. I can forgive and I can show gratitude. I choose to build character through my morals and values and good habits. I can grow. I can choose to label myself with positive attributes and demonstrate them to myself and to others. I am able. I am who I am and I like who I am.

A Little Something You Might Want to Try
Taking Responsibility for Myself

You can complete this now, if you think you are ready, or you can wait until you have read the sections that follow.

Create your own Self-Declaration of Independence:

- Use "I" statements
- Use positive words and statements only
- Take responsibility for all aspects of yourself
- Be honest, realistic, and sincere
- List only what you are able and willing to do, to have, and to be
- Start your personal Declaration of Independence with "I, (insert name here), do solemnly declare that…

A GOOD SWIFT KICK

(motivation)

This thought bumped me up to my next discovery in this pinball game of life: motivation. Instead of leaving the rhetorical question "Why bother?" unanswered, I figured that given my new positive attitude, I ought to give consideration to a proper response. I thought of what, indeed, would motivate me to bother. Before I could provide myself with an adequate answer, I pondered the meaning of motivation and where it came from. The dictionary defines motivation as "an act of motivating" (thanks a lot) or a call to action. All the results of my research of motivation were geared toward employment-related goal-setting. When all was said and done, I began to see motivation as an invisible force that nudges—sometimes catapults—me toward a desired outcome through my own commitment and perseverance; in turn this would satisfy a need, want, or desire. Another way of wording this is, if I need, want, or desire something bad enough, I'll pursue it, or else I didn't really need, want, or desire it bad enough as much as I thought I did. I also learned that "self-motivation" is redundant; all motivation comes from within *me*. Others may inspire, support, influence, or reinforce me, but only *I* can motivate myself. Consequently, waiting to be motivated is tantamount to waiting forever.

I needed a good swift kick in my derriere and I needed to do it myself. Sure, it's not always easy and, sure, sometimes you end up folding yourself into a pretzel but, like anything that is worth doing, you must make the effort. I often used to expend more energy in coming up with excuses *not* to do something than it would have taken just to do it in the first place. So for someone with such a disposition, I had to organize my thoughts systematically in order to get my motivation in gear.

A Little Something You Might Want to Try
Motivation #1

Make a list of various things that motivate you. This would include things you find interesting, inspiring, uplifting, and anything that you believe would be in your best interest.

A Little Something You Might Want to Try
Motivation #2

1. Create a to-do, to-have, and to-be list by drawing a table with three columns. The first column heading should be TO DO, the second column heading should be TO HAVE, and the third column heading should be TO BE.
2. Make it an ongoing list, adding on as soon as an idea enters into your head.
2. Ask yourself what blocks you from even the smallest step? For example, negative payoffs, laziness, negative past experiences, excuses, waiting to hit rock bottom, emotions (fear,   anger), etc.
4. If you are feeling stuck, ask yourself:
   - Do I want it bad enough?
   - Why do I want it?
   - Is it my own choice?
   - Is it for myself?
   - Am I committed to make the effort?

LET'S *NOT* DO THE TIME WARP AGAIN

(focusing on the here and now)

Being an avid time traveller did not make me happy; it made me anxious. Since too frequent visits to the past made me guilty and trips to the future were fraught with worry, I realized I needed to spend more time in the here and now. As with all of my new changes on my Journey Within, I had to make a deliberate effort to avoid a time warp and stay put. It was clear that I needed to be aware more than ever since it was so easy for my mind to slip back in time to when I did stuff I regretted, or tumble forward in time, thinking, "What if this or that happens?"

A Little Something You Might Want to Try
Focusing on the Here and Now

1. Write down a statement that appears to be a "past" statement or a "future" statement.

2. Rephrase (and rewrite) the thought to maintain focus on the here and now. In other words,
   - Replace "woulda/coulda/shoulda" with "Can I do anything about it now?"
   - Replace "What if . . . ?" with "What is the probability that . . . ?" or, "Understanding the possible consequences and repercussions, can I do something about it now and if so, what?"

3. Repeat this every time you find yourself in the future or in the past, that is, every time you find yourself ridden with guilt or rattled with anxiety.

REALITY CHECK

(how real or realistic is the situation?)

As with time travel, I found that I frequently needed to check on my dimension of reality. Sometimes the most bizarre things seem so real; other times the most mundane aspects of life seem ridiculous. Both are shimmering, quivering, translucent, ethereal. Can I reach out and touch it or will my hand go through it? Is this a languid daydream or a terrifying nightmare?

Sometimes it is okay to bask in the warm light of imagination. But on those occasions when my thoughts become a muddle, when life becomes a struggle, making decisions becomes difficult, and moving forward is seemingly impossible, I need a reality check.

Whenever I feel stuck, confused, indecisive, doubtful, or immobilized, I say to myself whichever of the following fits:

Really?

Get real!

Reality bites.

How realistic is this?

A Little Something You Might Want to Try
Reality Check

1. How do I feel (e.g. stuck, confused, indecisive, doubtful, immobilized, other)?
2. Why am I feeling this way?
3. Does this issue make sense?
4. What is my approach in dealing with this situation?
5. Is this approach realistic?
6. If not, how could I better manage?

FOOL PROOF

(evidence and intent)

One of the tasks I had in my Social Services job in the *real* world was being a fraud investigator. In order to put together a case that would stand up in court, I had to provide evidence and prove intent. If someone was in receipt of welfare assistance but contravened the rules and regulations of eligibility by, say, having an undisclosed bank account which exceeded the allowable assets, it was my responsibility to obtain records of the bank account and balances (evidence) and demonstrate through copious file notes that said account was intentionally not made known to the case worker (intent).

I realized that the same principle holds true for my thoughts: whenever a rogue or unwanted or destructive thought pops into my head, I need to ask myself, "What evidence do I have to show that this thought is true or valid?" and "What is my intent by having this thought?" or "What do I intend to do with this thought?" If, for example, I found myself in a situation where I did not succeed in a job competition that prompted the thought, "I'm a real loser!" I would inevitably find little evidence to support that thought; moreover I would likely find evidence that proved the opposite, such as, "I have succeeded in other job competitions including the one that secured my current position." In reflection, what did I intend to do by entertaining this thought? Being brutally honest with myself, I intended to rationalize my embarrassment of not succeeding in the competition and I intended to wallow in self-pity, which would then justify my not moving forward and not learning anything from the experience. To restate this in a more positive light, the inability to provide evidence and the realization of the proof of intent was enough to let go of the negativity and move forward.

It's called "burden of proof" for a reason.

A Little Something You Might Want to Try
Evidence and Intent

1. Detail the situation.
2. Identify your feeling(s) regarding the situation.
3. Regarding the situation, what resultant thoughts automatically occur to you?
4. State the evidence that show these thoughts are valid.
5. State the evidence that show these thoughts are not valid.
6. What is your intent by having these thoughts?

HOW PERCEPTIVE!

(perception and keeping things in perspective)

Perception is a reality and reality is but a perception.

The Journey Within was really a joyride on carnival bumper cars. The next thought I drove into was the notion that there really is such a thing as perception, and that reality may be perceived differently by individuals, groups, or societies, based on the myriad variables which influence perception. Consequently, I began to understand that my thoughts are perceptions which are coloured by my variables. These variables include, but are not limited to, age, sex, culture, socio-economic status, life experience and observations, influence of others, sensory experiences, etc.

I am asked, "Why the goofy grin?" when I smile at a stalk of celery. Could it be because it reminds me of the love I gave and the care I took, feeding celery to the school hamster when I brought it home for a weekend in grade two? I breathe a sigh of gratitude when I acknowledge that my opinions are being heard by someone I admire and respect, and that person is perplexed by my response. I redden with a flush of disbelief if someone pays me a compliment. I am puzzled when a friend expresses awe at the vast amount of space in my rather modest home.

Usually, I don't pay too much attention to how I perceive the world, unless my perceptions are being challenged, or questioned, or merely brought to my attention. It may be someone expressing a differing point of view; I may have read something which caused me to acknowledge that I never thought of it that way before; I may have an out-and-out confrontation with someone insisting I am wrong. Whenever there is incongruence between me and the world, me and another person, or even between me and myself, I have discovered the importance of taking a moment to check my perception.

I would come to understand my perception through the following exercise, which would then allow me to reinforce my perception, alter my perception, or even agree to disagree and move on.

As far as keeping things in perspective is concerned, all I need to do is, for one brief moment, imagine my life differently, with more of a struggle, having less, being less, and doing without. It could always be worse, that is (keeping a positive spin on things), I could always perceive my world and my circumstances to be better than they might be or might otherwise have been.

A Little Something You Might Want to Try
Perception

1. What is the issue?
2. What is your perception of the situation?
3. Identify the incongruence(s) i.e. what seems off?
4. Why are you perceiving it this way? i.e. what are the variables which are causing you to perceive it this way?
5. If another person is involved, how does the other person perceive it?
6. What are the variables of the other person(s) perception?

A Little Something You Might Want to Try
Perception

1. What is the situation/circumstance and what is your perspective?
2. How could the situation/circumstance be worse, more difficult, less enjoyable?
3. Reflecting on this imaginary perspective, how do you feel now about the current situation/circumstance?
4. Taking this one step further, can you make improvements to the situation/circumstance? If so, how?

CONTROL FREAK . . . NO MORE!

(what is within my control?)

The next rung on the ladder of my Journey Within was to discern the things in life over which I had control and the things over which I did not have control. This was an especially important consideration whenever I was feeling stuck, anxious, angry, immobilized, and virtually any other negative emotion. I realized that, ultimately, if the issue was within my control, I could then determine what to do about it. If the issue was not within my control, I could abandon feeling responsible for it, not own it, let it go, and move on.

A Little Something You Might Want to Try
Control

1. What is the issue?
2. Is the issue within your control?
3. If so, can you acknowledge ownership of it?
4. If not, can you let it go?
5. If not, why do you think you are holding onto it?

"FUHGET ABOUT IT!"

(the unlearning process)

Up to now, I had learned virtually everything I could about being negative and self-deprecating; this elicited a wide range of interpretations, from whimsical and endearing to obnoxious and miserable. Believe me, there was a whole lot of stuff I learned about myself, others, and the world, which was full of crap.

I realized that if I were going to do anything to improve the quality of my life, I would have to *un*learn just about everything.

A Little Something You Might Want to Try
Unlearning

1. Ask yourself if the thought was stated clearly and understood fully. If not, "Forget about it!" Start over.
2. Ask yourself if the thought was fostering a positive attitude. If not, "Forget about it!" Start over.
3. Ask yourself if the thought was creating positive feelings. If not, "Forget about it!" Start over.
4. Ask yourself if the thought was truthful and honest. If not, "Forget about it!" Start over.
5. Ask yourself if the thought was congruent with your morals, values and beliefs. If not, "Forget about it!" Start over.
6. Ask yourself if the thought was taking you where you wanted to be. If not, "Forget about it!" Start over.

TRY AND TRY AGAIN

(failure and success: it's okay to learn from my mistakes)

Scarecrow: "Oh, I'm a failure because I haven't got a brain!"
Dorothy: "What would you do with a brain if you had one?"
Scarecrow: "Why, if I had a brain, I could…"

The fact that I have failed (and often) doesn't matter, really, I discovered in the next chapter of my Journey Within. What I do after I have failed, and what I have learned after I have failed, is what really matters. Once I realized and believed this, I wouldn't just overcome shame, embarrassment, disappointment, defeat, depression, and self-deprecation, I slowly began to view failure as that respected teacher I alluded to in Part I.

Failure, has taught me a whole lot o' lessons: perseverance, humility, acceptance, possibilities, and choices; correct, alter, change, or relinquish what I am doing; how to be less selfish, less self-centered, and more giving. Even how to survive. Failure is strengthening my character.

And I can now look at myself in the mirror and say, sincerely, "Being a failure can be cool!"

By failing at something at least I know I have tried. If I would have avoided trying for fear of failure, as I had done so many times before, I would never have known if I would have succeeded, and I would never have given myself the opportunity to learn, to grow, to change, to experience, and to move forward.

If all else failed in my attempts to understand failure, I took comfort in understanding that everyone has failed at something. I'm really not alone in failing. And I learned that to have learned from failure is, in itself, a success.

So, nu, what is success?

The first image that I conjured up when thinking of success is some form of fame and fortune. Though these may be outcomes of achieving success, they are not success in and of themselves. That is why, I suppose (as previously stated), there are so many rich and famous people who are miserable and disillusioned with their lives.

Success, I discovered, is being satisfied with who you are, with what you think, with how you feel, and with what you do. To be successful, therefore, requires:

- setting and accomplishing goals,
- looking forward to life's struggles and challenges.
- having a sense of direction and purpose,
- learning about life and doing the best you by continually developing, improving, growing, strengthening and evolving.
- realizing your full potential.
- creating and maintaining a set of standards, values, morals, and beliefs to commit to and to live by.
- working hard, using time constructively and effectively.
- building good relationships.
- having a positive attitude toward life.
- accepting responsibility appropriately.
- being kind, considerate, and respectful toward others and bringing out those qualities in others as well.
- looking for the good in others.
- seeing life as a series of opportunities and possibilities, and just generally accepting life.

Since success, like failure, comes only as a result of trying, there is nothing else to do but try and try again.

A Little Something You Might Want to Try
Failure and Success

1. Describe the failure or what you believe you have failed at.
2. Is this truly a failed attempt at something or are you just feeling sorry for yourself? If the latter, try to relate that feeling to something concrete and specific.
3. Identify any other feeling associated with this sense of failure.
4. What, specifically, in your attempt to do this, failed?
5. Why, specifically, do you think this attempt failed?
6. If you feel like giving up, ask yourself: is it the feeling associated with the failure or something more specific (such as lack of knowledge, time, skills, tools, etc.) that is preventing future attempts?
7. Can you do something (specific) to gain whatever you may be lacking (such as gaining the knowledge, making the time, acquiring the skills, utilizing the tools, etc.)?
8. What did you learn from the failed attempt? What could be done differently in your next attempt? List your options.
9. Acknowledge that the lesson learned from the failure is, in itself, a success. Once you have done this, reward yourself for the success of having learned from the failure.
10. Proceed to try again, using what you have learned. Repeat this process, where required.

SO WAS FRANKENSTEIN'S MONSTER

(human nature)

It was a difficult lesson for me to learn that people may be hard-wired differently. Not everyone in the world, it seems, is miserable and struggling to climb out of the abyss. Not everyone yearns to break the chains that bind him to his circumstances. Not everyone despairs over the conditions of his environment. Some people are perfectly content to be miserable. Some people are happy clams living in rags and shambles. Still others seem to have been born into the world wearing rose-coloured glasses.

What do they know that I don't?

It has been suggested by sages, heretics, and pop-psych gurus that our lives have been pre-ordained, that our souls have selected our parentage prior to our birth, based on genetics and circumstances, to enable us to learn or re-learn lessons for the soul's development. At first I thought that, if this were true, my soul must be either stupid or masochistic. On this Journey Within, however, I decided that the best approach would be for me to embrace who I am, genetics, circumstances, warts and all. I would change what I wanted to change or what I could change, keep the rest, and revel in it.

The key to this strategy, for me, was not to use "I was born that way" or "It's just the way I am" as an excuse not to pursue improvements to the quality of my life. That is to say, being hard-wired a certain way should not prevent me from stepping out of my comfort zone, meeting new challenges, challenging my limitations, and creating new experiences for myself.

A Little Something You Might Want to Try
Human Nature

1. Divide a page into two columns or use the chart below.
2. Make a list in Column A of all the attributes you like about yourself (see note).
3. Make a list in Column B of all the attributes you do not like about yourself (see note).

   <u>Note</u>: These attributes could relate to your physical appearance, your personality traits, your genetic predisposition, things you do, things you say or tell others, your morals, your values, your circumstances, etc.
4. Can anything in Column B be changed? If so, highlight.
5. If so, are you willing to make the changes?
6. If yes, how? Create a 'to do' list for each of those attributes that can be changed. List the unwanted attribute in one column and the steps to change the unwanted attribute to the desired attribute.
7. If no, why not?
8. For those areas in Column B cannot be changed, why not (for example are there limitations, time, cost, energy restraints, comfort issues, realistic considerations, etc.)?

   Once you have done so, move to Column A.
9. At the end of this exercise, you should have only a column A.

I AM GUMBY!

(elasticity: how much am I prepared to endure?)

When my youngest daughter was about four years old, she discovered this great expression for something that was too far away and beyond her grasp. "Daddy," she said, "it's too reachy!" I would encourage her to lean forward or bend or stretch to get hold of whatever it was she wanted to get hold of. When she finally did get the object in her little hands, she giggled with delight, "It's *not* too reachy!"

I thought about this in relation to my life, that if I wanted something, I need to bend, stretch, and flex just a little more. The physicality of it felt good and it was good for my body.

Then I realized the same principle applied to my mind and my spirit. They, too, needed to be exercised to keep in shape.

By testing my beliefs, learning new things, and stimulating my thoughts, I began to understand that:

- I am very elastic; I can stretch, bend, and expand and I will not break in two,
- I can prevent mental and spiritual atrophy by continually exercising them,
- I have more endurance than I give myself credit for, and
- There is very little in life that is too reachy.

A Little Something You Might Want to Try
Elasticity

1. Identify at least five things you believe are too difficult or impossible to do (such as: something you wish to acquire, a discussion you wish you could have, an activity you wish you could engage in, an acquaintance you wish you could make, a relationship you wish you could cultivate, a moral or value you wish you could adopt, etc.).

2. What makes these things so difficult?
    - Is it a feeling (e.g. fear, embarrassment)?
    - Is it a limitation or lack of something (e.g. skill, talent knowledge, physical ability, access, etc.)?
    - Is it unrealistic (e.g. flying without an airplane or an assistive device, having an intimate relationship with a movie star of choice, etc.)?

3. If the thing you wish you could have, do, or be is 'have-able', 'do-able', or 'be-able', are you willing to step out of your comfort zone?

4. If so, create a plan of action (using small steps—see section on setting goals) and follow your steps.

5. Reward yourself for your accomplishments, for testing your limits, and for doing something that is not normally comfortable for you.

6. Add to the list as necessary and repeat exercise.

GET OUT THE WINDEX
(clarity)

As I was travelling along the dimly lit corridors of my Journey Within, it was apparent that I needed to clean the cobwebs from the corners of my mind. As long as those fuzzy, wispy webs blocked, distorted, or otherwise clouded my view, I would not be able to find what I was seeking. Whatever I was thinking, I needed to have a clear vision of it. With whomever I was conversing, I needed to clarify the issues. Regardless of what I was feeling, I needed to clearly understand why I was feeling that way. However I was behaving, I needed to be clear about my actions and their consequences.

A Little Something You Might Want to Try
Clarity

1. Identify the thought and write it down.
2. Have you covered, in your statement, all the particulars, that is, who, what, where, why, when and how? If not, do so.
3. What are the feelings associated with the thought?
4. Are they congruent with the thought and the behaviours?
5. What are the behaviours associated with the thought?
6. Are they congruent with the thought and the feelings?
7. Look at your statement and analyze each word as it pertains to the thought.
     - Are you saying what you are intending to say or mean?
     - Is it relevant to the overall thought?
     - Is there a more appropriate word?
     - Can you eliminate any unnecessary words?
8. Are you being honest with yourself about the thought?
9. Rewrite the new statement.
10. Does this new statement make sense?
    Is it what you intended?
    Is it clearer than the previous statement?
    If it is not clearer, repeat the process.

LIFE IS A SCHOOLROOM
(life lessons)

I have noticed, over a period of time, that if I am dissatisfied with a thought, plagued by an unwanted feeling, or uncomfortable with any action I have taken, I seem to be faced with the same or similar circumstance until such time that I come to a resolution regarding the thought, cast off the unwanted feeling, or find a way of behaving more appropriately. When I was scared to death at the thought of public speaking, I would find myself having to speak in front of a group of people. If I wanted to avoid certain people, I would suddenly find myself in their company. If I was bored or lonely, I would find myself all alone and with nothing to do.

I realized that each and every time I encountered something that would diminish the quality of my life, or prevent me from moving forward, or left me with unresolved issues, I would find myself in the schoolroom of life, repeating the lesson over and over until I got it right.

Each time I had an "Aha!" moment, the lesson was learned and I graduated, ready for the next lesson.

A Little Something You Might Want to Try
Life Lessons

1. Define the circumstance.
2. About which thought, feeling, or behaviour am I uncomfortable?
3. Do I need to change anything? How can I change it?
4. What lesson can I learn from this circumstance or experience? Or, what lesson am I supposed to be learning?

LIFE IS A CIRCUS COMPLETE WITH A TRAPEZE AND A HIGH WIRE
(balance and vibrations)

Life hangs in the balance, literally.

In this leg of my Journey Within, I discovered that balance is the way of managing opposing forces: good and bad, light and dark, fast and slow, serious and funny, right and wrong, hard and soft, black and white, strong and weak, creative and destructive.

I could hear the barker's raspy call as I approached the Big Top in the circus of life: "Step right up, folks; the show is about to begin. Watch in amazement as the one-thousand pound elephant balances on a little ball! Gasp in awe at the trapeze artists swinging back and forth thirty feet off the ground! Shudder in anticipation as the balancing stick sways from side to side with each dangerous step forward on the high wire!"

I began to notice balance in everything. I also noticed that balance isn't stationary or stagnant; it is the constant movement from one force to its opposite. This is called a vibration: the ba-bong ba-bong ba-bong beat of your heart, the patterned pace of inhaling and exhaling, the rhythm of sex, the up and down motion of gravity, the rapid movement of the eyes of someone who is in a deep sleep, the repetition of waves lapping the shore, expansion and contraction. Vibrations are found in every aspect of life. Collectively, vibrations are energy. Energy is life.

It came to my attention that I needed to expend my energy to maintain balance which, in turn, would enable me to maintain my life. I was finding a balance in what I ate in order to be healthier. I began to exercise, too. This principle also applied to my emotions. If I was feeling sad, I would seek out ways to recapture happiness. If I was passionate or super-excited about something, I could calm down and exercise restraint if the situation called for it. If I was bored, I could quell the boredom by engaging in activity. When I was suffering spiritually, I began to follow a path that would broaden my spiritual perspective. I saw that if I did not keep up the vibration, if I did not seeking a balance, and if I did not using my energy, it felt as though my lifeblood was being sucked out of me. I was totally drained, lethargic, and lost.

When I was able to keep the vibration going, I was able to live my life more fully, becoming more complete, fulfilled, accomplished, and satisfied. This seems to hold true for all aspects of life. Physically, I recognized that I need to take care of my body to make sure it functions better and to make sure I don't croak. If I don't exercise my muscles, they will wither away. Through my increased knowledge of balance and vibrations, I realized that this concept also applies to my digestive system: input and output; there is input and output for my thoughts, feelings, and behaviour as well, which affect my physical, intellectual, and spiritual well-being:

- Input—what I consume; output—what my body absorbs, stores, eliminates, and utilizes
- Input—what I read or what I watch on television; output—what I do with that information
- Input—how I develop my beliefs; output—how I express my beliefs

It is all balance, vibrations, and energy.
I wasn't just *at* the circus; I was a *part* of it!
Life is, indeed, a balancing act.

A Little Something You Might Want to Try
Balance and Vibrations

1. Draw a graph. At one end of the bottom horizontal line, write a word, phrase or statement (the simpler the better) that best describes your thought, feeling, behaviour, or circumstance. At the other end of the bottom horizontal line, write its polar opposite.

2. Along the vertical line on the left, write the numbers 1 to 10 in ascending order and evenly spaced. These represent the degree of intensity from low to high.

3. Using this graph, you can identify where you are in terms of the thought, feeling, behaviour, or circumstance and in terms of the degree of its intensity. Mark an 'X' at that spot on the graph.

4. Give yourself a time reference (for example, an hour, a day, or a week). Within that time of reference, mark an 'X' for each one (that is to say, an 'X' for each day of the week, or each hour of the day, etc.). By the end of your time reference, you should have a number of 'X's all around the graph. Ultimately, the closer to the centre of the graph, the more balanced is the thought, feeling, behaviour, or situation, and the more levelled the intensity.

CLOAK AND DAGGER:
THE OTHER SIDE OF THE LOOKING GLASS

(relationships)

Curiouser and curiouser! On my Journey Within, I stumbled into an area that seemed totally familiar but not yet thoroughly explored: relationships. I was on the other side of the looking glass!

In short order, I realized I couldn't investigate relationships with respect to happiness on my Journey Without because it was really an internal thing, that is, other people can't make you happy (perhaps they can instigate and influence) just as they can't *make* you feel *any* emotion. Only *you* can make yourself feel happy.

But why? And how? And where do other people fit in?

Well, for me, it started with deep-rooted beliefs I had about myself as revealed in my Starting Point. Based on my opinions and in my assessment of myself, taking into account my life experiences and other people's assessments of me, I developed a deep-rooted belief about who I am. Since most of my self-assessment was negative, it produced many negative and hurtful emotions, such as anger, sadness, self-pity, loneliness, etc. Feelings of being rejected, abandoned, and ridiculed were everywhere and they hurt. At least, I believed these feelings to be true as a continuing process of my self-assessment (even if they weren't true). I then acted on these feelings by doing whatever it took not to have fun or not to interact: avoiding, expressing anger, not getting to know people, making up stories and scenarios as to why people wouldn't want to be my friend or lover or soul mate, and acting in a way that wasn't the real me so that I would be liked or would make a good impression.

It wasn't until I realized what I was doing that I was able to change it: I was overdressing myself.

Yes, I was overdressing myself in self-assessments, in all the ways in which I thought I was not good enough: cute, rich, smart, sexy, powerful. In all the ways I thought I didn't measure up. In all the ways I had self-imposed or unrealistic expectations of myself. That was my first layer of clothing. But I wanted to keep it out of sight . . . after all, who really wants to don their insecurities for everyone to see? So I put on a second layer of clothing, which represented all the things I should be: well-educated, successful, a devoted husband, a loving father, a role model. But there was also a third layer of clothing, all the things I would like to be: wise, giving, caring, philanthropic, positive, happy. The fourth layer of clothing was all the things I thought others thought of me. The next layer was the jaded view I had about the world, which was an extension of all the other layers of clothing. Further to this were the additional layers of emotions and behaviours, culled and expressed from all these thoughts. Then there was the outer layer of clothing, my finest suit: it was what I wanted people to see.

At this point I was carrying the weight of a hundred pounds of clothing and I felt like I was suffocating!

What does all this have to do with relationships, you ask? Well, each person I involved in my life came with layers of clothing, too. He/she/ they had their own false self-assessments, thoughts of who they should be, what they would like to be, how they thought the world saw them, and how it all coloured their outlook on life and the people in them, to all varying and changing degrees. They, too, were grossly overdressed. So much so that, when we interacted or formed a relationship, we were too buried under all that clothing for me to see the real them or for them to see the real me. In fact, there was yet an additional layer: how we all viewed one another over and above how we saw ourselves or how others saw us. Could we really see one another underneath all those layers of clothing? No, only the outer layer was visible. And *that* may not even be seen since we all only see what we want to see, or see what we project the others in the relationship should be wearing.

I now get why I was so confused!

So how do you really get to the authentic person beneath all those layers of clothing? It's easy! Simply take off all your clothes!

I started rather tentatively by removing one layer at a time. To begin, I had to shrug out of the notion that I was revealing my true self and not the false, imagined self. All of those negative things I said about myself were just erroneous deep-rooted beliefs; they were not real. Likewise, I had to strip away the idea that I should be someone or something other than whom or what I was, what I should be, or the *un*attainable expectations of who I would like to be. I also removed my incorrect assumptions and unchecked perceptions of what I thought others thought of me. This enabled me to peel off my negative world view.

By removing all my clothing, I was allowing the other person to see the authentic me and reform their assessment of me, based on who I really am. They, too, then have the opportunity to get naked by removing all of their own layers of clothing so I can know them and love them for their true selves. By no longer being encumbered by the weight of my false beliefs as represented by the layers of clothing, I not only undressed, but cast aside all the emotional drama and resultant behaviours that went with it.

I stripped down and was naked! Go ahead, world, take a good look! I'm naked!—perhaps obsessed with nakedness, but still—I'm naked and free! I'm me and I have created my own happiness for myself and for my relationships!

A Little Something You Might Want to Try
Relationships

1. On a scale from one to ten, one being 'can do without' and ten being 'can't do without', rate the importance of the relationship.
2. What makes the relationship as important or unimportant as you think it is?
3. What is the situation within the relationship that is in question (be specific)?
4. Ask the other person what he/she sees is the situation within the relationship that is in question. How does this compare to yours?
5. What thoughts does this situation within the relationship elicit?
6. Ask the other person, what thoughts does this situation within the relationship elicit? How does this compare to yours?
7. What feelings do this situation and these thoughts within the relationship elicit?
8. Ask the other person what feelings do this situation and these thoughts within the relationship elicit. How does this compare to yours?
9. What behaviours do this situation, these thoughts, and these feelings within the relationship elicit?
10. Ask the other person what behaviours do this situation, these thoughts, and these feelings within the relationship elicit. How does this compare to yours?
11. Since you cannot change others (but only influence them), how can you change yourself in this relationship in order to make improvements (such as communication [including what you say as well as what you hear and how you listen], compromise, control, attitude, empathy, etc.)?

12. What character traits do you need to bring out in yourself that would foster an improved relationship? Go back to the relationship and employ your new-found knowledge.

FEELING GOOD FEELINGS

I spent so much of my life dwelling on negative thoughts and behaviours which, of course, elicited negative feelings. But I wanted to feel good. I wanted to experience the more pleasurable and rewarding feelings life had to offer. I did not want to blow my stack, flip my lid, toss my cookies, be a shrinking violet, turn green with envy, red with rage, white with fear, gray with shock, yellow with cowardice, or feel blue.

Because I knew very little about feeling good feelings, I decided to make a list of some of those key emotions I considered to be 'good' ones, and to try my best to experience them. These included: thankfulness/gratitude, feeling useful, feeling wanted, feeling unique, feeling a part of something, hope, courage, humility, love, joy, awe, letting go/release, and acceptance/peace. In order to do something, I needed to actually think of something or do something to attain the experience.

There is something reverential, spiritual, when experiencing positive emotions, and it feels good. There is also a kind of overlap amongst many of these good feelings. For example, when you are awestruck, humility creeps in. When you are accepting, there is a certain amount of love that encroaches. When you are grateful, it augments feelings of hope.

In addition to this, there are varying degrees of intensity with feelings. Interestingly, the more the feelings are experienced the more intense the feelings become, and the stronger the craving. Also, it is old news that there is scientific proof regarding these feelings in relation to the release of chemicals in the body. It stands to reason, then, that the pursuit of good feelings parallels addiction to drugs. The difference is that seeking natural experiences to attain these feelings is not artificially induced, does not have bad side effects, is not harmful to your health, and does not create an external dependency.

For each of these positive emotions, I needed to discover:

- What is the feeling, and what is its definition?
- Why pursue the feeling?
- How is the feeling experienced and what can I do to acquire the experience?

So, off I went on my Journey Within to explore, experience, and understand these feelings . . .

FROM THE BOTTOM OF MY HEART

(thankfulness and gratitude)

Being thankful and showing gratitude is much more than just being humble or deferential. Sincere gratitude stems from a heightened awareness, a drop of awe, and a dash of humility.

I never really thought of what I had but, instead, dwelled on what I didn't have. This way of thinking inevitably induced a bout of whining and complaining. And what did whining and complaining get me? At best, I felt exhausted. At worst, it created an ongoing cycle of more whining and more complaining, without resolution of the issues. As I learned the hard way, no one likes to be in the company of a whiner; all it served to do was to alienate me from others. And, believe me, I complained a lot! Sometimes I complained even when I didn't have much to complain about. In the greater scheme of things, my complaints were pretty dumb, petty, frivolous, and prevented me from moving forward with my life.

I discovered that, if I think about what I actually do have, the resultant behaviour would likely be a sincere expression of gratitude. Since expressing gratitude gave me a sense of fulfilment, closure, and reinforced my new positive attitude, it helped to lift me out of my depression and prevented me from taking life for granted.

Expressing gratitude feels good.

A Little Something You Might Want to Try
Thankfulness and Gratitude #1

1. Create a chart with three columns, one for **People**, one for **Places**, and one for **Things**. Complete the list with as many things as you can think of and indicate **why** you feel gratitude for these people, places and things. Note: **things** can be intangible (such as freedom, the circumstances of life you were born into, the ability to see, etc.).

2. Review the list whenever you have the urge to complain or if you are feeling depressed.

3. Where possible, find those individuals you recorded in the **People** column and express your gratitude (in person or in writing). Don't forget to tell them *why* you are thankful.

A Little Something You Might Want to Try
Thankfulness and Gratitude #2

1. Try to go for a week without complaining.

2. If you do make a complaint, write it down.

3. If you go for a day, a half-day, an hour, or whatever time period you choose without making a complaint, reward yourself.

4. Review your list of complaints. Determine which are resolvable and create an action plan.

5. If you believe your complaints are not resolvable, rephrase the complaint from what you don't have to what you do have.

I HOPE SO!

(hope)

Having surrounded myself with feelings of hopelessness for most of my life, it came as quite a surprise that I first tuned into a sense of hope when I said to an ill acquaintance, rather robotically, "Hope you're feeling better soon." At first the words seemed hollow, but after thinking about what I had said, I realized I really did want this person to feel better. It was my hope for him that he feel better. I had hope!

What was this 'hope' that I had felt?

It seemed to me that I not only strongly desired, but also truly believed that there could be a positive outcome in this situation.

In feeling hope for myself, on those rare occasions when I felt hopeful, it was usually borne of desperation to fill a need at any cost. I never did figure out where my sense of hopelessness originated, or why I always seemed so desperate. I was emotionally nourished as a child and never neglected; I didn't really experience loss (my parents' marriage was intact, nobody close to me passed away in the first couple of decades of my life, and I lived in the same comfortable and familiar house for my first twenty-one years); I wasn't abused or harmed (maybe teased or made fun of from time to time).

Can a little boy experience burnout? I'm not sure, although I always felt defeated, asking myself, "What's the point?" or asserting, "I can't."

With my new positive approach to life, I'm beginning to see how hope can be borne of optimism, even in the face of some stark realities. For example, instead of watching the grains of sand filter with ever-increasing speed to the bottom of the hourglass, I must not only focus on the fact that there is still some sand left in the top half, but also recognize there is still time to make every speck of it count. Or, as corny and clichéd as it is, I can refuse to see the proverbial cup as half-empty and begin to see it as half-full, as well as figure out what the hell is in the damn cup. I can foster the feeling of hope by doing things, like setting goals and working towards them and overcoming barriers, accepting challenges, taking opportunities, and making things happen.

The outcome: hope for me, hope for you, hope for the world.

Hope feels good.

A Little Something You Might Want to Try
Hope

1. Take inventory of those less fortunate than you (e.g. patients in a hospital), and do something for them to have a reason to hope.
2. Read to someone who is sight-impaired. Spend time with an elderly person and engage him/her in conversation. You can also benefit by learning from their wisdom and life experience.
3. Do something for someone in a third world country (such as, adopt a child or a village).
4. Invest in someone's idea.
5. Do something eco-friendly e.g. save the whales, trees, atmosphere, etc.
6. Be there for someone in need, in crisis, in despair. Volunteer on a crisis phone-line or at a distress centre.
7. Donate time, money, energy, support, etc.
8. Pick a goal and follow steps to achieving it. Support others with *their* goals.
9. Help another person to have hope by sincerely identifying something positive about him/her.
10. Do something to effect change for the better.

"I'M JUST A DANDY LION!"

(courage)

Some would argue that courage is an act, not an emotion. In the context of my meagre life experience, courage refers to the feeling associated with acting courageously. This includes:

- acquiring an inner strength and resolve in the face of adversity, pain, or grief
- managing—even overcoming—fear, or acting even in spite of fear
- voluntarily leaving behind a certain level of comfort and moving into some unknown territory
- confronting uncertainty, possibly danger
- demonstrating restraint
- speaking your mind
- taking a stand for yourself and for others

I remember creeping timidly, apprehensively, onto a diving board, one foot placed tentatively and deliberately in front of the other, until I reached the edge. A thousand thoughts raced through my mind as my skinny little eight-year-old frame shivered and wobbled on the plank. It's hard to know for sure what was the moment of truth, that decisive instant that sent me spiralling toward my impending demise, as the solid surface of the water rose up to meet my belly with more of a thud than a splash. As I gurgled and glugged to the surface, I thought to myself, I did it! I dived!

I was a courageous little boy. But somewhere between pre-pubescence and mid-to-late life I wimped out, avoided, retreated, and even hid from life. Again, why this happened I'm uncertain. I suppose I preferred feeling comfortable, safe, and secure, and so I stopped doing stuff. I spent a lot of time watching TV instead of interacting with people, pursuing goals, or articulating and defending my point of view.

Over time, I noticed that only when I forced myself to act through desperation did I become aware of the courageousness of which I was capable. The death of a parent, my son's car accident, the decline and decay of some of my relationships, the deterioration of my spirit and dissolution of my energy, all these circumstances needed to change swiftly and dramatically in order to ensure I didn't self-extinguish. I needed to rediscover that courageous little boy inside of me and consciously work toward re-establishing my courage.

So here is a "twelve-step program" I try to practise in order to calculate, claim, and cultivate my courage (Note: this may be easier to do once you read the section on Behaving Well):

1. Identify the circumstance and decide to do something—anything—that is, take action.
2. Evaluate the situation. Are you being courageous or foolish by taking action with respect to the situation?
3. Understand the overall vision.
4. Implement the decision by setting goals and taking small steps.
5. Ensure your external supports are in place (that is, people who are trustworthy and supportive).
6. Persevere. Learn from failure and move forward.
7. Commit to it and believe in it. Believe in yourself. Stay focused. Be aware.
8. Step out of your comfort zone and find ways of facing your fears. Look forward to discovering new things.
9. Embrace fears optimistically and enthusiastically. Or, at least, work at overcoming them. Ask yourself, "What am I fearing?" and "Why?" Pretend (if necessary) until action becomes habit.
10. Challenge yourself and never give up or give in.

11. Let your conscience guide you. Stand by your morals and values and demonstrate them.
12. Feel the courage within you. Immerse yourself in the feeling.

Courage feels good!

A Little Something You Might Want to Try
Courage

1. Think of something you have always wanted to do but didn't due to fear. Draft a "small steps to goal" chart toward achieving this goal. (See section on setting goals). Determine the risks along the way and decide if it is worth taking the step. Note that it does not mean you are cowardly if there is imminent danger and you decide not to follow through.

2. Follow the "twelve-step program" to courage:
    1. Identify the circumstance and decide to do something—anything—that is, take action.
    2. Evaluate the situation. Are you being courageous or foolish by taking action with respect to the situation?
    3. Understand the overall vision.
    4. Implement the decision by setting goals and taking small steps.
    5. Ensure your external supports are in place (that is, people who are trustworthy and supportive).
    6. Persevere. Learn from failure and move forward.
    7. Commit to it and believe in it. Believe in yourself. Stay focused. Be aware.
    8. Step out of your comfort zone and find ways of facing your fears. Look forward to discovering new things.
    9. Embrace fears optimistically and enthusiastically. Or, at least, work at overcoming them. Ask yourself, "What am I fearing?" and "Why?" Pretend (if necessary) until action becomes habit.
    10. Challenge yourself and never give up or give in.
    11. Let your conscience guide you. Stand by your morals and values and demonstrate them.

12. Feel the courage within you. Immerse yourself in the feeling.

3. Do at least one small thing out of your comfort zone.

4. Select something painful in your life and develop a plan to work through it.

5. Attend a Toastmaster's group or a town hall meeting, or write a speech and present to a group.

6. Determine a moment when you need to stand up for yourself or for someone else and say something on your or their behalf.

"I AIN'T GOT NO SATISFACTION"— WAIT A MINUTE, YES I DO!

(feeling satisfied, useful, unique, and included)

There are three feelings I initially planned on addressing separately, but I soon realized, on my Journey Within, that they all had a common denominator: feeling satisfied.

The first of these is feeling useful. It is the sensation you get from having a success, an accomplishment, or from undertaking a purposeful life. It is fulfilment, satiation. It is knowing that your life has meaning and that there is a reason to live.

The second of these is feeling unique. This is not filling the need for attention, recognition, or approval but, rather, being your own person, developing your own talents, your own skills, and embracing your individuality and idiosyncrasies.

The third of these is feeling a part of something. This means a sense of belonging, a connectedness, feeling wanted and included.

Feeling satisfied in any of these three areas requires two components:

- A positive attitude
- A desire to take action

In other words, these are feelings that can be cultivated by how you think and by what you do.

So how do you get to feel satisfied?

With a positive attitude, determine what is meaningful to you, how you can be useful, and what you consider an accomplishment. Then do it.

With a positive attitude, determine what makes you unique, what skills you have developed, what talents you possess, and where your interests lie. Then act on it.

With a positive attitude, determine what makes you feel like you belong, how you would like to feel included, and what kind of relationships you would like to have. Then pursue it.

Easier said than done, for sure, but check out the section on "Behaving Well" before you think I've lost my mind.

A Little Something You Might Want to Try
Feeling Satisfied

1. Choose one thing that would be meaningful to you e.g. read a book, do a puzzle, build a model airplane, and complete it. How does it feel?
2. From your list of talents/skills, complete something that is unique to you. How does it feel?
3. Join a group e.g. bowling league, meet-up group, club, organization with interests common to yours, something that involves other people, and interact. How does it feel?

"WOULDN'T IT BE LOVERLY?"

(feeling love)

"What can I get for you, love?" asked the waitress.

"I'd love a cup of coffee," the woman at the table next to me replied. She turned to her friend and said, "I love your dress! Is it new?"

"Yes, my lover bought it for me from this lovely little boutique for Valentine's Day."

The diner's radio chirped, "All you need is love . . . love . . . Love is all you need."

"Gotta run."

"Okay. Love you. Bye-bye!"

I felt like being clubbed and dragged into a cave.

There are different kinds of love: there is romantic love, sexual love, object love, erotic love, auto-erotic love, experiential love, experimental love, puppy love, parental love, love for one's child, one's country, one's God.

There is loving someone, being in love, being a lover, being a lovechild, being a love god, being love-sick.

Love can be a feeling of affection, a friendship, fellowship, kinship, or a deep emotional attachment.

Love can cause you to do an act of kindness or to behave in weird and unusual ways.

Many (if not most) songs contain the word 'love', and most books, plays, and movies have love as a central or secondary theme.

Love can be expressed through a kind word, a hug, a kiss, a sexual encounter, or a generous act.

Love can be true, sincere, misguided, star-crossed, guarded, secret, inhibited, or forbidden.

Love can be fleeting or it can last a lifetime. Love can be abundant and love can be elusive. Love can grow.

Love can be given and love can be received.

Love is one of the most clichéd, overused, and abused words in our lexicon.

But I still want it! I still want to feel it, to experience it, to fall in it! To be in it!

Because love feels good!

A Little Something You Might Want to Try
Love

1. Determine what kind of love you are seeking (one at a time). Be honest with yourself.
2. Determine with whom you want this experience.
3. Determine how you want to experience this.
4. Take action accordingly, by finding different ways of expressing/ declaring your love e.g. doing something romantic.

JOY RIDE
(feeling joy)

I kept having this insidious daydream—a daymare, really—which recurred in an assortment of settings and circumstances: a woman whose face and form I did not recognize ran toward me, at me, and whacked me on the side of my head with her oversized purse.

"Ow! Who are you?"

"Don't you know who I am?" she asked, perplexed. "I am Joy."

I did not know who Joy was; I did not know *what* Joy was, even though I had been seeking Joy for much of my life.

Trying to find a definition of joy that fit with my wispy idea of joy was no more difficult than trying to fit the last piece of a jigsaw puzzle on the edge of a picture when the piece has no straight sides. I found the following descriptors of joy:

- Experiencing the present moment
- Being immersed in your senses
- Sharing happiness with others
- Being in tune with yourself
- Being aware of life's small pleasures
- Having appreciation for other people, places, and things
- Being able to say "Where did the time go?"
- Having a momentary wave of elation
- Experiencing anything life has to offer
- Being open and mindful to nature and beauty
- Finding inner strength and peace, even solitude
- Rekindling playfulness and reclaiming your childhood enthusiasm for life
- Having and maintaining optimism
- Building and expending energy

- Being in a state of bliss, exuberance, rapture, ecstasy, and euphoria

I decided to take all of these definitions and wrap them up into one big bundle of joy. After all, they not only describe what joy is but offer the 'how to' as well.

Joy feels good.

A Little Something You Might Want to Try
Joy

1. List your experiences and circumstances for today.
2. For each one, ask yourself if you experienced each of the afore-mentioned descriptors of joy:
    1. Experiencing the present moment
    2. Being immersed in your senses
    3. Sharing happiness with others
    4. Being in tune with yourself
    5. Being aware of life's small pleasures
    6. Having appreciation for other people, places, and things
    7. Being able to say "Where did the time go?"
    8. Having a momentary wave of elation
    9. Experiencing anything life has to offer
    10. Being open and mindful to nature and beauty
    11. Finding inner strength and peace, even solitude
    12. Rekindling playfulness and reclaiming your childhood enthusiasm for life
    13. Having and maintaining optimism
    14. Building and expending energy
    15. Being in a state of bliss, exuberance, rapture, ecstasy, and euphoria
3. If you answer 'yes', you can enjoy the memory of the experience.
4. If you answer 'no', ask yourself why not and what could you have done to change it?

TOO BIG FOR MY BRITCHES
(feeling humility)

As a young kid, I used to get positive reinforcement for my major accomplishments. When I would wrap my legs around my neck and exclaim enthusiastically, "Look what *I* can do!", I would be lavished with praise. When I could count to ten unassisted, my mother clapped her hands together with pride and joy, and shouted, "He's going to be a doctor!"

I don't know exactly when it happened, but there came a time in my young life when things suddenly changed, and I was no longer rewarded for my endearing precocious behavior. "You're getting too big for your britches!" my father admonished, leaving me to wonder what a britch was and why I didn't even know I had one. My mother put me in my place with far more eloquence by reminding me, "You're just a fart in a windstorm!"

What was I supposed to infer from *that*?

I gravitated toward feelings of insignificance possibly because of the number of times I was ignored, told to shut up, and that whatever I said was unimportant and didn't matter; or probably because I didn't understand the concept of humility. This entailed letting go of the need to be right, to show off, to clamor for attention, to hide my shortcomings, and to exaggerate or embellish my accomplishments. I needed to understand that there is something far greater in this world than I without diminishing my significance or self-worth.

Being humble meant recognizing and showing appreciation to others, listening, giving credit and gratitude freely, allowing myself to be approachable and available, and being more accepting of others and their ideas.

In order to practice humility, I therefore needed to:

1. Stop talking and start listening *and* start paying attention
2. Decide to be happy instead of being right or always having to win
3. Be helpful to others and without expecting something in return
4. Acknowledge the individuality, creativity, and potential in others
5. Admit to not understanding something and recognize my shortcomings
6. Apologize for being wrong when I am wrong
7. Adhere to my morals and values
8. Express gratitude
9. Provide positive feedback and not be critical; be positive, encouraging and supportive
10. Accept a compliment with a simple "Thank you" and don't brag about my accomplishments
11. Allow myself to learn from others without believing I have to know it all or should have known it all
12. Be more respectful, which includes saying "You're welcome" or "My pleasure" when being thanked, and perhaps "I'd be honoured/delighted!" when being asked for help
13. Be assertive, not timid or aggressive
14. Be more forgiving and don't hold grudges
15. Be inclusive
16. Give credit where credit is due and give others the benefit of the doubt
17. Respect the fact that others are entitled to their opinions, even if I disagree with them
18. Continue to practise humility every day

Being humble makes me feel good.

A Little Something You Might Want to Try
Humility #1

Follow each of the seventeen steps and complete as a checklist:

1. Stop talking and start listening *and* start paying attention
2. Decide to be happy instead of being right or always having to win
3. Be helpful to others and without expecting something in return
4. Acknowledge the individuality, creativity, and potential in others
5. Admit to not understanding something and recognize your shortcomings
6. Apologize for being wrong when you are wrong
7. Adhere to your morals and values
8. Express gratitude
9. Provide positive feedback and not be critical; be positive, encouraging and supportive
10. Accept a compliment with a simple "Thank you" and don't brag about my accomplishments
11. Allow yourself to learn from others without believing you have to know it all or should have known it all
12. Be more respectful, which includes saying "You're welcome" or "My pleasure" when being thanked, and perhaps "I'd be honoured/delighted!" when being asked for help
13. Be assertive, not timid or aggressive
14. Be more forgiving and don't hold grudges
15. Be inclusive
16. Give credit where credit is due and give others the benefit of the doubt
17. Respect the fact that others are entitled to their opinions, even if I disagree with them
18. Continue to practise humility every day

A Little Something You Might Want to Try
Humility #2

Examine your day.

a) Did you feel the need to be right?

b) Did you show off, seek attention, hide or ignore your shortcomings, or exaggerate or embellish something?

c) Did you show apprehension in expressing gratitude, listening, giving credit, or being available, tolerant, and accepting?

d) If so, why?

AWESOME, DUDE!

(feeling awe)

When I look back on the time before I was imposed upon by the rules and restrictions of adulthood, I recall the hours I spent gazing in fascination at ants, busy at work creating sand hills in the sidewalk cracks, at the shapes and designs of passing clouds, feeling a breeze in my hair (now long gone), listening to the rustle of the autumn leaves from my bedroom window, the buzz of bees on a hot summer day, and the howl of a lone wolf on a cold winter night. I recall the imagined sensation of flying through the air, speed and altitude controlled only by my thoughts of how fast and how high I would dare to go. I recall the thrill of discovering the beauty of Echo Gulch, a drainage ditch through which I could peer into another world filled with mystery and wonder.

Some people would say I was odd.

I would say I was awed.

I realized I needed to reconnect with that wide-eyed, open-mouthed little guy who used to be fascinated with just about everything. I needed to leave behind my boring, little life filled with mundane, insignificant activities, and actually experience awe.

Experiencing awe is uplifting and humbling at the same time. Experiencing awe is discovering things in life that are curious, wonderful, amazing, moving, mysterious, beautiful, horrific, paradoxical, innocent, shocking, uplifting, mesmerizing, and inspiring, and can move me to tears or to fits of laughter.

Awe can a bleeding sunset, or the sun at dawn peeking over the horizon, ocean waves crashing against a rocky shore, or the parched and cracked desert earth, the night sky illuminated with forks or sheets of lightning, or the view from a mountaintop.

Awe can be a tornado twirling its way down a main city street, a thrilling roller coaster ride at the amusement park, a horrendous car accident that you inevitably slow down to witness, the implosion of a skyscraper, the wail of sirens warning of an impending disaster.

Awe can be the recollection of a childhood memory, the recantation of a survivor of war, a revelation or an epiphany, an inspiration, a sudden awareness, comprehension, bewilderment, discovering the unknown, and recognizing just how much of life is not known or what is still to be revealed.

Awe can be the innocence of a child at new discoveries, the beauty of a human face, the horror of a human deformity.

Awe can be works of art, haunting music, an inspired play, a great movie, a fascinating photograph, an optical illusion, and scientific or technological discoveries.

Awe can be a moment of déjà vu, an inexplicable experience, a creation, desatruction, a paradox, a brand new colour never before seen, and even in the surreal nature of a dream.

Awe can be history, or life on other planets, or awe can be what is happening right now.

All so poetic I could feel my eyes rolling to the back of my head. But why the drive to pursue the feeling of awe? Well, it balances out my feelings of insignificance; it tempers the ego of my significance; it stimulates my imagination; it pushes me toward humility; it keeps me grounded; it offers me experiences that are natural, unnatural and supernatural (so that next time my wife tells me I'm not natural I can only thank her); it allows me, even for a brief moment, to understand that there is more to life than me; it gives me an opportunity to be more appreciative and more aware of the world around me.

Experiencing awe makes me feel good.

A Little Something You Might Want to Try
Awe

1. Select an area of interest or expertise, for example, photography. Go to a neighbourhood or area and take pictures of exceptional architecture or landscape, of interesting people or of a theme.
2. Watch a lightning storm and listen to the ripples of thunder.
3. Stimulate the senses by going to a movie, reading a book, looking at a photo or a work of art, attending a concert, dining in a gourmet restaurant, etc.
4. Seek out fascinating natural phenomena.
5. Find a place of solitude.
6. Imagine, for example, a new colour, a new invention, being able to fly, having x-ray vision, your very own custom-made amusement park, etc.
7. Go geocaching or on an adventure of discovery.
8. Put your mind in another time and another place and enjoy the unfolding fantasy as you create it.
9. Examine works such as Escher or a study on optical illusions. See a magic show.
10. Create a scrapbook of memories.
11. Attend an inspiring lecture, sermon, or discussion.
12. Learn something entirely new.
13. Read stories of inspiration, such as "Chicken Soup for the Soul" books.
14. Examine anything of interest to you mentioned in this section on Awe.

I DON'T WANT TO BE A SNAKE IN THE GRASS ANYMORE

(feeling forgiveness)

What the heck is forgiveness and why should I want to forgive?

Well, I saw myself as a slithery snake with a thick, leathery skin, squirming and sliding my way through the crabgrass of life. I was wretched, nasty, and unforgiving. I hissed at friends who may have said something offensive or unpleasant, perhaps years and years ago; maybe they said something hurtful or sarcastic or ignorant. I did not forgive them. Instead, I developed a thick skin of anger, resentment, and bitterness, which protected me not just from these people, but from others and from life in general. But my thick skin was burdensome and I was miserable.

When I couldn't stand it anymore and I finally decided once and for all I've had enough and I was ready to forgive, the negative feelings and the reasons I had for being so began to fall away. I started to molt, losing that thick, burdensome skin and I began to feel lighter and less encumbered. That was when I began to heal from my sorrow, my anger, my bitterness, and my wounds (even the self-inflicted ones). My relationship with those people also began to heal.

But how did I shed my thick skin, especially when I feel so hurt? How did I forgive, and how did I know when I was ready to forgive?

Well, my skin became so thick and heavy that I just couldn't stand it anymore. The defining moment for me was that I realized the issue or circumstance occurred so long ago that wasn't able to clearly recall what happened in the first place. The original issue had become distorted and blurred and unrecognizable and forgotten over time. I realized that perhaps it wasn't as important as I once thought it was, or it wasn't relevant to my current life circumstances, or the grudge just wasn't worth the energy I was expending anymore. It was time to let go of all the bad feelings that were weighing me down and it was time to shed my thick skin. I didn't want to be a snake in the grass anymore.

After all, forgiveness feels good.

A Little Something You Might Want to Try
Forgiveness

1. List those that have wronged you or have done a disservice.
2. How have you been wronged or what is the disservice?
3. How has it affected you?
4. When did this happen?
5. Is it still relevant?
6. If yes, how?
7. Is it still as important as it once may have been?
8. If so, why?
9. Does the person even know about it or to what degree it has impacted on you or how you feel?
10. If yes, how do you know they know?
11. Is there something you feel you need or want from the other person?
12. If so, what?
13. Can you try to see the situation from the other person's perspective?
14. Describe what you think he/she sees.
15. Do you accurately remember the incident?
16. If yes, describe in detail.
17. What is it about the incident that bothers you?
18. Are you benefitting by holding onto the grudge?
19. If yes, how?
20. Can you let go? Can you forgive? If yes, do so. If not, why not?

AT LAST!

(feeling acceptance and peace via patience and tolerance)

How can you feel acceptance of something if you aren't accepting?

How can you feel peaceful if you are not at peace?

Is acceptance synonymous with resignation? Is peace the same as passivity?

These are the questions that had impeded my progress along the Journey Within, since peace and acceptance were the next destination I wanted to experience and perhaps incorporate into my life.

When I think of acceptance I think of receiving, allowing, welcoming. I feel a sense of purification by whatever I have allowed myself to receive. I am allowing myself to receive a big fat hug from everyone and everything. I feel compassionate, empathetic, expansive, magnanimousness, and just plain good. Acceptance means disengaging from the struggle of resistance, to just let things happen without the encumbrance of emotion, and to abandon the desire to be right or even to express an opinion. Acceptance is to be able to say "it is what it is".

There is no judgment with acceptance. There are no conditions, no restrictions, no boundaries. No thoughts, feelings, or behaviours of the past or the future to impact or influence.

Similarly, when I think of feeling peaceful, I think of being calm, of being restful, of having very few internal or external distractions. I think of growing dreadlocks and proclaiming, "Irie, mon" to everyone. I feel refreshed and content. The voices in my head are quiet or, at least, less irritating or, at least, not quite so loud. Worries are few. Wants, needs, desires, cravings, and obsessions have dissipated. There is no panic, no regrets, no hurry, no sense of being overwhelmed. By being at peace I can give up the fight, especially the fight against myself.

It appears that there are several paths that can lead to acceptance and peace. For me they have been difficult ones to navigate, primarily due to the detritus of negativity that has often blocked my way. Two of the paths that have been especially significant for me are patience and tolerance, since I had rarely been able to demonstrate either of these particularly well.

How did I know I was impatient?

I became frustrated easily. I watched the clock. I could feel anger bubbling up inside of me. I didn't want to listen. I was anxious to get my point of view out there at any cost. I often lost focus and lost my train of thought. I became impulsive. I made rash decisions. My hands were often clenched into fists or else I was tapping my fingers. I would pace a lot and nag others to hurry. Little things as well as things not in my control would make me irritable.

How did I know when I was intolerant?

I didn't listen to others; I tuned them out. I discounted or disregarded others' concerns and opinions. I looked for differences between me and other people and focused on them, even made fun of or acted superior to others who were not like me. I would ignore or ridicule things that I did not understand or were not part of my experience. I was dismissive.

I was, indeed, an asshole.

And I didn't like myself very much.

So I decided to practise behaviours that were foreign to me, which required copious amounts of effort. I had to:

- Be a bit more humble and realize the rest of humanity did not revolve around me.
- Be aware: of what I am thinking and why; of what I am feeling and why; of how I am acting and why.
- Catch myself wishing time would speed up, hoping people would just go away, thinking that others, along with their thoughts and ideas, are simply not as important or relevant or good as I am.
- Catch myself feeling angry, frustrated, irritable, superior, inferior, overwhelmed, rushed, anxious, or depressed.

- Catch myself pacing, clock-watching, finger-tapping, yelling, making rude, derogatory, or dismissive remarks.
- Be in the moment.
- Determine what was within my control and what was not.
- Listen without speaking until it was my turn.
- Count to ten. Even remove myself from the situation. Think it through before returning.
- Keep things in perspective and keep in mind what is really important.
- Take small steps; compartmentalize.
- Understand that others have their own experiences in life; ask questions if I do not know or do not understand, where appropriate.
- Create a quiet place in my head; visualize and build a safe place, an ideal getaway, somewhere to go whenever I begin to feel overwhelmed.

When I did these things, I noticed that intolerance morphed beyond tolerance and into appreciation and acceptance. Impatience transcended into a peaceful calm.

Acceptance and peace feel good.

A Little Something You Might Want to Try
Acceptance and Peace

1. Explore and participate in Mindful Meditation.
2. Practise letting go by understanding the feeling and the circumstances surrounding the feeling. Does the issue or thought that generated the negative feeling matter in the greater scheme of things?
3. Identify signs of impatience and intolerance.
   - Why is the thought so important to you?
   - Can it be managed differently? If not, why not?
4. Follow each of the following steps:
   a) I realize the rest of humanity did not orbit around me.
   b) I am aware: of what I am thinking and why; of what I am feeling and why; of how I am acting and why.
   c) Catch myself wishing time would speed up, hoping people would just go away, thinking that others, along with their thoughts and ideas, are simply not as important or relevant or good as I am and STOP! Work it through.
   d) Catch myself feeling angry, frustrated, irritable, superior, inferior, overwhelmed, rushed, anxious, or depressed and STOP! Work it through.
   e) Catch myself pacing, clock-watching, finger-tapping, yelling, making rude, derogatory, or dismissive remarks and STOP! Work it through.
   f) Be in the moment.
   g) Determine what was within my control and what was not.
   h) Listen without speaking until it was my turn.
   i) Count to ten. Even remove myself from the situation. Think it through before returning.

j) Keep things in perspective and keep in mind what is really important.

k) Take small steps; compartmentalize.

l) Understand that others have their own experiences in life; ask questions if you do not know or do not understand, where appropriate.

m) Create a quiet place in your head; visualize and build a safe place, an ideal getaway, somewhere to go whenever you begin to feel overwhelmed.

EMOTION MANAGEMENT 101
(understanding and managing feelings)

One of the most important lessons I've learned about feelings on my Journey Within, in addition to the recognition and understanding of them, is how to manage them.

Having realized that emotions are a response to a thought or an action, and having understood that they are a measure of how circumstances are weathered, I have also come to know that they need to be managed appropriately.

Positive emotions are the ones you want to feel more frequently, more intensely. Negative emotions are those you'd just rather not experience if you didn't have to. As stated earlier, I discovered that feelings can be suppressed, expressed, or let go.

Suppression is temporary by nature. If utilized inappropriately, it can lead to avoidance of an issue, poor communication, a delay in taking action or finding a resolution, physical ailments, stress, and sometimes even an explosion. Suppression of feelings can also be used appropriately. For example, if you are in the middle of a job interview or an exam, you might want to suppress your anxiety about getting the job or failing the exam. Or you might want to suppress feelings of love toward someone until your job interview or your exam has ended.

Likewise, expression of an emotion has its time and place. To better manage the expression of an emotion, it is necessary to determine if it is a feeling you want or not, that is, if it is a positive or negative feeling. Negative emotions are best managed by finding an alternate means of expression that are less destructive to you and to others. Rather than yelling, screaming, crying, hitting others, breaking things, and committing crimes, you may want to consider punching pillows, going for a jog, writing in a journal, preparing and rehearsing what you want to say to someone, or even painting a picture. Positive emotions are best managed by demonstrating them to yourself and to others by the actions that you take: a hug, a nod of acknowledgement, giving your time and attention, offering support or a word of encouragement.

There are times when you need to yell and scream and cry and lash out. There are times when it is important, even necessary, to sing and dance and play, to squeal with delight and shout with joy, to drop your jaw and say "Wow!", and to laugh without restraint. However you look at it, expressing how you feel is not only to allow yourself to feel the feeling but to become acquainted with it, acknowledge it, understand it, and hug it for all its worth. Then let it go.

I spent the better part of my Journey Within trying to figure out how to release a feeling. Most of the books I've read on the subject tell you to let go of the feeling without telling you how to do it, which is most unsatisfying and extremely frustrating—yet another feeling to release!

What, I thought, do I need to do to let a feeling go? Well, I need to:

- Ask myself, "What am I feeling?" and acknowledge the existence of the feeling.
- Identify the feeling by describing it and naming it.
- Understand what I am feeling. Ask myself, "Why am I feeling this way?"
- Consciously determine what I want to do with this feeling: do I want to suppress it? Express it? Do I want to embrace it? Hug the shit out of it? Do I want to drop it like a hot potato? Let it go?
- Do something about the feeling. Take action. If I want to experience the feeling, I must be in the moment and immerse myself in it. If I want to let the feeling go, I must do something to release it. For example, if I am feeling shame, maybe I need to state my feeling aloud, perhaps publicly, perhaps assign

appropriate responsibility, perhaps offer an apology, or forgive someone, forgive myself. If I am angry at someone, I might want to find some cathartic means of expression in a non-destructive way, or I might want to take a step back and then write down clearly the reasons for my anger and confront the person without acting out.

Something to think about, something to do.

I discovered another aspect of managing my emotions: I had to be willing to tear down the thickly layered walls of protection that I'd built around myself over the years; just like forgiveness, I discovered that I was a snake in need of shedding my layers of skin; I was an onion in need of peeling back the layers of onion skin to reveal my soft, sweet, fragrant middle (well, forget this metaphor… sounds gross). I had to allow myself to be vulnerable and exposed (appropriately, of course). That meant I had to:

- Cast off my sarcasm
- Throw away my cynicism
- Shrug off my self-deprecation
- Swallow my pride
- Get rid of my secrets
- Stop putting on airs
- Avoid being aloof
- Avoid avoidance
- Chuck the martyrdom
- Refrain from the run-and-hide routine

I had to stand naked (again with the "naked"—note to self: see a therapist) and stand tall in front of the world.

I admit this task is daunting and time-consuming. I'm still working at it but it is proving to be well worth the effort. By doing this, I am enabling myself to feel my feelings and to manage them effectively.

A Little Something You Might Want to Try
Managing Emotions

Practise all the following points previously listed in this section:

1. Ask yourself, "What am I feeling?"
2. Identify the feeling. Describe it. Name it.
3. Acknowledge its existence.
4. Understand the feeling. Ask yourself, "Why am I feeling this way?"
5. Consciously determine what you want to do with this feeling: do I want to suppress it? Express it? Do I want to embrace it? Do I want to let it go?
6. Take action.
7. Get rid of sarcasm.
8. Get rid of cynicism.
9. Get rid of self-deprecation.
10. Get rid of pride.
11. Get rid of any secrets.
12. Get rid of putting on airs.
13. Get rid of being aloof.
14. Get rid of avoidance.
15. Get rid of martyrdom.
16. Get rid of the run-and-hide routine.

BEHAVING WELL

As I have led you through a melee of mixed metaphors and as we have forayed through a jungle of jumbled analogies, we found ourselves in a quagmire of thoughts—*my* thoughts. Most of these thoughts were borne of early experiences and my feelings associated with them. They then developed and mutated into the kind of behaviours that have kept me from moving forward in life.

Now, passing from thinking well and feeling well on my Journey Within, it comes as no surprise that I must also behave well. So, here I am with my little carpenter's toolbox to continue to reconstruct a life of worth, to build an edifice of character that will rise like a phoenix from the ashes of my Starting Point and my Journey Without. After all, if I have determined that my overall vision is to improve the quality of my life, then aspiring to attain, as my goal, a reasonable level of characteristics I deem to be worthy of a life of quality naturally follows.

Where to begin? There are so many branches on this tree of life!

Well, if my goal, at this stage of my Journey Within, is to behave well, then logically (when have *I* ever been logical about anything?) I should start by behaving, that is, taking action. I must work hard to get to where I want to go. I need to examine my moral make-up, the values I have come to endorse, protect and uphold. I need to employ various workable strategies to demonstrate, practise, and refine my behaviour. I need to play the hand I was dealt, but understand that I can choose the game. In other words, I must understand that I am in control of building my own character; I am the architect of my own life, after all. I need to make some difficult yet necessary choices, and to exchange old habits for ones that are newer, better, and in keeping with improving the quality of my life. I need to develop an effective way of communicating with others, water my garden and watch my relationships blossom, and dig out those toxic relationships that threaten to overgrow and kill off the healthy ones. I must not only clean house, but I must ensure that the support beams of my house are structurally sound. I need to see what I want for my life and give that to others. After all, I am not living in isolation. I need to make decisions, commit to them and, with my overall vision in mind, I need to work toward my goals one small step at a time. I need to develop strategies to ensure I think and step outside the box by taking some calculated risks. Nothing ventured, nothing gained. I must find a reason for doing all of these things, for recreating a whole new me, and I want to have fun doing them as I go along. I want to do for others as well as for myself and for all my efforts, I want to party like there's no tomorrow!

So, I am tugging on my wedgie and holding on to my trunks! Here I go down the slippery waterslide of life,

Behaving Well . . .

LOOK, MA, I'M AN ARCHITECT!
(building character)

One of my biggest discoveries on my Journey Within was the realization that, in order to improve the quality of my life, building character is the cornerstone in the construction of a better life. The foundation is a firm belief in the attributes I assign to my character. My morals and values are the bricks and mortar that hold the construction of my walls together.

Okay, so I have this idea that I want to rebuild my edifice to be solid and safe. In determining how to go about this reconstruction, I needed to use my own thoughts, knowledge, and intuition, along with information and influences learned from parents, friends, teachers, and many others. My most useful tool in building character is my level—my emotional level, that is—that keeps my walls straight.

First, I needed to understand the difference between values and morals. I determined that values represent the things I believe are most important to me, the things I hold most dear. Morals are my code of conduct based on conscience, that is, how I choose to behave. Together they give strength and order to my emotional and spiritual construct.

To start, I thought of an experience or an influence, for example, helping an old lady across the street. I then used my emotional level to gauge this trait which, in turn, assigned an attribute to it, such as, kindness and, having consulted my conscience, I decided that being kind is good. I identified this behaviour as an act of kindness and I adopted it as one of my values. Then I began to seek opportunities to practise this behaviour to reinforce this piece of my character. By continually measuring the effect of my behaviour (my moral) with my emotional level I can reinforce the soundness of my structure. Because the behaviour made me feel good, happy, proud, satisfied, etc. then

I decided to keep the notion of kindness as one of my values. Had the behaviour made me feel uncomfortable, ill-at-ease, self-conscious, embarrassed, angry, etc. (or had the little old lady bonked me on the head with her purse), then I would have had to discard this value because it would not have built character—in fact, it may have destroyed my structure.

Consequently, I discovered that if I act in ways which are contrary to my moral code of conduct, my emotional level will show that my walls are not straight because something doesn't feel right. It's like that icky feeling I get akin to shame and embarrassment if, for example, I hold refraining from gossip as one of my values and then I open my big mouth and let something slip. If I don't act in accordance with my moral, then how valuable is my value? How well-built is my character?

It is also important to note that character sometimes requires renovations. With time, experiences, influences, and changes in points of view, some of my values had changed as well and it was necessary for me to reconstruct my character to keep my bricks lined up and my mortar intact. Making these renovations, I discovered, comes at a cost: time, money, effort, and comfort; I found it was well worth the investment.

A Little Something You Might Want to Try
Building Character

1. Create an ongoing list of values (what you hold dear).
2. Create an ongoing list of morals (how you behave).
3. Add, delete, modify, change, or alter for improvement, ensuring that your morals are compatible with your values.

STRATEGIC DEPLOYMENT
(strategies for appropriate behaviour)

I found that I could deploy different strategies to ensure that I was behaving appropriately. Usually, the simpler the strategy, the better, because the strategy was clear, concise, and got right to the heart of the matter.

Most often, using my emotional level to measure the strength of my conviction was sufficient. However, if that did not work well, if I was experiencing negative feelings of any sort, all I needed to do was to ask myself if the behaviour I was exhibiting was working well, working in my favour, getting me what I wanted, and leaving me feeling better about myself. If I could not answer 'yes' to these questions, I needed to change my behaviour.

A Little Something You Might Want to Try
Strategies for Appropriate Behaviour

1. Identify your various behaviours.
2. What is the reading in your emotional barometer for each of these behaviours?
3. Do you need to change any of your behaviours? If so, how?
4. Make the changes, as appropriate.

CUSTOM DESIGNING MY OWN LIFE
(identifying and prioritizing various aspects of my life)

I knew I had a lot to work on in order to improve the quality of my life. I had to not only identify all the different areas needing improvement, but also I had to prioritize them (since each area of my life was clamouring for attention). It was overwhelming.

The first thing I needed to do was to brainstorm to come up with a list of the various areas of my life, regardless of whether or not I believed they required improvement. The list, of course, went on and on to the point of being ridiculously long. So I decided to group together certain areas that had common elements and yet not lose track of some of the important specifics, by making notes of people, situations, and issues alongside the areas of concern. I then decided to narrow down my list to the top ten areas that seemed to feel most urgent. Next, I required a suitable metaphor, one that would give me the most meaningful representation of those areas of my life: a line graph representing the continuum of my life was, well, too linear. A wheel of life was unoriginal and too overdone. A pie chart just made me want pie. So I opted to see my life as my dream house and I was the interior designer. Each room would be an area of my life. I could look at the rooms of this house and decide how I was going to design each room and how much I would fill it with quality furnishings and decorations.

I concluded that my house would be a ten-room mansion, each room a different area of my life. I then drew the floor-plan of the house and labelled each area. The areas that I chose for myself, at this particular point in my life, were: finances, housing, social life, retirement/ vocation, relationship with spouse, leisure and recreation, health and wellness, family, learning, and spirituality. I then took a pencil crayon and coloured in each room; the lighter the shade, the more I needed to decorate that particular room. Ideally, my house would be well-decorated to the fullest and most balanced if each of the rooms were shaded in with the darkest shade. Having completed this, the visual representation showed me which areas needed the most work, so at least I knew what I was dealing with. I then had to decide if I wanted to multi-task by working on decorating many rooms at once, a little bit at a time, or if I wanted to concentrate on just one room and finish decorating it before moving on to the next. I chose to multi-task simply because this is what works best for me.

A Little Something You Might Want to Try
Identifying and Prioritizing Various Aspects of Your Life

1. Select a metaphor that works best for you or use the one in this section if you like.
2. Identify those areas of your life of which you would like to improve the quality.
3. Create your model.
4. Select your method of prioritization and fill in the model.
5. Select your method of approach.

NATURAL SELECTION
(making choices)

I came to the realization that everything I do is a choice that I alone am responsible for. These choices are how I define myself. They are who I am. Whenever I would make excuses for the choice I made, namely, "I can't", "I don't have the time", "It's too much bother", "I'm too tired", "I feel like crap", "It's snowing outside", etc., I was denying responsibility for my choices and thus not taking ownership for my own life.

The list of choices that I have made in my life is endless because absolutely everything in life is a choice: getting out of bed in the morning, screaming at my kids to get ready for school, going to work, avoiding the class reunion, driving along that particular road, wearing those metallic blue shoes, ignoring that homeless man in the bus shelter, and on and on. There are some (albeit few) events and circumstances in one's life that occur which may be beyond one's control where there is no choice, or there is limited choice, such as: action taken by others, the forces of nature, etc., but of course there is a choice of how to respond to those events and circumstances. For example, I did not have a choice in being robbed, but I did have a choice to report it to the police, to buy better locks for my front door, and to speak with someone about my feeling violated. I discovered that it wasn't so much what the event was that occurred, but how I chose to deal with it that mattered.

I also realized that not making a choice is a choice. Whenever I chose not to take action I have actually made a choice. Sometimes, by not taking action, I had given someone else the opportunity to take action on my behalf, and sometimes not always for my benefit. I remember deciding not to go on a job interview, and someone else (obviously) got the promotion. It demonstrated to me that there are consequences to not making choices, just as there are to making choices.

I learned that making choices would give me the experiences that I needed to take responsibility for my own life and how to deal with events and circumstances that came my way.

What I choose is who I am. I am defined by the choices I make. My choices also affect my potential (and what I do with it), my ability to learn and accomplish things, what I believe, and where life takes me.

Most importantly, I discovered that life is a freedom, a privilege, and an opportunity. I learned that I don't *have to* do things (if I choose not to do anything). I *have the opportunity to* do things.

A Little Something You Might Want to Try
Making Choices #1

1. Begin by designating one hour of your time. Force yourself into awareness for everything you think, feel, and do. List them.
2. Re-evaluate each of these as they occur, by restating them as choices. Write them down.
3. Review and ask yourself:
   - "Would I choose differently?"
   - "Am I benefitting by this choice?"
4. Take two—redo the scene with your new choice.
5. Repeat as often as necessary.

A Little Something You Might Want to Try
Making Choices #2

1. In the span of a day, record all the not-so-insignificant choices you have made (even things you have chosen *not* to do).
2. What are the consequences of each choice?
3. Are the consequences in your best interest? Write YES or NO beside each.
4. If NO, can you choose differently? What have you learned?
5. If YES, what is your new choice for each? Follow through.
6. Review this whenever you are uncomfortable or unsure about making choices.
7. Repeat as often as necessary.

A Little Something You Might Want to Try
Making Choices #3

1. Keep a list of all the excuses you make for not doing something, not following through on something, or not making new choices.

2. After a week, review your list. Are your excuses valid reasons or just excuses? If the latter, what consequences are you trying to avoid?

3. How can you make the choice resulting in a positive outcome?

STRINGING MYSELF ALONG:
(good habits)

There came a time when I was compelled to examine my behaviour more closely in order to determine if my actions were bringing me closer to my goals or moving me away from them. In doing so, I noticed that some of my behaviours were repetitive—so much so, in fact, that they often became habits. When I was a younger version of me, I remember having a hangnail which, by virtue of the fact that scissors were not readily accessible, I bit off. It started innocently enough, but then it happened again and then again. Before I knew it, I noticed myself gnawing at my fingernails, especially when I was nervous, anxious, or impatient. By the time my fingers were raw, bloody stumps, I suspected I had developed a bad habit.

It was around that same time that I began to venture out without my parents in tow, exploring neighbourhoods I had never seen, discovering new landmarks, and experiencing local flavours. I would walk all over the place; the fresh air and the exercise made me feel good, too, and before too long I had developed another habit, this time a good one.

I might say that I am a creature of habit, but that just might lead one (including me) to believe that the behaviour just happens and that I am not responsible for it. Au contraire, my behaviour is my choice—good or bad—and I own it regardless of how many times I repeat it.

I realized that I learned my habits; I wasn't born with them. This was an important lesson for me to learn, because it meant that the habits which I didn't want I could change, and the habits I did want I could keep. Furthermore, the habits that I didn't want I could change by replacing them with habits I did want. Instead of noshing on chips and cake and cookies and candy, I forced myself to munch on raw vegetables, berries, and nuts. Over a period of time (during which I went nuts, ironically, with cravings for anything but nuts), I eventually decreased my habit of reaching for junk food, and my habit of choosing a healthier snack became second nature. The key to this for me was not to stop the bad habit cold turkey, but to replace it with a better habit.

A Little Something You Might Want to Try
Habits

1. Make a list of habits you want to change (bad habits).
2. Why do you want to change them? i.e. what are the consequences of keeping these bad habits (referring to both long- and short-term outcomes)?
3. With what can these bad habits be replaced?
4. Create a plan for each of these.
5. Practise.

LIGHTS, CAMERA, ACTION!

(taking action; hard work; keeping busy)

Taking action is, by definition, behaving. I learned that taking action gives direct experience, allows growth and development, brings interaction to life, and defines who I am.

Taking appropriate action or, if you will, behaving well, therefore, helps to build character. Building character and achieving goals requires constant hard work. Working hard to achieve and excel is definitely an attribute worthy of striving to attain. Whenever I do something half-assed, I feel mediocre; I even feel like a fraud. When I work hard at something, I end up feeling good about myself and what I have accomplished. It gives me the motivation and determination to work even harder. Working harder makes me feel good about myself and gives a sense of meaning and fulfilment to my life.

That is not to say that I can't have fun while I'm keeping busy and working hard. In fact, if I'm not enjoying some aspect of what I am doing, it makes working hard even harder to do. Consequently, I have been putting forth an effort to seek out the challenges and enjoyment when I am doing something.

It must also be noted that there are different ways to keep busy: mindless fun, intellectual stimulation, exercise, daily chores, purposeful tasks, relaxation, and major projects. By taking action such as any of these, I discovered I don't have the time, the inclination, or the desire to ruminate about loneliness, weariness, injustice, failure, worry, should have's, what if's, 'poor me!', 'why bother?', and 'I can't!'.

There rarely seems to be a quick and dirty way to take action to accomplish something. It usually requires self-discipline, which often includes: setting boundaries and restrictions, sacrifices, risk-taking, delayed gratification, putting forth effort, and using time wisely and productively. But, in the end, it is all worth it. And I can bask in the light of my achievement for having taken action and for having worked hard.

A Little Something You Might Want to Try
Taking Action, Working Hard, Keeping Busy

1. If you are encountering an obstacle, an impasse, a difficult choice, an upsetting behaviour, an unattainable goal, a failure, a loss, an unwanted moral, value, or character trait, or a disturbing thought, ask yourself, "What is it that I am doing: mindless fun, intellectual stimulation, exercise, daily chores, purposeful tasks, relaxation, major projects, etc.?"

2. Then ask yourself, "How is this working for you?"

3. Have I taken appropriate action? What is the action I have taken? Does it make sense? Could I be doing something more, something better?

4. Is doing what I am doing worth it?

5. Have I put forth an effort? Am I enjoying what I am doing?

6. Have I taken the easy road to mediocrity? Is it just good enough? Have I done all I can do? Have I worked as hard as I can? Have I put my heart and soul into it? Have I done the best I can do and utilized my full potential? Am I challenging myself?

7. Do I feel good about myself and my achievement? Have I maintained my integrity?

COMMUNICATING WELL
(developing and maintaining good communication)

I had travelled such a long way on my Journey Within, and I was so parched that I could hardly speak. I saw a structure up ahead. I moved towards it and saw that it was a well. "Talk to me!" a voice implored imperiously from deep within the bowels of the well. I leaned over the rim of the well and asked, "Who...who are you?" It replied, "I am... Communicating Well!" (wah-wah).

So I decided to dip the bucket and drink the water to slake my thirst for knowledge of how to communicate well.

Up to now I thought my communication skills were fairly polished. But when I took a look at all the information I could find on effective communication and measured it against the status of my relationships, present and past, I discovered I had a lot to learn and a lot to improve.

Once again, I started with forcing myself to be aware of everything I said and everything I did in each of my relationships. I kept a log of how I listened (or didn't listen), what I said (or didn't say) both verbally and non-verbally, and what the response was and how I perceived it. Then I assessed the effectiveness of the communication. This wasn't too difficult since saying the wrong thing or making an improper non-verbal gesture would usually bite me in the ass sooner rather than later. Once I knew the communication to be ineffective, I could then work on finding a solution for better communication.

Here's an example of how it worked:

My wife said to me, "Stop biting your nails. It bugs me!" She flailed her hands in disgust.

I folded my arms, lifted my chin and said (shouted, actually), "Oh, yeah? Well you always jut out your jaw and bear your teeth like a wild animal! Besides, I don't bite my nails… I just manicure them with my teeth!"

"F___ you!" she retorted. I grinned broadly, as she stomped out of the room with her jaw a full minute ahead of her.

That didn't go quite as I had hoped.

What the heck happened?

Well, first, I wasn't really *listening* to what she had to say; I was focused on the fact that I had just been put down—again—and so I was already formulating my response almost before the words were out of her mouth. I was listening to the criticism but not the message. Second, what I *said* back to her was a deliberate attack, telling her she *always* did this (even if it really wasn't as often as I claimed it to be). Then I discounted her message by trivializing her feelings, making light of the situation. What I *didn't say* was the truth about how I was being treated, how I would like to be treated (my issue), and acknowledging her concern in some way. Also, my non-verbal communication represented anger and defiance (folded arms) and an air of superiority (tilted chin). And yet I made a point of attacking *her* non-verbal behaviour. Third, I *perceived* that I was being scolded like a child, *my* perception, not something she had stated with clarity and certainty. I made the assumption that she was looking for a fight (which may or may not have been the case) and I gave her one. Also, knowing how upset she was (by the cursing), I grinned at her like a Cheshire cat, which was incongruent with the interaction and was obviously mean-spirited.

What could I do to improve the communication next time? First and foremost, I had to remind myself that I cannot change her (or anyone else's) behaviour—I could only change my own. And, perhaps by changing mine, I could influence her to make a change in her behaviour. Next, I could have started by acknowledging her concern. "You get really annoyed when I bite my nails." Then, perhaps I could let her know my feelings about it: "I don't like it either, but I can't seem to stop." I could even take it a step further and include her by asking her if she has any suggestions on how I might stop biting my nails. I could keep my arms unfolded and lower my chin, but keep my eyes focused to show her I am engaged and listening. And I could get rid of that "F___ you, too, sweetheart!" smile. The objective is to focus on the issue and engage in meaningful dialogue.

I knew this was far from a quick and dirty approach to improving my communication skills; it is, in fact, a continuous and ongoing exercise. It seems to be worth it, so far.

So, based on an exhausting review of my interactions with various people in my life, here is an inexhaustible and ever-growing list I made for myself of things to ask myself in order to communicate effectively. Am I:

- Acknowledging the other person and his/her concerns?
- Telling the other person what s/he does right or offering suggestions of what could be done, if asked?
- Checking my perceptions to ensure the other person understands correctly or that we are both on the same page?
- Looking for and finding the good in people and supporting them as sincerely as possible?
- Encouraging and nurturing others?
- Asking for what I want in a direct and straightforward manner?
- Being clear and concise?
- Staying focused on the issue?
- Using "I" statements? Saying "When you... I feel...; in the future I would like..."?
- Understanding what the other person is asking of me?
- Negotiating for what I want, taking the other person into consideration, and considering a sacrifice or a compromise where appropriate?

- Praising the other person sincerely, even if it is only for bringing the issue to my attention?
- Being attentive and listening to what is being said, as well as what is not being said?
- Being aware of my non-verbal communication: the tone of my voice, my stance and posture, what I am doing with my appendages, what my facial expressions are conveying?
- Ensuring that my non-verbal communication is congruent with my verbal communication?
- Making time to discuss the issue, or negotiate a better time if now doesn't work?
- Refraining from insisting that I am right and the other person is wrong?
- Focusing on the other person's issues; putting aside my own internal dialogue; holding off from planning my next response while the other person is stating his/her concerns?
- Refraining from being sarcastic, conveying hostility, or creating tension?
- Using constructive tactics; staying away from as guilt, fear, martyrdom, worry, and intimidation?
- Making no assumptions and not jumping to conclusions?
- Avoiding the words "always" or "never"?
- Stopping myself from telling the other person that it is his/her fault or pointing a finger?
- Ensuring I do not act as if I am a terrible person (looking for sympathy)?
- Careful not to sulk, pout, withdraw, interrupt, respond with something irrelevant, say nothing, or act out?
- Bringing up only relevant issues and things I am not reminded of from the past?
- Not acting defensively, admitting to any wrongdoing or involvement if I am wrong or involved?

- Stopping myself from saying "what's the point?" or "why bother?"?
- Paying attention to the other person's feelings?
- Refraining from offering unsolicited help, advice, opinions, or from trying to "fix" the other person's problem?
- Prohibiting myself from (at least, without evidence), calling names, swearing, or insisting the other person is the one with mental problems?
- Refraining from counterattack with criticism?
- Being careful not to ramble, use words or sentences with hidden meanings, say what I don't mean, or apologize without meaning it?

A Little Something You Might Want to Try
Developing and Maintaining Good Communication #1

Over a selected period of time, create your own communications log. Identify with whom you are communicating, what the issue was (try to describe the interaction verbatim and in detail), how you listened (or didn't listen), what you said (or didn't say), how you communicated non-verbally, and what your perceptions were. Determine what worked and what didn't work. How could you be more effective in your next communication?

A Little Something You Might Want to Try
Developing and Maintaining Good Communication #2

Review the following statements (previously listed in this section). Consider each point and how it does or does not apply to you. In other words, identify if the statement is true or false. Why?

1. I acknowledge the other person and his/her concerns.
2. I tell the other person what s/he does right or offer suggestions of what could be done, if asked.
3. I check my perceptions to ensure that I am understanding correctly or that we are both on the same page.
4. I find the good in people and build them up honestly.
5. I encourage people, being nurturing and supportive.
6. I ask for what I want in a direct and straightforward manner.
7. I am clear and concise.
8. I stay focused on the issue.
9. I use "I" statements; try saying "When you... I feel...; in the future I would like..."
10. I understand what the other person is asking of me.

11. I negotiate for what I want, take the other person into consideration, and consider a sacrifice or a compromise where appropriate.

12. I praise the other person sincerely, even if it is only for bringing the issue to my attention.

13. I am attentive and listen to what is being said, as well as what is not being said.

14. I am aware of my non-verbal communication: the tone of my voice, my stance and posture, what I am doing with my appendages, what my facial expressions are conveying.

15. I ensure that my non-verbal communication is congruent with my verbal communication.

16. I make time to discuss the issue or negotiate a better time if now doesn't work.

17. I do not insist that I am right and the other person is wrong.

18. I do not focus on my own issues; I do not pay attention to my own internal dialogue; I do not plan my next response while the other person is stating his/her concerns.

19. I am not sarcastic, nor do I convey hostility, or create tension.

20. I use constructive tactics and stay away from guilt, fear, martyrdom, worry, and intimidation.

21. I make no assumptions and do not jump to conclusions.

22. I do not use the words "always" or "never".

23. I do not tell the other person that it is his/her fault or point a finger.

24. I do not act as if I am a terrible person (looking for sympathy).

25. I do not sulk, pout, withdraw, interrupt, respond with something irrelevant, say nothing, or act out.

26. I do not bring up irrelevant issues or things I am reminded of from the past.

27. I am not defensive, refusing to admit any wrongdoing or involvement if I am wrong or involved.

28. I do not say "what's the point?" or "why bother?"
29. I do not ignore the other person's feelings.
30. I refrain from offering unsolicited help, advice, opinions or from trying to "fix" the other person's problem.
31. I do not accuse (at least, without evidence), call names, swear, or insist the other person is the one with mental problems.
32. I do not counterattack with criticism.
33. I do not ramble, use words or sentences with hidden meanings, say what I don't mean, or apologize without meaning it.

A Little Something You Might Want to Try
Developing and Maintaining Good Communication #3

Create your own list for effective communication.

CLEANING HOUSE
(re-evaluating unhealthy relationships)

Scrubbing away and flushing out all the poisons in my environment was essential to my good health and well-being. Likewise, cleaning house made me feel good. Getting rid of unwanted clutter made me feel better.

I determined that eliminating the toxic people in my life would also make me feel better. I took a look at some of my relationships to determine who was toxic and toss them out of my life: a co-worker who continually talked against people behind their backs—in the garbage! People from my past who always belittled or discounted me—out the door with them! Those who prevented me from growing and learning and being a better person—flush them down the toilet!

That is not to say that I automatically and arbitrarily eliminated everyone who has ever hurt me, offended me, compromised my values, or otherwise pissed me off. If that were the case I would simply have just reinforced my loneliness, and my house would be clean but sparse. What I had to do first was to take a good look at the relationship and determine its intrinsic value, that is, if it was strong, salvageable, or irreparable. I also had to determine who else would be affected by my housecleaning. For example, if I found an in-law to be toxic, I would have to figure out if I could discard that person from my life and, if not, how my reduced involvement with that person would affect my wife (considering that how it would affect her would affect *me*!). Ultimately it was a matter of minimizing the ongoing damage, hence minimizing the toxicity and reducing the clutter. Also, by doing some housecleaning, I could have the space to refill my house with cleaner stuff and positive people.

A Little Something You Might Want to Try
Re-evaluating Unhealthy Relationships

1. Make a list of all the people in your life.
2. Indicate if you want to keep them in your life?
3. Why are they involved in your life in the first place? What do they contribute to your life.
4. How toxic is this person?
5. Can this person be eliminated from your life?
6. Who else will be affected if you eliminate this person from your life, or if you reduce the amount of time spent with this person?
7. What will you achieve by eliminating this person from your life, or by reducing the amount of time spent with this person?

Neil Katz

"SOMEONE TO WATCH OVER ME"
(developing support systems)

Much of my life I was feeling unloved and lonely. This always made the task of looking after myself, physically, emotionally, and spiritually, extremely difficult. What made it even harder was that, by the time I was a grown man and able to articulate my needs, I couldn't very well tap somebody on the shoulder and say, "Lift me up. Carry me. Nurture me. Support me. Help me." They'd think me quite the whack job. And the last thing I needed was to be rejected, laughed at, or ignored. So, I thought I could *do life* all on my own.

Nevertheless, I knew that if I were to grow up to be a non-hermit, I would need to develop some form of external social support.

Once I worked on eliminating as much of the toxic people from my life as I could, then I had to reconstruct my external supports. But I wondered how to go about doing this. First, I had to understand what it meant to have an external support system. I figured this out based on what I knew was missing from my life. So I sought out:

- someone who could be kind, considerate, caring, and empathetic,
- someone who I could trust and with whom I could share personal information freely,
- someone who could accept me for who I am, and wouldn't interfere or try to change me, but would, instead, offer help, insight, and encouragement when needed
- someone who could understand my values and morals,
- someone who would be fun to be with,
- someone with whom I could be my weird, goofy self, without my having to wonder or worry about being humiliated, chastised, or ignored, or fear repercussions,

312

- someone who would be honest with me, give me feedback, advice (when asked for), and give me that kick-ass ass-kick when needed,
- someone who could be a sounding board and let me vent when I need to,
- someone who would be there and available when needed, and
- someone who would give a damn.

Is this too much to ask?

I suspected this undertaking would have to include more than just one person since, having reviewed this list, I guessed that not everyone could be all things to me. So I needed to determine who to include in my list of social supports, each with his or her own criteria. I made a list, a pool of possible support resources, even if they didn't yet exist, which included: old friends, new friends, family members, various relatives, teachers, leaders, pets, employers, employees, colleagues, intimate partners, gym mates, classmates, and individuals from groups I attend. If ever I would have professional supports (such as therapists, social workers, psychiatrists), I could put them on my list as well.

My next step was to match the list of what I needed for an external social support to specific individuals from my list of possible social supports. I also had to understand if the support was mutual or mutually exclusive. As well, I needed to keep in mind that relationships change over time, and therefore my list of supports needed to be flexible. Finally, I had to realize that if I didn't want to hear the answer, I shouldn't ask the question.

A Little Something You Might Want to Try
Developing Support Systems

1. Make a chart of three columns. In column 1, make a list of all possible supports.
2. In column 2, indicate the contribution the support has made to your life.
3. In column 3, state whether the relationship or need is reciprocal.

HE SHOOTS! HE SCORES!
(setting a vision, big goals, and small steps)

One of my longer stays on my Journey Within was at the point where I had to take a look at what I needed in order to be happy and successful and improve the quality of my life. I needed to have a goal, and I needed to know how to reach that goal. It was therefore necessary for me to understand first what my overall goal was, because if I didn't understand this, I was merely floundering, a fish out of water.

I knew the definition of a goal, so I didn't look it up, but having checked out the internet on *setting goals,* I came up with over eight million sites. I suspected that there must be a whole lot of people wanting to know the same thing: how to set goals. Each of the sites I selected offered a slightly different version of the same information. So I picked out those points that seemed to be most significant to me, and I came up with a composite guide to goal-setting. This is what worked best for me:

1. First, I made an agreement with myself to write everything down, as tedious as that was. I figured this would be important to do, at least for clarity, recall, reinforcing my commitment to follow through, check-listing, and reviewing.

2. I realized I had to be clear about what I actually wanted to accomplish in life. It was all very well and good to say my goal was to be happy (don't we all?), but that just left me in the mist, unable to see the paths ahead of me. In order to clear the fog, I had to develop an overall vision to see the big picture that I will have created for myself, and to understand what I will have won the Lifetime Achievement Award for.

3. To create my vision, I then chose a big-picture timeframe that gave a clear vision, but not too off in the distance so that my

vision was remote and blurry. I needed to focus my timeline binoculars. I chose a ten-year vision.

4. To continue creating my clear vision, I decided to identify three general areas of life that would help me to gain a better understanding of what this vision would consist of: the types of things I want *to do* with my life, the sorts of things I would like *to have*, and the kind of person I would strive *to be*. I made three columns and wrote down all the things I ever wanted to do, to have, and to be. Since these would be things I wanted to accomplish, I decided to write them as I envisioned them, by

   • ensuring I used 'I' statements,
   • keeping the statements positive,
   • writing them as though they have been achieved.

The lists were inexhaustible but I stopped when I became too exhausted to continue. Below is a sample of what I came up with:

TO DO	TO HAVE	TO BE
I have published a book.	I have a comfortable home.	I am in excellent health.
I have created my own artwork.	I have many loyal friends.	I have maintained my integrity.
I have learned to speak Dutch.	I have a good financial portfolio.	I have gained self-confidence.
I have completed a successful career.	I have four great kids.	I am at peace with myself spiritually.
I work at a satisfying volunteer job.	I own a castle in Europe.	I am accepting of others.
I travel to interesting places.	I wear smart clothes that fit well.	I am an astute philosopher.
I go to the gym three times a week.	I own many interesting books.	I have been a social worker and a teacher.

| I attend mindful meditation classes. | I have my own bowling shoes. | I have good communication with my wife. |

5. Next, to further clarify my vision, I identified those goals with common elements and grouped them together like I did when creating my rooms, as follows:

GROUPS	TO DO	TO HAVE	TO BE
HEALTH/ FEELING GOOD PHYSICALLY	I go to the gym three times a week.	I wear smart clothes that fit well.	I am in excellent health.
CAREER/ SERVICE	I have completed a successful career. I work at a satisfying volunteer job.		I have been a social worker and a teacher.
FINANCES		I have a good financial portfolio.	
SHELTER		I have a comfortable home. I own a castle in Europe.	

PERSONAL GROWTH	I attend mindful meditation classes.	I have many loyal friends.	I have maintained my integrity. I have gained self-confidence. I am at peace with myself spiritually. I am accepting of others.
LEISURE TIME	I have published a book. I have created my own artwork. I travel to interesting places.	I have my own bowling shoes.	I am an astute philosopher.
EDUCATION	I have learned to speak Dutch.	I own many interesting books.	
FAMILY	I have four great kids.		I have good communication with my wife.

6. I then had to make a clear and concise statement about my overall vision in each of these categories. They were kind of run-on and ungrammatical, but they at least captured the essence of my vision. For example:

    a) By going to the gym three times a week and wearing smart clothes that fit well, I am able to maintain excellent health and feel good about myself.

b) I have completed my career as a social worker and I have taught classes of my own creation; now I am providing service by working at a satisfying volunteer job.

c) Now that I am retired, I am receiving a full pension and I have a good financial portfolio.

d) I have a comfortable home, living in a clean environment, and I own a castle in Europe.

e) I have built my character to include integrity and self-confidence; I have many loyal friends, and I am accepting of others; I am at peace with myself spiritually with the aid of attending a mindful meditation class.

f) I have published a book, created my own artwork, travelled to many interesting places, have my own bowling shoes for the occasional informal leisure night out, and enjoy philosophizing with my friends.

g) I continue to learn from the many interesting books that I own, including the Dutch language.

h) I have four great kids with whom I spend my time, and I have learned how to communicate well with my wife.

I now have a clear vision of what my life will be like in ten years.

7. By creating my vision I had also created some of my big picture goals. Still, I found that I had to further refine these goals by asking myself some tough but necessary questions; these questions helped me to get a clear grasp on my goals and make them more manageable:

1) Do I really want to accomplish this goal?

2) Is this goal specific enough?

3) How do I measure the progress of this goal?

4) Is this goal attainable?

5) Is this goal within my control or within my ability to achieve?

6) Is this goal realistic?

7) Is this goal relevant to my vision?

8) Is this goal consistent with my values and morals?

9) Do I have a clearly defined timeframe for achieving this goal?

10) Do I have a plan for periodic evaluation for my goal to determine if my overall goals and priorities have changed over time?

8. At first glance I was overwhelmed by the number of goals I wanted to achieve and by the competing priorities. I took a good look at each of my categorical goals and prioritized them as best I could, based on the following criteria and considerations:

1) What is likely the most urgent goal at this time?

2) What is likely the most interesting goal at this time?

3) What is likely the most easily achievable goal at this time?

4) What goal is likely to have the most impact on my life at this time?

5) What will likely incorporate taking the least number of risks/dangers by undertaking the goal at this time?

6) What will likely have the most positive or acceptable consequences by undertaking the goal at this time?

9. Based on the answers to these questions, I then developed and wrote down my list of priorities on a scale from one to eight (based on the number of the goals I had identified, one being the most and eight being the least) for my goals, which looked something like this:

Goal	Question 1	Question 2	Question 3	Question 4	Question 5	Question 6
a	5	2	2	3	3	3
b	1	7	1	4	4	5
c	2	8	7	5	8	6
d	6	5	8	7	7	7
e	4	3	3	2	1	4
f	7	1	6	6	5	2
g	8	6	4	8	2	8
h	3	4	5	1	6	1

After completing the chart I then tallied the numbers under the questions for each goal (horizontally). The results were as follows: a = 18; b = 22; c = 36; d = 40; e = 17; f = 27; g = 36; h = 20. I ordered my goals from lowest to highest number, thusly: e, a, h, b, f, c, g, d. I compared the two goals with the same number and determined that c ranked higher on my list of priorities than g. Consequently, the first goal I would tackle would be to focus on the development of my character, my social circle, and my spirituality.

10. Having selected my number one priority goal, I realized that it was fairly broad and it required being broken down into smaller and more manageable steps, organized in a way that would lead me in the most direct manner toward my goal. And they really were steps, which I represented diagrammatically, like this:

GOAL: I have published a self-help book by 31/12/13

STEP 5: find an editor or book publisher by 31/03/13

STEP 4: find a legal rep by 28/02/13

STEP 3: review, edit, and complete final draft by 31/01/13

STEP 2: finish writing first draft, one topic at a time by 31/08/12

STEP 1: list and research all topics to be discussed by 28/02/12

In order to create these steps, I went through the same process by asking myself the same questions in #7 and #8 for each goal, breaking down the steps even further to ensure I could manage them.

11. Finally, I had to give the dog a bone, me being the dog. I needed positive reinforcement to reward myself every time I completed a step—nothing over the top—just some small gesture of self-acknowledgement and recognition to give me a boost up to the next step, even if the achievement of completing the step was reward in itself. Also, I thought it would be neat to have the reward relate to the goal—a positive twist to 'let the punishment fit the crime'—but if this couldn't be done, it didn't really matter as long as I gave myself the reward. At first, I thought this concept was just a bunch of new age hokum (does hokum come in bunches?), but I tried it and I liked the idea because it really helped me to motivate myself. For example, when my goal was to retire from my job of thirty-three years, not only did I decide I was going to attend a retirement party the Social Services Division made for me and enjoy it, I also decided to treat myself and my wife to a vacation. This not only reinforced my decision to have retired and encouraged me to move onto my next goal, it also allowed me to be recognized by my colleagues by participating in an event that was both memorable and enjoyable.

12. Once I was able to achieve my goal I decided it would be best to evaluate or review my accomplishment by asking some more questions:
    a) Was I successful in achieving this goal? More importantly, was I successful in my performance/actions regarding this goal as opposed to its outcome?

b) What did I learn from my success/failure?

c) Did the completion of this goal take me on a new path or lead me to other new goals?

d) Did I achieve my goal too easily? Should I make my next goal more challenging?

e) Was the goal to difficult to achieve (i.e. time, skill, cost, effort, obstacles, etc.)? What could I do next time to make achieving my goal a little easier?

f) Was there any discrepancy with the questions in #7 and #8?

g) Do I need to make any changes to my next goal or in the steps it will take to get there? If so, what are they?

h) Do I need to reprioritize my goals?

i) Am I still in keeping with my overall vision?

j) What has achieving this goal done for me?

A Little Something You Might Want to Try
Setting a vision, big goals, and small steps #1

Create your own vision by:

1. committing to writing everything down
2. selecting an overall timeline
3. brainstorming, and using the previously identified format/chart to record all the things you want to do, to have, and to be, ensuring 'I' statements are being used, keeping the statements positive, and writing them as though they have been achieved.

A Little Something You Might Want to Try
Setting a vision, big goals, and small steps #2

Using the previously identified format/chart, identify those goals with common elements and group them together, using your own categories. Use the headings for your columns:
GROUPS, TO DO, TO HAVE, TO BE.

A Little Something You Might Want to Try
Setting a vision, big goals, and small steps #3

Create your own statement for each group of goals, using the previously identified format/chart.

A Little Something You Might Want to Try
Setting a vision, big goals, and small steps #4

Answer the following questions for each of your goals:

1) Do I really want to accomplish this goal?
2) Is this goal specific enough?
3) How do I measure the progress of this goal?
4) Is this goal attainable?
5) Is this goal within my control or within my ability to achieve?
6) Is this goal realistic?
7) Is this goal relevant to my vision?
8) Is this goal consistent with my values and morals?
9) Do I have a clearly defined timeframe for achieving this goal?
10) Do I have a plan for periodic evaluation for my goal to determine if my overall goals and priorities have changed over time?

A Little Something You Might Want to Try
Setting a vision, big goals, and small steps #5

1. Review the questions listed in this section.
2. Based on the answers to these questions, develop your own list of priorities on a scale from one to eight (based on the number of the goals you have identified, one being the most and eight being the least) for your goals, by using the previously identified format/chart (Column 1: Goal (a—j); Column 2: Question 1; Column 3: Question 2; Column 4: Question 3; Column 5: Question 4; Column 6: Question 5; Column 7: Question 6).
3. After completing the chart tally the numbers under the questions for each goal (horizontally).
4. Order your goals from lowest to highest number.

A Little Something You Might Want to Try
Setting a vision, big goals, and small steps #6

Select the goal highest on your list of priorities, using the previously identified format/chart.

A Little Something You Might Want to Try
Setting a vision, big goals, and small steps #7

For each step you take, identify a reward to give yourself and follow through.

A Little Something You Might Want to Try
Setting a vision, big goals, and small steps #8

Answer the following questions:

a) Was I successful in achieving this goal? More importantly, was I successful in my performance/actions regarding this goal as opposed to its outcome?
b) What did I learn from my success/failure?
c) Did the completion of this goal take me on a new path or lead me to other new goals?
d) Did I achieve my goal too easily? Should I make my next goal more challenging?
e) Was the goal to difficult to achieve (i.e. time, skill, cost, effort, obstacles, etc.)? What could I do next time to make achieving my goal a little easier?
f) Was there any discrepancy with the questions in #7 and #8?

g) Do I need to make any changes to my next goal or in the steps it will take to get there? If so, what are they?

h) Do I need to reprioritize my goals?

i) Am I still in keeping with my overall vision?

j) What has achieving this goal done for me?

MATHEMATICALLY SPEAKING
(making decisions and making commitments)

I noticed that it was all wonderful and momentous to have made a decision at all, considering that, for much of my life, I questioned and fretted over everything. Just as a goal without a timeline is merely a dream, making a decision without implementing it is nothing more than a brain fart.

I thought about my New Year's resolutions, and how disappointed and frustrated I was when they did not come to fruition. Something didn't add up. There was something missing in the equation for implementing a decision, that is, following through, that is, taking action.

Although, as I've established, my math skills leave a lot to be desired (not a negative, just a fact), I do know that making a decision + good intentions = brain fart. Likewise, making a decision + x = taking action. I knew the answer to the equation!: x = commitment.

How do you commit to something and follow through? Having researched here are the top ten suggestions:

1. Make a plan. Identify the big picture, the major goal(s), and the small steps.
2. Complete a risk assessment.
3. Give yourself timelines for both the small steps as well as the goal itself.
4. Give yourself a consequence if you don't follow through.
5. Make your tasks fun and try to enjoy the process.
6. Get others to support you and cheer you on (use your list of external resources).
7. Invest time or money or effort or any combination of these, as needed.
8. Learn from any failed attempts, modify your plan, and start again.
9. Give yourself a reward for following through.

10. Just get off your lazy ass and do it!

I'm partial to the last one myself.

At any rate, I came to the conclusion that brain farts don't exactly get you what you want. So I decided to add commitment to whatever decision I was planning to make, and I was then able to take action to reach my goal. Perhaps I'm not as mathematically challenged as I thought.

A Little Something You Might Want to Try
Making Decisions and Commitments

1. Make a plan. Set your vision, big goal and small steps, using the "To Do, To Have, and To Be" chart.
2. List the Goal # and the corresponding statement.
3. Using the previously identified Step Chart, proceed to list the steps needed to reach the goal set.
4. Complete a risk assessment.
5. Give yourself timelines for both the small steps as well as the goal itself.
6. Give yourself a consequence if you don't follow through.
7. Make your tasks fun and try to enjoy the process.
8. Get others to support you and cheer you on (use your list of external resources).
9. Invest time or money or effort or any combination of these, as needed.
10. Learn from any failed attempts, modify your plan, and start again.
11. Give yourself a reward for following through.

GOING OVER THE FALLS IN A BARREL
(taking risks and embracing challenges)

Being a timid and shy sort of guy, I was not much of a daredevil. Consequently I missed out on many opportunities and life experiences.

That is not to say I didn't do things with reckless abandon. In my youth, one Hallowe'en night, I tricked and I treated in full drag queen regalia. But my future bride was by my side every step of the way, hiding in the shadows of suburbia. For a time, I created and taught courses for the District School Board Continuing Education Program. But the classes were small and the duration of the program relatively short. I white-water rafted through the treacherous river that separates Israel and Jordan. Except that the white-water was actually brown-water and the river wasn't all that treacherous... it was shallow, mud, really, only three feet deep.

In each instance, my reckless abandon was actually deliberate, calculated, strategized and planned to the point of sanitizing the risks right out of the undertaking. And to some extent, the enjoyment.

In my own private daydreams, the thrill of skydiving, ballooning, and parasailing excited me to no end. I was obsessed with the idea of becoming a famous actor, a skilled philosopher, and a daring explorer. These daydreams, however, always exploded in a puff of orange smoke each time I seriously entertained them, and consequently they were never realized.

That got me to wondering why this was happening and why I was so reluctant to take risks: pure unadulterated fear! So much so, in fact, that by not taking risks, I was putting the quality of my life at risk.

Having discovered, at this point of my Journey Within, that I needed to approach the issue of risk-taking with logic, care, and intelligence, I also realized that I needed to balance this with the simple pleasure of just "doing it". Taking action involved understanding my goal or objective by acquiring knowledge about the risks, what some alternative actions or choices might be, determining what the internal and external influences and impacts are, what could be the consequences of taking the action, and when would be the best time to take on the risk which could impact on the action.

I also needed to overcome my reluctance to approach anything remotely sounding like a risk, including the word 'risk'. To risk something meant the possibility of losing something; it meant something potentially dangerous. It meant the likelihood of surrendering something. But then, its synonyms were just as scary: taking a chance was too unstable; facing a challenge was too confrontational; to hazard or to venture meant something was at stake. So I needed to accept risk for what it was (although I did end up preferring the term "to embrace a challenge").

By asking myself some serious questions before taking a risk (you'll find those questions in *A Little Something You Might Want to Try* which follows), I would better-equipped to make a sound decision about the current risk, and more comfortable and confident about future risks.

I left no stone unturned when it came to taking risks.

A Little Something You Might Want to Try
Taking Risks and Embracing Challenges

Ask yourself the following questions whenever you are faced with taking a risk or embracing a challenge:

1. What the hell am I doing? In other words, do I clearly understand what I want to achieve? Have I planned out the details as much as possible, or do I just want to take the plunge unprepared? Do I actually have a plan? Do I have a plan B? What information do I need to know or gather, and what resources do I need to have in place before embracing the challenge? Who is there for me? Is there anything preventing me from moving forward with my plan?

2. Why the hell am I doing it? In other words, what is urging me on, prodding me to take the risk? Will I commit to follow through? Does the risk fit in with my overall vision? Or is it a smaller piece of a bigger picture?

3. What the hell is at stake? In other words, what exactly am I risking? Is it important to take the risk? Is it required that I take the risk? Why am I even taking the risk? What is my motivation? Will I follow through? How does this risk fit in with the bigger picture of my life, my overall vision? Am I committed? Am I flexible? Am I realistic? Am I enthusiastic? What are my responsibilities? What are my limitations?

4. What the hell is my fear factor, the acceptable level of paranoia? In other words, who is against me? Who is my competition? Have I overlooked any potential or existing problems that would make me think twice about taking the risk? Am I scared? Should I reconsider? What might I be sacrificing by taking the risk? Is there anything about this risk that is not within my control? Is taking the risk my own choice, or am I being forced into or

obligated to taking the risk? Or do I *perceive* that I am being forced into or obligated to taking the risk?

5. What the hell was I thinking? In other words, what are the possible consequences of taking the risk? What are the consequences if I don't take the risk? What could change by taking the risk? What may result if I decide not to follow through or delay taking the risk? Is it too late to change my mind?

6. What the hell happened? In other words, do I have the tools necessary to evaluate the risk and if I actually achieved what I set out to do? What have I learned from the experience or from the process?

DO YOU VALIDATE?

(validation)

I remember rushing into the store with my parking ticket. I asked the store clerk, "Do you validate?" She gave me a big hug and said, "You are a worthwhile human being!"

Up to now my Journey Within has taken me to places where I am learning to behave well in reference to myself. But *I* am not the only one with whom I interact, and so another measure of how well I behave is in relation to other people. When I first thought about this notion, I was flooded with a wave of thoughts of conformity, surrendering my identity, and phoniness, as well as feelings of loneliness, insignificance, and not belonging. I was almost boomeranged back to my starting point.

With my new-found awareness and change of attitude, however, I could see that there were other ways I could approach this concept. The breakthrough for me was to ask myself: "Based on my own values and morals (keeping in mind that not everybody shares the same moral code or has adopted the same values), how would I like to be treated?" And immediately I answered myself, "With dignity, respect, kindness, empathy, loyalty, and honesty. In a way that would allow me to feel appreciated, included, and acknowledged." Ultimately I would want to be seen, to be heard, to matter or, in other words, to be validated.

I used to think that it would be a case of reciprocity if the relationship were solid: if I validate others then I would be validated in return. I realized that this is not always so, and for a variety of reasons, such as:

- The other person is not in the same head space as I (e.g. s/he is going through a crisis)

- The other person does not share the same values and is not guided by the same moral code as I
- I have not made it clear to the other person what I want or need from him/her
- There are differing perceptions, perspectives, or opinions between me and the other person.

Remembering that I cannot control others but that I can control how I respond to them, I decided that I would not seek out validation; instead, I would offer validation to others as a part of my goal of building character to achieve my overall vision of improving the quality of my life. This would empower me to do for others and not get all bent out of shape if I were not validated in return. It would also encourage me to be more assertive, that is, if I wanted or needed something from someone, I could ask for it.

Next, I had to determine *how* to validate someone. How do I demonstrate to another person that they matter, that they are worthy, without coming across as a know-it-all or without sounding superior, hoaky, insincere, or condescending?

I identified five main areas to validate another person:

1. Be present and in the moment. Am I thinking about something other than what the person is saying to me? Am I thinking about my own point of view? Am I thinking about my own next statement or how to help solve the other person's problem? If the answer is yes to any of these questions then I am not present and in the moment.
2. Pay attention and listen carefully to what is being said, how it is being said, and what is not being said.
3. Acknowledge what is being said: the thoughts, the feelings, the behaviour.
4. Determine what is being asked of me. Am I being asked for an opinion, for information, for advice, for confrontation, for

an explanation, for clarification, for assistance, for suggestions, for a critique, for references, to identify alternatives, to be a sounding board, or simply to be there to allow the other person to vent?

5. Show appreciation and express gratitude, where appropriate.

A Little Something You Might Want to Try
Validation

1. Are you present and in the moment?
2. Are you thinking about something other than what the person is saying to you?
3. Are you thinking about your own point of view?
4. Are you thinking about your own next statement or how to help solve the other person's problem, even before they finish their explanation?
5. Are you paying attention and listening carefully to what is being said, how it is being said, and what is not being said by the other person?
6. Have you acknowledged what the other person said, including their thoughts, feelings, and behaviours?
7. Have you determined what is being asked of you (such as: an opinion, clarification, advice, confrontation, explanation, assistance, suggestion, critique, reference, identifying alternatives, being a sounding board, or someone to vent to, etc.)?
8. Have you shown appreciation and express gratitude, where appropriate?

I DID IT ON PURPOSE!

(living a purposeful life)

I had to ask myself why I was pursuing goals in the first place. To what end? Ultimately, it seemed to me that I was seeking goals to establish clarity, seek truth, become authentic and acquire direction. Most importantly I learned that, for me, pursuing a goal gave my life purpose, a reason to be and continue being. In turn, my goals had to be purposeful or else they were just filler.

It seems to be instinctive, this pull toward finding meaning in life, at least, I believe it to be so. Having attempted to discuss this with some people, though, I have received responses ranging from enthusiastic agreement to denial and anger, to amused bewilderment, to blank stares. I had to go with what felt right for *me*, that the quest for a purposeful life is a strong instinct.

Reflecting on Viktor Frankl's theory on Logotherapy, this strong desire to find meaning, is of great significance which can be found by creating a work or doing a deed, experiencing something or encountering someone, and developing an appropriate attitude toward unavoidable suffering.

I thought long and hard about this and decided I would understand it better if I put it in my own words (to give it more personal meaning) in relation to my personal goals. Therefore, there is meaning in:

- Creating something,
- Doing a deed (hopefully a good one),
- Experiencing something,
- Encountering someone,
- Developing an attitude to manage even the worst case scenario.

This, however, cannot stand alone. It is necessary to add qualifiers to the above points. Only when I add my own values and morals is a sense of purpose given.

This was actually beginning to make sense to me. It was all starting to come together: these statements explained why it was so important to interact with others and not be a loner, to gain direct experiences by doing things and not to be so passive and uninvolved, to be creative and add depth and dimension to the world, to do a deed that would benefit, if not all of humankind, at least one human being, and to see my life, and life in general, in the best possible light, even in the worst possible circumstances, because of the worst possible circumstances, and in spite of the worst possible circumstances.

This is the 'how' and the 'why' to the notion of improving the quality of my life.

A Little Something You Might Want to Try
Living a Purposeful Life

In keeping with the notion of doing something creative, doing a 'good' deed, having direct experience, having an interaction with someone, and developing and maintaining a positive attitude to manage even the worst case scenario, try each of the following as often as possible, even on a daily basis:

1. Identify one humorous or amusing thing that occurred today.
2. Practise fifteen minutes of peace (mindful meditation, finding a place of solitude, etc.)
3. Engage in one kind act of selflessness.
4. Offer someone a genuine compliment.
5. Create/study one beautiful drawing or photo.
6. Devote at least fifteen minutes of your day to physical exploration.
7. Devote at least fifteen minutes of your day to intellectual exploration.
8. Devote at least fifteen minutes of your day to emotional exploration.
9. Devote at least fifteen minutes of your day to spiritual exploration.
10. Engage in one creative endeavour.
11. Focus on developing or improving one character trait.
12. Create one thought record.
13. Engage in fifteen minutes of environmental consciousness.
14. Learn or read one new thing.
15. Enjoy a good conversation with an old friend or a new acquaintance.

REINVENTING MYSELF

(becoming the person I want to be)

I am starting to see that potentiality is the blueprint for my life and has always been there waiting for me to develop it in my own unique way. Having decided upon the importance of incorporating, building, and refining those character traits that activate my potentiality, I set out to define who I am, who I want to be, and who I can be.

Remembering that, for decades, I chose to label myself as a loser, a slacker, a fool, as someone who was anxious, depressed, fearful, cowardly, bashful, jealous, awash in self-pity, and easily embarrassed, someone who would lie, blame, complain, and hold a grudge, and someone who had low self-esteem, little confidence, and no self-worth, I realized that I needed to shed those labels, to say goodbye to that loathsome image in the mirror, and reinvent myself.

But how?

I figured that if I could list all of my negative characteristics so succinctly, I could just as succinctly list all of the positive ones.

So I made a small list of one hundred seventy-two words (see *A Little Something You Might Want to Try* that follows).

Yet again I was overwhelmed (I get that way a lot!) by the vast potential within me waiting to be realized. As a result, I decided to take only those top few descriptors that resonated with me at the moment. I gave careful consideration to them, and figured out how to build on them and incorporate them into my life. I began to understand that the only way to do this was to take action.

The three characteristics that I selected were: being resilient, being authentic, and having integrity.

To me, being resilient meant that I could bounce back in the face of adversity, that rather than surrender, I could persevere freely and with joy, abundance, and enthusiasm. The concept of resilience reminded me of a punching bag clown I used to have as a kid. No matter how often it got knocked down it would always right itself again. Not that I see myself as a punching bag—at least, not any longer—nor as a clown, but the fact that it—I—would be able to bounce right back, and do so because I could, because I wanted to, and to give it my all, was a very appealing concept. Certainly, I would need to call upon my pool of strengths to see me through and, by doing so, would allow me to utilize my new positive attitude, my awareness, my courage, and my resolve to deal with any situation that came my way.

Being authentic meant being true to and about my unique self. I could allow myself to be who I am by expressing myself freely without the worry of what others might think or say about me. I could finally forgo denying who I am, keep what I like, and discard or make changes to the rest of me. There would be no trying to impress others, no phoniness, no pretenses, no having to live up to someone else's expectations. I could do this as well with joy, abundance, and enthusiasm. And I could celebrate my authenticity.

Having integrity meant that I could maintain the whole of who I am, even in the face of adversity, that I could understand that behaviour results in experience, qualifying my experiences positively through my attitudes and values, and know that I am the sum of my experiences. I could and must stand by my beliefs, and (although the expression mildly turns my stomach) I must walk the walk and talk the talk.

A Little Something You Might Want to Try
Becoming the Person I Want to Be

Your personal characteristics might just as well be positive, confidence-building ones rather than negative, self-effacing ones.

Below is a list of words (adjectives) which may or may not describe who you are. That is for you to decide. Some may describe these adjectives as positive qualities however that may not necessarily be the way you would describe them.

The idea is to break away from how you see yourself based on how you have been described over the years by yourself or by others and to define your own attributes, perhaps even identify those qualities you recognize as needing change.

1. Circle in red those words which you feel adequately describe you.
2. Circle in blue those words which you feel are applicable in certain situations.
3. Do not circle those words which you feel do not adequately describe you.
4. Review the list and the choices you have made.

There is no right or wrong. After all, take away the adjectives and what's left?

I AM

In exploring your relationships and the kind of individuals you would like to have in your life, you may want to try the word circle again but substituting I AM for YOU ARE and select the subject(s) of your choice.

Feel free to add to the list if you so desire.

WORD LIST

DIGNIFIED	WARM	RESOURCEFUL	CAREFUL
INVENTIVE	ACCURATE	UNEXCITABLE	CONSCIENTIOUS
PRUDENT	AGGRESSIVE	ATTRACTIVE	CAUTIOUS
TENACIOUS	DELIBERATE	COOPERATIVE	CHARMING
INTELLIGENT	EFFICIENT	BOLD	CONFIDENT
PROGRESSIVE	LOGICAL	BROAD-MINDED	CHEERFUL
TEACHABLE	REALISTIC	COOL	CLEAR-THINKING
ZANY	TRUSTING	FLEXIBLE	COMPETENT
DISCREET	INDEPENDENT	MODERATE	COMPETITIVE
KIND	PLEASANT	RESPONSIBLE	CLEVER
PURPOSEFUL	STEADY	HONEST	INTROSPECTIVE
THOROUGH	VERSATILE	SPUNKY	ANALYTICAL
INTELLECTUAL	ALERT	SOCIABLE	FORGIVING
PRECISE	DARING	NATURAL	KNOWLEDGEABLE
TACTFUL	EMOTIONAL	MODEST	SUPPORTIVE
WITTY	LOYAL	RETIRING	CONSISTENT
DOMINANT	REFLECTIVE	HELPFUL	ASSERTIVE
LEISURELY	TRUSTWORTHY	OUTGOING	MOTIVATED
QUICK	IMAGINATIVE	SINCERE	CONSIDERATE
THOUGHTFUL	PERSEVERING	FORMAL	PAINSTAKING
PRACTICAL	VERBAL	ROBUST	AWARE
WISE	CURIOUS	ORIGINAL	CREATIVE
ACADEMIC	ARTISTIC	TRUTHFUL	ENTHUSIASTIC
ADVENTUROUS	COURAGEOUS	FRANK	COLOURFUL
ADAPTABLE	ENERGETIC	OBLIGING	INTERESTING
DETERMINED	MATURE	PRIVATE	JOLLY
EAGER	RELAXED	FRIENDLY	PROFESSIONAL
LIGHT-HEARTED	UNAFFECTED	OPEN-MINDED	CLEAN
QUIET	HUMOROUS	SELF-CONTROLLED	REASONABLE
TOLERANT	PATIENT	GENEROUS	HAPPY
EASY-GOING	FAIR-MINDED	GENTLE	INSIGHTFUL
WHOLESOME	METHODICAL	GOOD-NATURED	YOUTHFUL
ACTIVE	RELIABLE	OPTIMISTIC	UNUSUAL
AFFECTIONATE	UNASSUMING	ORGANIZED	UNIQUE
APPROACHABLE	HELPFUL	SENSITIVE	SELF-RELIANT
LIKABLE	FAR-SIGHTED	SERIOUS	SENSUAL
RATIONAL	METICULOUS	ORIGINAL	LOVABLE
TOUGH	RESERVED	CONSERVATIVE	INVOLVED
INDIVIDUALISTIC	AUTHENTIC	EMPATHETIC	BUSINESS-LIKE
POISED	FIRM	CALM	SEXUAL
STRONG	MILD	CAPABLE	ARTICULATE
AWESOME	JOYFUL	ACCEPTING	ATTUNED
RESILIENT	INTEGRAL	UNDERSTANDING	WITTY

5. Explain why the red-circled words describe you. Give an example for each.

6. Explain under what circumstances the blue-circled words describe you. Give an example for each.

7. Explain why the uncircled words do not describe you. Give an example for each.

LIGHTEN UP

(finding humour, being less serious and more silly)

"I have a severe disability... I was born without a sense of humour."

That was my opening line for my comedy routine at the *Laughing Like Crazy* showcase performance. Me, the most depressing, awkward, and pessimistic person in the universe. I was volunteering at the Mood Disorders Association of Ontario when I saw a flyer for one of their programs: a unique and interesting way to improve your mood through humour. I struggled for sixteen weeks, along with twelve other participants, to find my funny bone—not an easy task, considering up to that point I had rarely laughed at anything. I gave glassy-eyed stares at performers in comedy clubs. I offered wide yawns amongst the howls of laughter of movie theatre audiences. If someone slipped on a banana peel, I would nervously move away for fear that I would somehow be blamed. If I did crack up at something that I found humorous, people around me would back off from the cackling kook who laughed when clearly there was nothing to laugh about. So, I threw myself into the challenge of writing my own material and performing in front of more than two hundred people. I was terrified!

It was wonderful! And I discovered that:

- I *did* have some kind of a sense of humour, whether others got it or not
- I was braver than I ever gave myself credit for, even at my scarediest
- I could kibbitz, be silly, allow myself to be scrutinized, and to stand up to hecklers by not worrying so much about what they thought of me
- I could open up a little more, even to strangers, and not be such a tight-ass

- I could allow myself to let down my guard and to feel like I belong
- I could seek out and find humour in everyday things, even the more serious stuff
- I could increase my self-esteem, self-confidence, and self-worth
- I could become more emotionally disentangled and reduce stress, anxiety, and depression
- I could better manage my life, my crazy thoughts, feelings, and behaviour, and the crazy situations in which I often found myself
- I could discover a new appreciation of others

From that point on, I have been spending more time paying attention to the lighter side of life.

A Little Something You Might Want to Try
Finding Humour #1

Write one joke every day and share it with someone.

A Little Something You Might Want to Try
Finding Humour #2

Review at least one situation you experienced during the course of a day, regardless of how emotional or boring or difficult or serious it was. What can you find in the situation that was funny or humorous or amusing?

OPPORTUNITY KNOCKS!

(philanthropy: acts of kindness, providing service,
and doing for others)

One of my most significant discoveries on my Journey Within was something I stumbled across quite by accident. I was waiting for a long while to accelerate into traffic when, finally, somebody slowed down and, smiling, waved me through. This is not only a commonplace story but pretty boring, right? And yet, I couldn't stop thinking about it: a stranger does a favour, a simple act of kindness for me, a stranger, and with a smile, no less!

What did this all mean, and why was I so stuck on something that, for me, would normally be so forgettable? Well, I suppose it was because:

- It was an action taken that was kind and considerate
- It was an act of giving to someone, one human being to another, without being asked
- It was an act given to a stranger, with no judgment, with no apparent ulterior motive, and with nothing expected in return
- It was done sincerely and happily

A flash of shame overcame me for all the unspoken apologies, for walking hurriedly past a homeless person, thinking, "I work hard for *my* money", for not saying thank you or giving a reasonable gratuity to a waitress who was obviously run off her feet, for those times I could have said "I love you" but didn't, for being angry at my generosity of a wedding gift when the dinner and reception were less than I expected, for averting my eyes or walking away from someone in need, for saying something hurtful directly to her, and for saying something hurtful behind his back, and for not asking "Can I help?"

For a week, I kept track (yet again with his lists!) of every time I said or did something that was unkind, thoughtless, or inconsiderate, or ignorant, or judgmental, or with ulterior motives, or expecting reciprocity, or did something grudgingly. My list was embarrassingly and horrifically long! This spoke volumes to my character and who I thought I was.

I began to think of how I could work on changing this character flaw, such as, saying a kind word, offering help and following through, doing a favour, taking positive action, maintaining a cheery disposition, providing service to others, paying it forward, giving back, and just giving. I also had to keep in mind that being philanthropic did not mean giving away what I could not afford to give, sacrificing what I did not have, sacrificing at the expense of others, and insinuating myself where I was not wanted.

Having browsed the internet, I was stunned by the number of sites related to acts of kindness and to philanthropic ideas. I was equally stunned by the number of people interested and invested in philanthropic acts. So I made yet another list of some ways I could philanthropize (?), and referring to my list until being kind, thoughtful, and considerate would become my way of life. This list included everything from volunteering at the Mood Disorders Association of Ontario, to reading a book to someone who cannot not read, to expressing gratitude to someone who once profoundly impacted on my life, to saying hello to a stranger in an elevator, to listening to someone else's problems, to asking someone about his culture, his experiences, his life, to telling my family how much I love and admire them, to dropping some change into the hands of a needy person, to offering to babysit, to teaching something to someone, to giving directions to someone who is lost or new to the city, to leaving a well-deserved tip to wait staff, to doing something ecologically sensible, to sending a greeting card, to donating my time for a community event, to bringing in treats for co-workers, and so on. The list is endless! And enjoyable! And rewarding!

A Little Something You Might Want to Try
Philanthropy #1

1. Using your awareness, keep track of every word uttered or every behaviour demonstrated that was unkind, thoughtless, inconsiderate, ignorant, judgmental, with ulterior motives, expecting reciprocity, or done grudgingly.
2. How could you change your words or actions in each of these situations to turn it into an act of kindness?

A Little Something You Might Want to Try
Philanthropy #2

Make a list of various philanthropic activities in which you may be interested (get ideas from others, from bookstores, social services agencies, websites on philanthropy, etc., or come up with your own ideas) and follow through. Have a positive impact on someone.

GIVE THE DOG A BONE
(celebrating successes, milestones, and life in general)

The annoying thing about clichés is the truth that lies within them. My first instinct, when somebody once told me I should celebrate my successes, was to throw him to the ground, extend my fist, and tell him to "celebrate *this*!" My successes felt trivial, almost insignificant. Then I thought about it (foolish me). Why do we celebrate birthdays, anniversaries, and retirement? Why do we have festivals and parties? Why do we have sports plaques, celebrity awards, certificates of merit, and comedy roasts? We engage in all these things to give honour, recognition, and acknowledgement to someone or to a group of someones for their achievements, their hard work, their milestones, and their life. The recipients of all this celebratory attention, in turn, feel humbled, grateful, important, satisfied, motivated, and uplifted.

Now that I am working toward being the opposite of that smug, cynical, and sarcastic person I once was, I figure I wouldn't mind feeling that way, too, as long as the praise and glory is sincere and as long as I truly deserve it and believe I deserve it.

I remember having a difficult time celebrating birthdays as a kid. After all, what was I really celebrating but a man-made construct on the same day, year-in and year-out, to commemorate the day of my birth? I didn't even do anything to deserve the honour. My parents did all the work. Once. In all honesty, how could I have accepted all that attention and all those gifts? I felt like a fraud whose anger and shame could only be quelled by whacking a piñata.

The same was true every year I celebrated a wedding anniversary. It was confusing: were we acknowledging the love we felt for each other, or were we partying because yet another year had gone by without killing each other?

Every year I would watch on TV the Oscars, the Emmys, the Tonys, and the myriad self-congratulatory award shows filled with glitter and glam, pretense and hokum. My only salvation was the doleful and sometimes hateful smiles of the award losers.

It wasn't until I retired from my thirty-three-year career that I began to really understand celebration. I was being honoured formally at a dinner and roast for more than three decades of hard work and contribution to society by colleagues, friends, and family (that is, people who mattered to me). And I had my Sally Field moment: "They like me! They really like me!" I actually felt the glory, the humility, the satisfaction, the gratitude, the importance, the motivation, and the upliftedness. I was soaring!

That was when I decided that celebrating successes had substance and validity. I also accepted the notion that I could celebrate all kinds of successes, big and small. I didn't even have to wait for someone to throw me a party; I could reward myself! I didn't need a twelve-piece orchestra playing every time I chose berries and oatmeal instead of a Grand Slam breakfast. I didn't need anything elaborate, expensive, or complicated. Just something that said: Congratulations! Good job! You did it! Keep going! You matter!

Generally, I tried for big successes—big reward; small successes—small reward. That way I wouldn't under- or over-value myself. Eating healthfully for a full week deserved a small piece of cake. Cleaning out the basement warranted a good massage or a long soak in a hot tub. Ending my career earned me a nice vacation. It's kind of like my own little rewards points system. And it seems to be working so far.

A Little Something You Might Want to Try
Celebrating Successes

Create a list of some of the things you would like to achieve or some milestones in your life and identify a reward for each.

GETTING TO KNOW ME:
THE INTROSPECTIVE PROFILE

(learning about myself)

Sometimes it seemed that the biggest obstacle for me to overcome was not necessarily thinking I knew who I was or what I wanted out of life, but not being too satisfied with the results. I discovered it was necessary to do a little inner probing to develop some introspective insight. This enabled me not only to identify and realize a wide range of goals I may otherwise never have known I had, but also to allow myself to acquire a clear understanding of how I saw myself, my perception of others, others' perception of me, and my perception of how others saw me.

There were no tricks to this exercise; it merely required total honesty and the willingness to give careful thought to the questions. The more detailed I was in my responses the more useful I found the exercise.

I initially completed this exercise on my own, writing out my answers as full and detailed as possible. It was easier to be truthful with myself without having someone looking over my shoulder. But I did realize that enlisting the assistance of someone with whom I would feel comfortable to ask the questions would keep my answers in check for honesty as well, especially if that person knew me well and if I trusted that person to record my responses exactly as stated in my own words. Sometimes hearing someone else ask these questions could motivate me to respond more thoroughly and concisely.

Most questions are in three parts: the first part is a question that is factual, or asks for one's thoughts or opinions. The second part of the question asks that one consider his/her feelings concerning the first part. The third part of the question relates to behaviour, more specifically, what changes one would make (if any) pertaining to the first part of the question.

Upon its completion this exercise should enable one to clarify any misperceptions that may exist of oneself and of others. Having completed this exercise myself left me with a well-rounded introspective profile of who I really am and what I really want out of life.

A Little Something You Might Want to Try
Learning About Myself: The Introspective Profile

1. a) What is your name?
   b) How do you feel about your name?
   c) Why/What changes would you make if you could?
2. a) What is your gender?
   b) How do you feel about your gender?
   c) Why/What changes would you make if you could?
3. a) Where do you live?
   b) How do you feel about where you live?
   c) Why/What changes would you make if you could?
4. a) Describe your health.
   b) How do you feel about your health?
   c) Why/What changes would you make if you could?
5. a) How old are you?
   b) How do you feel about your age?
   c) Why/What changes would you make if you could?
6. a) Describe your body.
   b) How do you feel about your body?
   c) Why/What changes would you make if you could?
7. a) Describe your lifestyle (e.g. marital status, children, fast-paced, laid back, etc.)
   b) How do you feel about your lifestyle?
   c) Why/What changes would you make if you could?
8. a) Describe your daily routine (including your work life/school life/home life)

b) How do you feel about your daily routine?

c) Why/What changes would you make if you could?

9. a) Describe your hobbies/interests/leisure time.

b) How do you feel about your hobbies/interests/leisure time?

c) Why/What changes would you make if you could?

10. a) Describe your social life.

b) How do you feel about your social life?

c) Why/What changes would you make if you could?

11. a) Outline a brief chronology of significant events that have occurred in your life.

b) Identify any patterns of thoughts, feelings, or behaviour with respect to the chronology of events that have occurred in your life.

c) What would you most readily change about your past and why?

12. a) List the significant people in your past (both positive and non-positive influences).

b) Identify your thoughts, feelings, and behaviours concerning these people.

c) If you could tell any of those people from your past something right now, what would you tell them?

13. a) When you were younger, what did you really want to be when you grew up?

14 a) What was the happiest experience you can remember?

b) What made it the happiest experience?

15. a) What was the unhappiest experience you can remember?

b) What made it the unhappiest experience?

16. a) What was the most embarrassing experience you can remember?

b) What made it the most embarrassing experience?

17. a) What was the funniest experience you can remember?

b) What made it the funniest experience?

18. a) What was the scariest experience you can remember?

    b) What made it the scariest experience?

19. a) What do you like about the way you think?

    b) What do you dislike about the way you think?

    c) Why/What changes would you make?

20. a) What do you like about the way you feel?

    b) What do you dislike about the way you feel?

    c) Why/What changes would you make?

21. a) What do you like about the way you behave?

    b) What do you dislike about the way you behave?

    c) Why/What changes would you make?

22. a) List your skills, attributes, talents, experience, strengths, and weaknesses.

23. a) What motivates you?

    b) How do you feel about these things as motivators?

    c) Why/What changes would you make?

24. a) List all you needs at all levels (as many as you can think of).

    b) Are these needs being met?

    c) If so, how? If not, how could you arrange for your needs to be met?

25. a) Make a list of your long-term and your short term plans.

    b) Are they really what you want?

    c) If not, what changes would you make?

26. a) List all the things about which you most often mentally argue with yourself.

    b) Can you identify any patterns or underlying themes? If so, what are they?

    c) Why/What changes would you make?

27. a) List those people with whom you most often argue.

    b) About what do you argue with these people?

    c) Why/What changes would you make?

28. a) List the things in or about the world that bothers you.

b) Can you identify any patterns or underlying themes? If so, what are they?

c) Why/What changes would you make?

29. a) Do you demand perfection of yourself?

b) How do you feel when you do not succeed?

c) Why/What changes would you make?

30. a) Do you expect/insist on approval or acceptance from others?

b) How do you feel when someone does not meet your expectations?

c) Why/What changes would you make?

31. a) Do you expect the world to be as you want it?

b) How do you feel when things do not go your way?

c) Why/What changes would you make?

32. a) Do you remember your dreams?

b) If so, what do you dream about?

c) Why do you thing you dream these things?

33. a) Do you see yourself as a moody person?

b) If so, in what ways?

c) Why/What changes would you make?

34. a) Describe your basic beliefs/convictions/morals/values.

b) Rate, on a one-to-five scale, the strength of your beliefs/convictions/morals/values.

c) What changes would you make?

35. a) What is your favourite colour?

b) What is your least favourite colour?

c) Why (for both)?

36. a) Do you ever feel trapped or stuck?

b) If so, in what way(s)?

c) Why/What changes would you make?

37. a) Make a list of all the emotions you have been feeling lately and also which have been elusive (happy, sad, excited,

embarrassed, anxious, aroused, angry, depressed, loving, resentful, longing, afraid, awed, etc.)

   b) What makes you feel this way?

   c) Why/What changes would you make?

38. a) List those things you would rather be doing.

   b) List the qualities of the kind of person you would rather be.

   c) Why/What changes would you make to do the things you would like to do and be the person you would like to be?

39. a) Create a priority list of the things most important to you.

40. a) Describe your views on: i) the world; ii) illness/injury; iii) aging; iv) old age; v) death.

41. a) Describe in detail all aspects of your wildest fantasy (including the ideal life for you, your goals, what you would like to achieve, what you would like to acquire, sex, your physical, intellectual, moral, and spiritual being, your view of the world around you).

42. a) List the contents of your personal time capsule.

43. a) If you had to leave behind a message to the world that would be heard and followed by all, what would it be?

44. a) Who are the people in your life at the present time?

   b) How do they fit into your life?

   c) What do you like about them? What do you dislike about them?

45. a) Who are your idols (real or not)?

   b) How do you feel about them?

   c) Why?

46. a) With whom do you not get along?

   b) What are the problems you are having with them?

   c) Why/What changes would you make?

47. a) List your significant others.

   b) How do you think your significant others see you?

   c) Why/If necessary, how could you rectify any misperceptions?

48. a) How do you think people in general see you?

    b) Why do you think they see you this way?

    c) Is this, perhaps, how you see yourself?

49. a) Review your list of your significant others.

    b) If you could tell them what you want from them, what would it be?

50. a) Review your responses to this exercise.

    b) What patterns or underlying themes have you discovered?

Using your list of significant others, ask a friend with whom you feel comfortable or take it upon yourself to approach each of these significant others and ask the following questions:

51. a) What is your relationship with _____?

    b) What do you like most about _____?

    c) What do you dislike most about _____?

52. a) Describe your communication/relationship with _____.

    b) What do you feel this way?

53. a) How does _____ think?

    b) Why?

54. a) How does _____ feel?

    b) Why?

55. a) How does _____ behave?

    b) Why?

56. a) Disclose a secret about _____ that would not jeopardize the relationship.

    b) Think of a secret about _____ that would jeopardize the relationship but do not disclose it. Why do you think it would jeopardize the relationship?

57. a) How do you think _____ sees him/herself?

    b) Why do you think _____ sees him/herself this way?

58. a) Is there anything you are now prepared to say or any message
    you are now prepared to give to _____?
  b) If so, what is it? If not, why not?

I NEVER METAPHOR I
DIDN'T JUST LOVE TO PIECES

(using metaphors in life)

If you have managed to stomach this book thus far, you know only too well that it is peppered with all sorts of metaphors. But why? For what purpose? And to what end?

A metaphor is a representation of a thing, an idea, a concept by an image, word, phrase, or description of another which gives a deeper meaning, or clarification, or illustration to the original. The intent, in the context of this book, is to assist in raising self-awareness, facilitate motivation, inspire creative thinking, excavate deeply rooted emotions, and examine behaviours for the purpose of improving the quality of one's life.

Metaphors are not to be confused with similes, which have a similar purpose as metaphors but usually draw a comparison to something, often employing words such as 'like' or 'as', such as 'Life is like a box of chocolates' or 'He is as happy as clam'.

Everything we say and do is filled to the brim with metaphors, some of which have become so ingrained in our speech and our thought processes that most of the time we are unaware of their existence. For example:

"My love soars to the heavens when I am with her. She is the light of my life. And I am her knight in shining armour. I asked for her hand in marriage from her father, but the sly old fox was suspicious and said, 'I smell a rat.' I told him that I have carried a torch for her for years. He asked, 'Will love put food on the table?' I told him that working the land was my bread and butter, that soon I'll be rolling in dough and that he can rest assured that his daughter will be draped in silk and dripping with diamonds. That was the straw that broke the camel's back. He almost tossed his cookies at my sugar-coated words and told me to get lost. I left his house with my tail between my legs and a well of tears behind my eyes. What a jackass! When I told her about the battle I had with her father, she said it didn't matter, that her love for me could not be destroyed. I jumped for joy and reminded myself that every cloud has a silver lining!"

Many metaphors have become commonplace and can be referenced from any subject, such as weather, cooking, sports, computers, space, time, family, even life.

Metaphors are found all over the place: all the world's a stage . . . , the light at the end of the tunnel, stepping out of the mist, the keys to success/happiness, a lightbulb going on or off, the flip of a switch, writing one's own script, playing the hand you are dealt, a brush stroke on the canvass of life, starting with a clean slate, a pot of gold at the end of a rainbow, the man in the mirror, the tree of life, a carpenter with his toolbox, on the other hand, the wheel of life, and on and on and on.

Metaphors can be inspiring, poetic, weird, imaginative, humorous, redundant, or just plain mixed up. Check out these, some of my favourites:

- "Her face was a perfect oval, a circle that had its two sides gently compressed by a thigh master."
- "She had a sultry, deep-throated laugh, like a dog about to throw up."
- "He was as tall as a tree—he was a six foot tree."
- "Even on his deathbed, the old man's mind was a steel trap, only rusted."
- "Her vocabulary was as bad as, like . . . whatever."
- "The feather glided gently down to earth the way a two hundred pound rock wouldn't."
- "The dancer extended her leg gracefully behind her, a dog at a fire hydrant."
- "He was a couch potato in the gravy boat of life."

- "He was so in love that whenever she spoke he thought he heard bells, like a garbage truck in reverse."
- "She scurried into the room, a centipede with ninety-eight missing legs."
- "Don't bite the hand that rocks the cradle."
- "He has a heart as big as gold."
- "He's not the brightest tool."
- "The grass is always greener under a rolling stone."
- "Try walking in my chair." Or "Try sitting in my shoes."
- "I turned a blind eye to everything I heard."

Everything in life has its metaphor. Everything in life is a metaphor. Life is: a roller coaster, a puzzle, a race, a journey (pathways, a maze, roads, a voyage), an adventure, a baseball game, hell, an uphill climb, a cabaret, a battle, a fairy tale, or anything you want it to be.

A Little Something You Might Want to Try Using Metaphors in Life #1

1. Think about your life as it is right now and create ten metaphors for it.

A Little Something You Might Want to Try Using Metaphors in Life #2

2. Think about your life as you would like it to be and create ten metaphors for it. Summon these metaphors whenever life throws you a curveball.

A Little Something You Might Want to Try Using Metaphors in Life #3

3. Review this book and identify all the metaphors you can find.

CONCLUSION

(okay, so this is where I decided to stop thinking)

Everyone has his own journey. Everyone chooses his own path, opens his own doors, burns his own bridges. Everyone has his own metaphor.

This book is the story of my journey, one I'm still experiencing. I began by presenting my credentials, albeit false ones, because I wanted you to believe (paradoxically) that I was perfect, that I had all the answers. I was going to state unequivocally and presumptuously how you should live your life so that you, too, could be perfect. All too quickly (after the first couple of paragraphs) I started to laugh at the absurdity of it all, at my own arrogance, and at my own lie. I was at the opposite end of the universe from perfect and I knew it. This got me to thinking about who I was, what I was, where I was, how I was, and why I was who I was.

I took a good look at my Starting Point which, I must clarify (if you haven't figured it out by now), was not the starting point of my life but the starting point of my journey. Hell, I didn't even leave the home I was born in until I was twenty-one years old! Up to that point I hadn't ventured any farther from Toronto than to Buffalo, New York. I never lived on my own—I leapt from my parental home to my matrimonial home. Aside from some summer employment and some self-made work teaching my own self-created courses for continuing education, I had only one main job in Social Services for the City of Toronto. I had my life experiences up to that point but they seemed trivial and unimportant. I felt trivial and unimportant.

Ever since I can remember I was uncomfortable with myself and my life. I glimpsed happiness on rare occasions and only then from afar, but I always felt that something was missing. Thus I began my journey, looking for what was missing.

Searching, always searching!

But what was I searching *for*? I used to think that I was chasing after the bluebird of happiness, that elusive feeling that seems to be the ultimate goal for everybody. What I've learned in my journey is that happiness, a feeling like any other feeling, is merely a by-product of a thought (kind of like the innards and eyeballs of a fast-food burger that may make the burger taste good but is not the essence, only the by-products). This feeling, in turn, may or may not influence my behaviour and perhaps my subsequent thoughts. To be happy I must think thoughts that will result in happy feelings and behave, that is, I must take action in a way that will elicit more happy feelings, keeping in mind that there are varying degrees of happiness as there are varying degrees of any emotion. Ultimately, therefore, the most direct route to happiness is through my thoughts and my behaviour.

At first, the search was external, the Journey Without. I looked toward other people, other things, and ideas not of my own making to point to where that damn bluebird had flown. Although this pursuit lead to new and eye-opening experiences, I still felt dissatisfied, disconnected, and disillusioned.

It was when I directed my search inward, my Journey Within, that things started to make some sense, especially when the search took me to the most significant question: "Do I like who I am or who I have become?" I realized that if the answer was 'yes' then I could continue to develop and grow; if the answer was 'no' then I could change how I think and I could alter how I behave.

By answering this question, I have been able to determine my life vision: to improve the quality of my life by continuing to build character, constantly evaluating my values and measuring them to my morals, testing the results, practising and re-evaluating, further developing and refining as I go along.

By undertaking goals to fulfil my vision, by doing, having, and being the best that I can do, have, and be, I am able to reinvent myself with artistic creativity.

It is important to underscore one key element throughout this journey: in pursuing the goals that led me to my ultimate life vision, I determined that I could not and would not damage anyone else along the way. To me, infringement on the rights of others would violate the very foundation upon which I was trying to build my character. In doing so, I would be damaging (if not destroying) myself.

There are many areas of thoughts, feelings, and behaviour I have not yet addressed, mostly because they are still being formulated in my mind and are ever evolving. Below are some I believe are worthy of consideration. Note that many are reflective of the duality of life discussed earlier:

- Take action and keep trying.
- Take a breather and reflect.
- Make every second count.
- Don't try so hard; just let it happen.
- Don't get caught up in perfection.
- Continue to find ways to constantly improve.
- Indulge in and express a zest for life.
- Take pleasure in the smaller things.
- Have the strength to weather whatever curve balls life throws.
- Respect the fragility of life.
- Enjoy life's freedoms.
- Understand life's constraints.
- Learn to enjoy my own company.
- Savor the company of others.
- Recognize similarities in others.
- Appreciate differences in others.
- Don't take things for granted.

- Explore my curiosity.
- Look for the best in people, especially the more difficult ones.
- Appreciate life's milestones.
- Learn from life's setbacks and pitfalls.
- Find your metaphor.

So is this the end of the road in my journey or just the beginning? I am reminded of that line in *The Sound of Music*, "If the Lord closes a door, some way He opens a window." I'm still a sap for corny movie dialogue.

The beauty of this tapestry of life is in the stitching—the tapestry grows, becoming expansive, richer, and more beautiful. There is an interconnectedness of all of these thoughts and ideas as the universe unfolds, for me and because of me, for everyone and because of everyone. Energy increases and vibrations are stronger. I am stronger. I am learning. I am renewed.

Life is a metaphor.

BOOKS AND WEBSITES THAT GAVE MY HEAD A SHAKE

(Bibliography and Reading References)

http://www.goodreads.com/author/quotes/27573.Leo_Buscaglia
http://www.meaningsoflife.com/Happiness.htm
http://www.self-improvement-mentor.com/philosophy-happiness.html
http://www.pursuit-of-happiness.org
http://plato.stanford.edu/entries/happiness
http://www.2knowmyself.com/Hormones_that_make_you_happy
http://www.bodywindow.com/endorphins.html
http://serendip.brynmawr.edu
http://www.holisticonline.com/hol_neurolinguistic.htm
http://www.myjewishlearning.com/practices/Ethics
http://innerself.com
http://www.ebonmusings.org
http://www.highonhappiness.com
http://www.randomactsofkindness.org
http://newconversations.net
http://www.nursingplanet.com
http://www.goodcharacter.com/index.html
http://www.differencebetween.net
http://www.motivation-tools.com
http://www.solveyourproblem.com
http://www.psychologytoday.com/articles
http://brainmind.com
http://www.mindtools.com
http://www.goodtherapy.org/types-of-therapy.html

373

http://www.helpothers.org/index.php
http://www.successconsciousness.com
http://helpguide.org/toolkit/emotional_health.htm
http://www.stevepavlina.com
http://www.buddhanet.net/e-learning/5minbud.htm
http://www.healer.ch/Chakras-e.html
http://www.kabbalah.info/
http://www.emoclear.com/
http://hinduwebsite.com/

A Complete Guide to the Tarot
Eden Gray © 1970
Crown Publishers, Inc., New York NY

A New Earth: Awakening to Your Life's Purpose
Eckhart Tolle © 1995
Published by Plume, a Member of Penguin Group (USA)

A Thousand Paths to Happiness
David Baird © 2000
Sourcebooks, Inc., Napersville IL

Abnormal Psychology—Current Perspectives
Curtis L. Barrett et al © 1972 by Communications Research Machines, Inc.
CRM Books, Del Mar CA

Attaining the Worlds Beyond
Rabbi Michael Laitman © 2003
Laitman Kabbalah Publishers, Thornhill ON

Awakening the Heroes Within—Twelve Archetypes to Help Us Find
    Ourselves and Transform Our World
Carol S. Pearson © 1994
Harper Collins Publishers, New York NY

Charlie Brown Series by Charles Schulz

Chicken Soup for the Soul (and other books in the Chicken Soup for the
    Soul series)
Jack Canfield, Mark Victor Hansen, Jennifer Read Hawthorne, Marci
    Shirroff © 1997
Health Communications, Inc., Deerfield Beach FL

Don't Know Much About the Bible
Kenneth C. Davis © 1998

Avon Books, Inc., New York NY

Don't Sweat the Small Stuff (series: including—And It's All Small Stuff, At
 Work, With Your Family, and For Men)
Richard Carlson, PhD. © 1997
Hyperion, New York NY

God Is a Verb
Rabbi David A. Cooper © 1997
Riverhead Books, The Berkeley Publishing Group, a member of Penguin
 Putnam, Inc., New York NY

I'm OK—You're OK
Thomas A. Harris, M.D. © 1967, July 1973
Avon Books, a Division of The Hearst Corporation, New York NY, by
 management with Harper and Row Publishers, Inc., New York NY

Kabbalah for Dummies
Arthur Kurtzweil © 2007
Wiley Publishing Inc., Indianapolis IN

Life 101—Everything We Wish We Had Learned About Life In School
 But Didn't
John—Roger and Peter McWilliams © 1991
Prelude Press, Los Angeles CA

Life After Life
Raymond A. Moody Jr., M.D. © 1975
Bantam Books, Inc., New York NY

Life Before Life
Helen Wambach © 1979
Bantam Books, Inc., New York NY

Life Between Life

Joel L. Whitton, M.D., PhD. and Joe Fisher © 1986
Doubleday and Company, Inc., New York NY

Life's Greatest Lessons—20 Things That Matter
Hal Urban © 1992
Simon and Shuster, Inc., New York NY (Fireside 2003)

Lifetimes: True Accounts of Reincarnation
Frederick Lenz, PhD. © 1979
Ballantine Books, a Division of Random House, Inc., New York NY

Living Your Past Lives: The Psychology of Past Life Regression
Karl Schlotterbeck © 1987
Ballantine Books, a Division of Random House, Inc., New York NY

Looking Out For #1
Robert J. Ringer © 1977
Fawcett Crest Books, a Unit of CBS Publications, Brooklyn NY

Man and His Symbols
Carl G. Jung © 1964
Dell Publishing Company, Inc., New York NY

Man's Search for Meaning
Viktor E. Frankl © 2006
Beacon Press, Boston MA

Men Are From Mars, Women Are From Venus—A Practical Guide for
    Improving Communication and Getting What You Want In Your
    Relationship
John Gray, PhD. © 1992 J. G. Productions, Inc.
Harper Collins Publishers, Inc., New York NY

Metaphor Therapy: Using Client Generated Metaphors In Psychotherapy
Richard R. Kopp © 1995
Taylor & Francis

Mind Over Mood—Change How You Feel by Changing the Way You Think
Dennis Greenberger, PhD. and Christine A. Padesky, PhD. © 1995
The Guilford Press, New York NY

On Death and Dying
Elisabeth Kubler-Ross © 1969
Macmillan Publishing Company, Inc., New York NY

Pathways to Recovery: A Strengths Recovery Self-Help Workbook
Priscilla Ridgway, Diane McDiarmid © 2002
University of Kansas School of Social Welfare

Pulling Your Own Strings
Dr. Wayne Dwyer © 1978, August 1979
Avon Books, a Division of The Hearst Corporation, New York NY, by
    arrangement with Thomas Y. Crowell Company

Risking
Dan Viscott, M.D. © 1977
Pocket Books, a Division of Simon and Shuster, Inc., New York NY

Secrets of Mental Magic—How to Use Your Full Power of Mind
Vernon Howard © 1964
Prentice-Hall, Inc., Paperback Library, a Division of Coronet
    Communications, Inc., New York NY

Social Psychology
Jonathan L. Freedman, J. Merrill Carlsmith, and David O. Sears © 1970
Prentice-Hall, Inc., Englewood Cliffs NJ

The Age of Ideology
Henry D. Aiken © 1956
Mentor Books, by the New American Library, Inc., New York NY

The Complete Guide to the Kabbalah—How to Apply Ancient Mysteries of
the Kabbalah to Your Everyday Life
Will Parfitt © 1988
Random House, London UK

The Dead Are Alive
Harold Sherman © 1981
Ballantine Books, a Division of Random House, Inc., New York NY

The Five Books of Moses
Moses Greenfield © 1986
Ateres Publishing

The Happiness Project
Gretchen Rubin © 2009
Harper Collins Publishers, Inc., Toronto ON

The Hero Within—Six Archetypes We Live By
Carol S. Pearson © 1986
Harper and Row Publishers, Inc., New York NY

The Individual and His Dreams
Calvin S. Hall and Vernon J. Nordby © 1972
Signet Books/ The New American Library of Canada, Ltd., Scarborough ON

The Life You Were Born to Live—A Guide to Finding Your Life Purpose
Dan Millman © 1993
An H. J. Kramer Book, published in a joint venture with New World
Library, Tiburon CA/Novato CA

The Power to Prevent Suicide: A Guide for Helping Teens
Richard E. Nelson, PhD. and Judith C. Galas © 1994
Free Spirit Publishing, Inc., Minneapolis MN

The Primal Scream

Arthur Janov, PhD. © 1970
Dell Publishing Company, Inc., New York NY

The Psychology of Motivation
Abraham K. Korman © 1974
Prentice-Hall, Inc., Englewood Cliffs NJ

The Secret
Rhonda Byrne © 2006 by TS Production Limited Liability Company
Atria Books, New York NY and Beyond Words Publishing, Hillsboro OR

The Sedona Method
Hale Dwoskin © 2003
Sedona Press, Sedona AZ

The Seekers' Handbook: The Complete Guide to Spiritual Pathfinding
John Lash © 1990
Harmony Books, New York NY

The Ten Commandments—The Significance of God's Laws In Everyday Life
Dr. Laura Schlessinger and Rabbi Stewart Vogel © 1998
Harper Collins Publishing, Inc., New York NY

The Third Force—The Psychology of Abraham Maslow
Frank G. Goble © 1970
Simon and Shuster of Canada, Ltd., Richmond Hill ON

Theories of Personality
Calvin S. Hall and Gardner Lindzey © 1957
John Wiley and Sons, Inc., New York, Sydney, London, Toronto

Visualization for Change
Patrick Fanning © 1994
New Harbinger Publications, Inc., Oakland CA

When All You Ever Wanted Isn't Enough—The Search for a Life That Matters
Harold Kushner © 1985 by Kushner Enterprises
Pocket Books, a Division of Simon and Shuster, New York NY

Your Erroneous Zones
Dr. Wayne Dwyer © 1976
Avon Books, a Division of The Hearst Corporation, New York NY, by
	management with Funk and Wagnalls

CPSIA information can be obtained at www.ICGtesting.com
Printed in the USA
LVOW10s0854110913

351848LV00007B/14/P

9 781452 574813